966
010 W9-BGI-619

Peacekeeping
in Sierra Leone

■ ■ ■

HISTORIES OF UN PEACE OPERATIONS
A project of the International Peace Academy

Peacekeeping
in Sierra Leone
THE STORY OF UNAMSIL

■ ■ ■

'Funmi Olonisakin

LYNNE
RIENNER
PUBLISHERS

BOULDER
LONDON

Published in the United States of America in 2008 by
Lynne Rienner Publishers, Inc.
1800 30th Street, Boulder, Colorado 80301
www.rienner.com

and in the United Kingdom by
Lynne Rienner Publishers, Inc.
3 Henrietta Street, Covent Garden, London WC2E 8LU

Library of Congress Cataloging-in-Publication Data
Olonisakin, 'Funmi.
  Peacekeeping in Sierra Leone : the story of UNAMSIL / 'Funmi Olonisakin.
    p. cm. — (Histories of UN peace operations)
  Includes bibliographical references and index.
  ISBN 978-1-58826-520-3 (hardcover : alk. paper)
  ISBN 978-1-58826-521-0 (pbk. : alk. paper)
    1. United Nations Assistance Mission in Sierra Leone. 2. United
Nations—Peacekeeping forces—Sierra Leone. 3. Sierra Leone—
History—Civil War, 1991—Peace. I. Title.
DT516.826. O45 2008
966.404—dc22

                                                                2007022728

British Cataloguing in Publication Data
A Cataloguing in Publication record for this book
is available from the British Library.

Printed and bound in the United States of America

5 4 3 2 1

Contents

Foreword

Terje Rød-Larsen
President, International Peace Academy

THE INTERNATIONAL PEACE ACADEMY (IPA) is proud to present *Peacekeeping in Sierra Leone: The Story of UNAMSIL,* by 'Funmi Olonisakin of the Conflict, Security, and Development Group, King's College London. This book is centered on a brutal civil war that shocked people around the world and a UN peace operation that served as both the catalyst and the testing ground for significant changes in UN peacekeeping. But the book is not intended to provide an explanation of the war nor an analytical study of the lessons learned for the UN. Instead, we seek to fill a gap in the literature by telling the inside story of the UN's engagement with the Sierra Leone conflict, from the first appointment of a Special Envoy in 1995 to the launch of the United Nations Mission in Sierra Leone (UNAMSIL) in 2000 and its withdrawal five years later. This is a story of gradually deepening engagement in the Sierra Leone conflict, spurred on by various factors including Security Council commitment, changing regional dynamics, and a desire to restore the UN's credibility following one of the worst humiliations in its history, when several hundred UN blue helmets were taken hostage by Revolutionary United Front forces in May 2000. By providing the real context behind UN decisions, from resolutions of the Security Council in New York to the day-to-day crisis management tasks of the mission leadership in Freetown, the book enhances our understanding of the UN's work in countries like Sierra Leone.

Peacekeeping in Sierra Leone is the first volume in the IPA's Histories of UN Peace Operations series, a project initiated by the UN's Department of Political Affairs and Department of Peacekeeping Operations, with the strong support of then Secretary-General Kofi Annan. It arose out of recognition that, for all the academic literature about UN peace operations, there was no guarantee the inside story of individual UN peace efforts would be told, and thus there would be real value in initiating a series to tell those stories in a consistent way over time. The International Peace Academy was asked to fill the gap by producing an ongoing series of histories that would capture UN perspectives, benefit from access to internal UN documents and personnel, and pay particular attention to the environment of opportunities and constraints within which major strategic decisions were made, while remaining fully independent and accessible to a broad audience. The IPA hopes that *Peacekeeping in Sierra Leone* will provide a learning tool for UN staff as they navigate the complex challenges of future peace processes, as well as insight and a point of reference for all those interested in the work of UN peace operations.

This book reflects the IPA's continuing engagement with issues related to peacekeeping and peacebuilding, the core competencies of the UN. Our proximity to the UN and working relationships with the Secretariat and member states continue to furnish us with a privileged understanding of the UN's work and a desire to place that knowledge in the public domain. In that spirit, this volume will be followed in the near future by similar histories of UN operations, such as the United Nations Verification Mission in Guatemala (MINUGUA) and the United Nations Operation in the Congo (ONUC), which we hope will lay the foundation for the Histories of UN Peace Operations series as a multiyear initiative. We are deeply grateful to the UN Secretariat for its ongoing partnership in this endeavor and to the project's donors—the governments of France, Ireland, the Netherlands, and the United Kingdom—for their generous support.

Acknowledgments

WRITING ON THE UNITED NATIONS' involvement in any complex emergency automatically predisposes the author to a huge debt of gratitude, which becomes all the more profound if the author has tried, as is the case here, to strike a balance between the interests of academics and the expectations of practitioners.

I am grateful to the International Peace Academy and the UN Departments of Peacekeeping Operations and Political Affairs for sponsoring the study that resulted in this book. At the IPA, Elizabeth Cousens was instrumental in bringing me on board for this project. I am grateful for her support and continued interest in my work. I want to thank especially Amy Scott, who accompanied me to Sierra Leone for the field study and coordinated the review process, making valuable input and editorial suggestions throughout; Vanessa Hawkins Wyeth for her dedicated editorial work; Alison Gurin, who painstakingly undertook the fact checking on documents and photos; and Adam Lupel, who coordinated the publication process. It has been a joy to work with them, and I want to thank them for their understanding even when I did not keep to deadlines.

A number of UN staff who, at different times, were involved in addressing the situation in Sierra Leone offered me their perspectives and insights into some of the complex actions (and sometimes inactions) of the organization during the difficult times of its involvement in the country. It is not possible to mention them all by name, but I want to express my profound gratitude for their support and interest in this study. I particularly want to thank Rei Zenenga, who read the manuscript with enormous interest and pointed out errors of fact; Margaret Vogt and Charles Anyidoho for their useful critique; Adriaan Verhuel, who shared his firsthand experience as desk officer responsible for monitoring the situation in Sierra Leone in the Department of Peacekeeping Operations (DPKO) at an important period in UNAMSIL's history; Sheila Dallas, who lived through different transitions in UNAMSIL and shared some of her personal experiences; General Martin Luther Agwai, who took time out of his busy schedule on several occasions to share his experiences; and Gebremedhin Hargoss, whose intimate knowledge of UNAMSIL helped me situate many of the stories collected along the way.

The field trip to Sierra Leone was made possible by the support of a number of UN staff in New York and in UNAMSIL, as well as Sierra Leonean friends and colleagues who facilitated our travel and various meetings. I am especially grateful to Jaiyeola Lewu, Fabiola de Freitas, and Yolanda at the DPKO. Jeannette Eno was very supportive in providing useful links to Sierra Leonean organizations.

I am also grateful to my colleagues at the Conflict Security and Development Group (CSDG) at King's College London and to other colleagues with whom I regularly brainstorm for their interest and support of the project. The fact that some of them were in Sierra Leone at one time or another during the country's civil war gave them particular insights that assisted me in this study. Specifically, I want to thank Abiodun Alao, Eka Ikpe, and Wale Ismail. Morten Hagen, as always, provided outstanding research support throughout. It would have been impossible to complete the study in time without Morten's dedicated research assistance. I deeply appreciate his commitment. In addition, I thank Brian Thompson, who was undertaking other work on Sierra Leone at the same time, for sharing the results of his work with me; and Zeedah Meierhofer-Mangeli, whose valuable comments helped shape my storyline for the book.

But above all, my greatest appreciation goes to the Sierra Leoneans, whose unpleasant experiences are recorded in this book. Despite these experiences, they maintained their dignity and their candor, and were ever so willing to share their stories with other people. My sincere thanks go to them.

Finally, to those whose contribution and assistance I have inadvertently given no mention, I offer sincere apologies.

Notwithstanding the valuable contribution and advice received from various sources in the course of this study, the responsibility for the contents of this book is entirely mine.

— 'Funmi Olonisakin

SIERRA LEONE

Introduction

AS THE UNITED NATIONS Mission in Sierra Leone (UNAM-SIL) prepared for its exit from Sierra Leone in December 2005, few could deny it had achieved a tangible measure of success. The sense of fulfillment experienced by its staff and leadership was palpable. Daudi Mwakawago, who steered the UNAMSIL ship through its final phase as the third of three Special Representatives of the Secretary-General (SRSGs), was full of pride as he addressed his staff for the last time: "Each one of you here should pat yourselves on the back for a job well done. There are peacekeeping missions that have been there forever, some are clocking 50 years with no end in sight. This one in six years has successfully ended its mission." He recapped the accomplishments of the previous couple years:

> The drawdown has been exceptional. We have successfully withdrawn one of the biggest UN peacekeeping forces, one time 17,500-troop strong, without any commotion. Last year some people felt that when UNAMSIL left, the people would be apprehensive. But we've done that in a very peaceful way and those personnel have been moved to other mission areas. We have handed security primacy to the Sierra Leone government. We've done that in Murray Town, Hastings, Bo, Kenema and Koidu.[1]

Similarly, UN Secretary-General Kofi Annan was like a proud father on his child's graduation day. On the last official day of the mission, he described how it had overcome "serious political and military challenges" to leave Sierra Leone "much better off today than it was five years ago."[2]

1

Against formidable odds, UNAMSIL had delivered on the key component of its mandate—the establishment of security—paving the way for the consolidation of peace and a return to normalcy.

The UN was not alone in this upbeat assessment of UNAMSIL's impact. In a BBC radio program on 22 December 2005, Sierra Leoneans and other Africans gave due credit to UNAMSIL for the stabilization and maintenance of a secure environment throughout Sierra Leone. In a public opinion survey carried out earlier that year, nearly 100 percent of respondents agreed that Sierra Leone's security situation had improved immensely due to UNAMSIL's presence.[3]

The evidence was apparent. In Freetown, the once deserted beaches of Lumley and Lakka were again alive with children playing and people—young and old—strolling without looking over their shoulders. The roads to Lunsar and Makeni were free from renegade soldiers and armed bandits who preyed on innocent civilians at will. From east to west, Freetown's streets were bustling with life, hawkers, pedestrians, and motor vehicles competing for space amid children walking to or from school, an image impossible to imagine during the dusk-to-dawn curfews of the war years. A city once devoid of a decent hotel was now awash with hotels and guest houses. Bintumani Hotel, once part of Freetown's claim to elegance and opulence but damaged by war and left fallow for years, was given a makeover by the Chinese.

Beneath the surface, however, the legacies of war were all around. The signs could be found in the hundreds of young people roaming the streets of Freetown, begging for handouts or searching for something to do; in the lack of opportunity structures within the overcrowded capital and under-populated villages; in the rampant prostitution among young girls and boys; and above all, in the abject poverty that predated the war and persists today. Many Sierra Leoneans expressed reservations about UNAMSIL's short-term focus and urged that the UN stay on to address the root causes of the conflict and help promote development in Sierra Leone.[4]

The UN's pride in UNAMSIL derived not so much from its belief that the job was entirely done, but more from the fact that UNAMSIL had overcome major obstacles to achieve results. It had become a model mission, and had been credited with several innovations, but only after an extremely difficult start, as reflected upon by Annan in his final report on the mission:

Given the unique history of UNAMSIL, I cannot but feel a deep sense of satisfaction as I submit this last report on the Mission. The trials and tribulations faced by the Mission during the crisis of 2000, the measures taken to reverse its fortunes, and its achievements between 2001 and today, are indeed remarkable. The Mission's recovery from the 2000 ordeal offers a wealth of lessons for current and future peace-keeping operations.[5]

His words stand as a reminder that just five years earlier, the mission's name had been synonymous with humiliation and failure.

▌ Freetown, May 2000

On 2 May 2000, as the last remaining Nigerian battalion departed from Lungi airport, completing the withdrawal of ECOMOG—the Economic Community of West African States Cease-Fire Monitoring Group—Sierra Leoneans were filled with appreciation, optimism, and apprehension at the same time.[6] Lungi was alive with applause and cheers from a crowd who had come to bid the Nigerians goodbye, for UNAMSIL had assumed full control of security on the ground.

In private conversations, ordinary Sierra Leoneans and government officials welcomed the UN presence in Sierra Leone but expressed concern about the ability of the United Nations to do what it would take to ensure security and stability in the country. West African regional forces, despite the challenges they faced, instilled greater confidence at the time. They had been tested on the ground and were feared by the Revolutionary United Front (RUF; pronounced *roof* by those who knew it intimately), the much-dreaded rebel group. Newly deployed, UNAMSIL was untested, and many feared that ECOMOG's withdrawal might tempt the RUF to desta-bilize the peace process.

Sierra Leoneans' worst fears were realized within two weeks of ECOMOG's withdrawal, as RUF hostility toward UNAMSIL intensified and escalated rapidly, resulting in a series of incidents that led to near total loss of confidence in UNAMSIL by the government and people of Sierra Leone. On 1 May 2000, in an RUF attack on the disarmament and demo-bilization site in Makeni, UNAMSIL military observers were taken hostage. By 3 May, the RUF had abducted almost fifty UNAMSIL sol-diers, with four killed. By 5 May, the number of UNAMSIL personnel reportedly held by the RUF had increased to over 300, and then within a few days to nearly 500. It was later revealed that the entire Zambian bat-talion, over 200 troops, had been forcibly disarmed by the RUF.

By this time, Sierra Leoneans were bitterly angry about the RUF's efforts to derail the peace process and the ease with which UNAMSIL troops had given in under the RUF's challenge. The security situation rap-idly deteriorated. On 8 May, bodyguards of RUF leader Foday Sankoh fired into a crowd who were demonstrating in front of Sankoh's residence in Freetown, killing some twenty protesters.

The lack of confidence in UNAMSIL produced strange bedfellows, bringing together renegade soldiers, bandits, armed civilians, and professional soldiers as Sierra Leoneans scrambled to defend their country against another RUF onslaught. The progovernment Civil Defense Forces (CDF) were deployed alongside their old enemies from the Armed Forces Revolutionary Council (AFRC), who in 1997 had joined forces with the RUF to oust the government but had subsequently distanced themselves from the rebels. Johnny Paul Koroma, leader of the AFRC, issued a rallying call to AFRC and former Sierra Leone Army (SLA) soldiers, who responded by the thousands to defend their country. This single act undid the progress achieved so far, for the AFRC had changed sides but not tactics. Weapons were put back into the hands of dangerous people, reviving dying monsters. As is often the case, the innocent would pay the price.

Beyond UNAMSIL and Sierra Leone, this series of events was a severe blow to the United Nations as a whole. The organization, which even if imperfect was largely looked upon as a guarantor of international peace and security and a protector of people facing humanitarian tragedy, was being publicly humiliated by a small, relatively insignificant force. As once again Sierra Leone became destabilized, the UN seemed unable to respond.

To worsen matters, the UN was widely criticized for its earlier inaction and failure to contain Liberian president Charles Taylor, considered to be the chief architect of instability in the Mano River area, which includes Guinea, Liberia, and Sierra Leone. It was an open secret that Taylor was a mentor to Foday Sankoh, and godfather to the RUF. Taylor kept the RUF lifeline sustained through a never-ending supply of weapons from across the border in Liberia, and Sankoh returned the favor by supplying Taylor with diamonds, which were sold in markets abroad. With his unique influence over the RUF, Taylor was by all accounts the major external impediment to the troubled peace process in Sierra Leone, and the UN now suffered the indignity of relying on him to secure the release of its peacekeepers.

Yet those who worked at the heart of the mission maintain that the crisis of May 2000 was the single most important factor in UNAMSIL's eventual success, and a necessary evil. Not only did the crisis shake the foundations of UNAMSIL, but it humiliated the UN as a whole, forcing its member states to scale up the mission's response. There were other factors at work in 2000 as well, including a revival of UN peacekeeping (exemplified by the missions in East Timor and Kosovo, which had been established the previous year) and pressure to avoid a double standard between responses to the "rich man's war" in Kosovo and the "poor man's war" in

Sierra Leone. Yet it was the need to "save" the UN that was the pinnacle factor, a powerful reminder that the UN's potential as an instrument of peace and security depends on the membership's desire to exercise it.

■ A History of the United Nations in Sierra Leone

This book tells the inside story of the UN experience in Sierra Leone and seeks to answer central questions raised by the events of May 2000. In the lead-up to those events, few would have predicted such a crisis in light of the Lomé Peace Agreement of 1999 and the semblance of security that existed in the country. What accounted for this disastrous and rapid deterioration? Then, in the aftermath, the UN was able to turn the situation around, and five years later UNAMSIL was ranked as a success alongside missions in Namibia, Mozambique, and Cambodia. What was responsible for this turnaround in UNAMSIL's fortunes?

This book is not a complete account of UNAMSIL, nor of the conflict in Sierra Leone, subjects on which there is already a wealth of literature.[7] The aim is instead to tell the story of the UN in Sierra Leone: why certain decisions were taken, what the opportunities and constraints were, and what it was like to be part of the mission on the ground. More fundamentally, my goal is to preserve the complex history of UNAMSIL—with all its personalities, political dynamics, and problems—for the benefit of future UN decisionmakers, and to bring it alive for the benefit of all who seek to understand the UN better.

Chapter 1 presents a quick tour of the environment in which the UN would later become embroiled. Sierra Leone was not a locale to which the world's powerful nations would typically and readily commit their resources. It offered no real attraction to most, and was not strategically important compared to some other African countries. This chapter explains the UN's slow, token response to the initial stages of the Sierra Leone crisis.

Chapter 2 describes how a new turn of events in Sierra Leone, Western Europe, and North America prepared the UN to take center stage in peacemaking efforts. In 1999, Sierra Leone provided an irresistible chance for the UN to raise its profile, especially as it was being outshined by other actors, such as the North Atlantic Treaty Organization (NATO) in Kosovo. What began as a need to respond to the "do something" lobby transformed into an opportunity to become a central player, the biggest fish in the West African pond. The UN took a chance in Sierra Leone. Yet it is not clear whether the planners considered all the risks, or chose the right balance between caution and more extensive engagement.

Chapters 3 and 4 go to the heart of the UNAMSIL story—the crisis of May 2000 and its immediate aftermath. Chapter 3 narrates the events and describes the people and factors at the core of the crisis. The chapter also looks at the role of the United Kingdom, particularly its "over the horizon" assistance strategy, which was initially praised by all for saving the day but proved to be a double-edged sword for UNAMSIL because of the negative publicity the mission attracted as a result.

Chapter 4 focuses on the dependence of the UN and regional actors on Liberian president Charles Taylor to resolve the May crisis. It highlights the personal and regional dynamics of the political situation into which the UN had inserted itself, and the UN's blindness to the Taylor factor for many years prior to the May crisis. Such blindness constrained the UN's room for maneuver in 2000. But the stark evidence of Taylor's leverage during the crisis encouraged the Security Council to take a more regional approach in its subsequent response to the conflict.

Chapter 5 focuses on the internal cracks and divisions within UNAMSIL as exposed by the May crisis. The importance of personalities and leadership, particularly at critical moments, was made apparent by a difficult relationship that escalated to a full-fledged dispute between Nigeria and India, now commonly referred to as the Jetley affair. The potential for contingents and their home governments to undermine a mission at critical moments is also discussed.

Chapter 6 focuses on how UNAMSIL recharted its course, to regain the credibility it lost and win back the hearts and minds of the population it was supposed to be helping. The response of the Security Council and Secretariat demonstrated the importance of leadership in steering a troubled mission like UNAMSIL toward success. The chapter also discusses the relationship between the Sierra Leone case and broader happenings within UN peacekeeping.

Chapter 7 describes the subsequent history of UNAMSIL and charts its evolution into a "model" peacekeeping mission to which UN staff wanted to be posted, and within which new ideas—such as a shift in the philosophy guiding mission drawdown—were tried. I conclude the story of UNAMSIL with a reflection on the real gains and lessons of this peacekeeping experience, both for the UN and for Sierra Leone, as well as an assessment of their implications for current and future operations, whether in Sierra Leone's immediate neighborhood or beyond.

■ Notes

1. *Africa Week* (special edition), January 2006, p. 26.
2. See http://allafrica.com.
3. Jean Krasno, *Public Opinion Survey of UNAMSIL's Work in Sierra Leone*

(New York: United Nations Department of Peacekeeping Operations, Peacekeeping Best Practices Section, July 2005).

4. "How to Make Peace Last," *Have Your Say: Africa,* BBC World Service, 22 December 2006.

5. See *Twenty-seventh Report of the Secretary-General on the United Nations Mission in Sierra Leone,* UN Doc. S/2005/777, 12 December 2005.

6. ECOMOG had been deployed to Sierra Leone since 1997.

7. See, for example, Ibrahim Abdullah, ed., *Between Democracy and Terror: The Sierra Leone Civil War* (Dakar: CODESRIA, 2003); Lansana Gberie, *A Dirty War in West Africa: The RUF and the Destruction of Sierra Leone* (London: Hurst, 2005); John L. Hirsch, *Sierra Leone: Diamonds and the Struggle for Democracy* (Boulder: Lynne Rienner, 2001); David Keen, *Conflict and Collusion in Sierra Leone* (Oxford: Currey, 2005); and J. Peter Pham, *The Sierra Leonean Tragedy: History and Global Dimensions* (Hauppauge, NY: Nova Science, 2006).

1 | Unattractive Terrain, Token Response

TO MANY POLICYMAKERS in Europe and North America and at the United Nations, Sierra Leone was the farthest place on earth in March 1991, when 100 rebel fighters, including Sierra Leonean dissidents and members of Charles Taylor's National Patriotic Front of Liberia (NPFL), invaded the country across its eastern border. This event did not appear on the radar screen in Western capitals, even as an afterthought. The rest of the world was preoccupied with brewing crises in the former Yugoslavia and the recent war in the Gulf.

Sierra Leone's neighbor Liberia had been at war for more than a year, though that crisis had not attracted the attention of the international community either. It was Liberia's West African neighbors, some of whom were themselves affected by the war, who mustered a response. Overwhelmed by the peacemaking effort in Liberia, the West African response in Sierra Leone was more limited. Only Nigeria (which had troops in Sierra Leone under a status-of-forces agreement), Guinea, and Ghana responded prior to the arrival of an Economic Community of West African States Cease-Fire Monitoring Group (ECOMOG) task force.[1] Not coincidentally, troops from these three countries also made up the bulk of the ECOMOG force. The task force was intended only to support the ECOMOG operations in Liberia, and to assist Sierra Leonean president Joseph Momoh in combat operations against the rebels and in the training of the national army.

Even without brewing crises elsewhere, Sierra Leone had always been unlikely to receive international attention beyond West Africa. The country was blessed with abundant natural resources, and its lush tropical rain forests and unspoiled beaches offered a potential for ecotourism; its flawless and highly sought diamonds were a constant source of attraction to

9

dealers, and its alluvial gold was rated among the best in the world. But its economic and strategic importance to Western Europe and North America was minimal. With a population of just under 5 million people, Sierra Leone did not constitute a sufficiently sizable market to matter in trade terms. And with the Cold War over, the only commodity that small states in Africa had previously been able to sell to secure great-power support—ideology—was no longer marketable. The people of this tiny West African country would have to sweat through their war alone.

▌ A War Waiting to Happen

Although the focus of this book is the UN in Sierra Leone, it is important to understand the background to the conflict and the UN's entry. When Sierra Leone became an independent dominion in 1961, it inherited a multiparty system of government from the British, over which its first leader, Sir Milton Margai, of the Sierra Leone People's Party (SLPP), presided as prime minister. Margai is widely remembered for his genuine efforts to build a united Sierra Leone and his promotion of good governance principles. Upon his death in 1964, his brother Albert took over the reins of power and rapidly reversed this process, taking Sierra Leone down a path of political corruption and mismanagement.

Albert Margai's rule by patronage, whereby only members of his favored ethnic group and network benefited from governance, quickly reinforced the division of Sierra Leone's party system along ethnic lines. Under his patronage, the Mende, a large and politically important ethnic group from eastern and southern Sierra Leone, came to dominate the ruling party, the SLPP. Northern ethnic groups, such as the Temne and the Limba, immediately gravitated toward the major opposition, the All People's Congress (APC). Sierra Leone was on its way to vicious ethnic politics.

The country's political situation deteriorated rapidly in 1967. Albert Margai's attempt to reverse the results of that year's elections, which were generally believed to have been won by opposition leader Siaka Stevens of the APC, culminated in a Margai-instigated coup. A countercoup in 1968 led to the inauguration of Stevens as Sierra Leone's democratically elected prime minister.

Despite his party's opposition to Margai's rule, Siaka Stevens did not improve on his predecessor's pattern of governance. His seventeen-year rule plunged Sierra Leone into a downward spiral of political chaos and economic collapse. He consistently intimidated and harassed political opponents, many of whom were executed, imprisoned, or sent into exile.

In 1977, Stevens declared Sierra Leone a one-party state, entrenched himself as president-for-life, and threatened those who challenged this state of affairs with treason charges.[2] Then, in pursuit of international relevance and prestige, and against all odds, he hosted the 1980 summit of the Organization of African Unity (OAU). In preparation, Stevens undertook huge capital projects, such as building the Bintumani Hotel and a prestigious housing complex, as described by John Hirsch in his book *Diamonds and the Struggle for Democracy*: "Stephens was duly elected OAU chairman but the hotel and the village [the housing complex] promptly fell into disrepair while the newly installed streetlights flickered out barely six weeks later. Wildly inflated contracts enabled those who were insiders on the scam to walk away with millions."[3]

The collapse of Sierra Leone's fledgling democracy was practically complete by 1985, when Siaka Stevens handed over the presidency to his army commander, Major-General Joseph Momoh. Despite initial promising signs and popularity, Momoh continued his predecessor's tradition of acute political corruption. Institutions of the state had been severely weakened by decades of sociopolitical exclusion and mismanagement. The parliament exercised no meaningful role under a harsh one-party rule in which the leader tolerated no opposition. Judges were co-opted and corrupted, while the military helped maintain the status quo by providing maximum protection to the regime. The civil service was littered with cronies and APC loyalists, many of whom were employed solely as a reward for previous acts of assistance to the party, albeit sinister or unpatriotic ones.

Momoh failed to revive the deteriorating economy, which had become heavily dependent on mineral resources rather than cash crops. By then, the country's supply of iron ore had been depleted, while large-scale diamond smuggling had begun. The state coffers were looted to feed the politics of patronage, which in turn shored up the regime, while control of natural resources was reportedly left in the hands of a few individuals.[4] The impact of this pattern of governance trickled down the system. With an empty state treasury, offices were gradually looted of equipment by unpaid civil servants without alternative means of livelihood.

The outbreak of war in Liberia in December 1989 spelled doom for Momoh's government and for the country as a whole. Under Charles Taylor's leadership, the NPFL invaded Liberia from Côte d'Ivoire. And the Samuel Doe regime's Armed Forces of Liberia (AFL) responded brutally, escalating the crisis into a full-blown civil war. Hit-and-run attacks by the NPFL against government officials in Nimba county incited AFL reprisal attacks against residents of the county accused of supporting the NPFL.[5] Within a few months, both parties were indiscriminately targeting innocent civilians. The war spread rapidly through the Liberian countryside, causing maximum damage and disorder, not to mention a massive loss of innocent lives.

The situation in Liberia prompted the Economic Community of West African States (ECOWAS) to establish an armed, cease-fire monitoring group (ECOMOG), which deployed thousands of troops in 1990. Momoh sent Sierra Leonean troops to participate in the monitoring force, and allowed it access to Lungi airport as an airbase. Momoh's support for ECOMOG, coupled with his earlier refusal to grant Taylor's request to operate an NPFL base in Sierra Leone, generated hostile reactions from the NPFL.

The common belief among West African experts is that it was in retaliation for such actions that Taylor provided support to the Revolutionary United Front (RUF), a group of Sierra Leoneans in exile, in their plan to invade Sierra Leone. The RUF's leader, Foday Sankoh, a former corporal for the Sierra Leone Army (SLA) who had been dishonorably discharged for a coup attempt against Siaka Stevens in 1971, had known Taylor since the 1980s. But Taylor had deeper motives aside from retribution against Momoh and loyalty to Sankoh, including access to valuable mineral resources in Sierra Leone and potential dominance over the Mano River region. In March 1991, the RUF, backed by the NPFL, invaded Sierra Leone from Liberia, marking the beginning of the war.

The NPFL-assisted RUF incursions served as a catalyst for war, but the prevailing governance conditions in Sierra Leone had forewarned disaster. One consequence of the governance breakdown in Sierra Leone was the emergence of youth as a formidable class. The educational system had been completely destroyed; university professors had either left in disillusionment or succumbed to the lure of the corrupt regime, accepting offers of political office. Schools were slowly dismantled and starved of resources. Only children whose parents could afford private education had access to good training. In the process, hundreds of thousands of young people were squeezed out of the educational system over time, with no access to good or even basic education.[6]

Under these circumstances, Sierra Leone was left to cope with a generation of uneducated and unemployed but functional illiterates, many of whom roamed the country's streets. They became a formidable social class with the potential for mobilization against the state, forming a ready pool of recruits available to the highest bidder. The RUF would come knocking, tapping this potential by offering what was for many young people an attractive alternative.

Ismail Rashid renders a compelling account of the process that produced this youth culture in Sierra Leone, stating that, as early as indepen-

Foday Sankoh, leader of the
RUF, in Freetown, April 2000.
Ryan Sloet © Reuters/CORBIS

dence in 1961, the "lumpen" or "potes" (terms for the dispossessed and socioeconomically displaced) were a relatively coherent social group with "prominent habits, dress culture, lingo and mode of behaviour."[7] In due course, the potes became an alternative to student halls. Even among the relatively few young people who had access to schools and made it to higher educational institutions, Rashid claims, there was general disgruntlement with the system, providing a common rallying point between the potes and young people who were higher-educated. The youth became the voice of the excluded, condemning the widespread corruption and the state's failure to provide for the basic needs of Sierra Leoneans, and advocating for sociopolitical change through recurrent student strikes and riots.[8]

Thus, although it has been argued that the war in Sierra Leone was caused by the war in neighboring Liberia, it is important to note that Sierra Leone already had a complete recipe for conflict. The RUF incursions into Sierra Leone in March 1991 only served to speed up the timeline of a drama for which the growing youth crisis at home provided ready fuel. Balancing these factors, Lansana Gberie argues in *A Dirty War in West Africa* that the RUF's war was driven not by local command and ideas and sensitivities—although there was a carefully choreographed attempt to create this impression—but by outsiders, principally Charles Taylor of Liberia. [But] This fact does not obviate the need to examine the conditions of pre-war Sierra Leone, the horrible neo-colonial failure [that] created the conditions for the development into a full-scale and highly destructive civil war and the emergence of a criminal warlord system with an invasion from Liberia by a petty army, largely foreign, which could easily have been crushed by any reasonably functioning state.[9]

■ The Face of War

At first, Sierra Leoneans did not all experience the war with the same intensity. The Sulima fishing community at the southernmost tip of Sierra Leone, at the border with Liberia, was the first to feel the full brunt. But just as Sierra Leone seemed like the far end of the earth for policy actors in Europe and North America, the war seemed remote when viewed from Sierra Leone's capital, Freetown, in the west of the country. Here, life continued as normal for many people. Lumley beach still had the same atmosphere of merriment during weekends; at its typical hut-shaped calypso bars, people drank and danced until the early hours of the morning. In the big hotels overlooking the beach and the water—and Freetown boasted three: Mammy Yoko, Cape Sierra, and Bintumani—it was business as usual.

Residents of Freetown only began to take notice as more people began to share in the sting of the battle raging between the rebels and government forces. Suddenly, the victims of the war were no longer anonymous. They were one's family and friends, or those of one's neighbors.

The rebellion intensified in brutality, first in the southern towns of Zimmi and Pujehun, as well as in the diamond-mining districts in the east, from Pendembu to Koindu and Kono. Then it slowly spread west toward the capital. The RUF was able to capture much of the southern and eastern districts, including the diamond-mining areas, because it confronted poorly trained and ill-equipped SLA soldiers.

In April 1992, young, disaffected SLA junior officers seized power in a bloodless coup that ousted General Momoh on the grounds that his APC government had failed to contain the RUF rebellion. The new government, led by twenty-five-year-old Captain Valentine Strasser of the National Provisional Ruling Council (NPRC), moved quickly to reverse the successes of the Taylor-assisted rebels. But while Strasser was initially able to regain some key rebel-held areas in the southeast, by early 1995 the RUF had gained back diamond areas as well as most of the countryside, and was advancing toward Freetown.

There were two main reasons for this reversal. First, the rebels had a sophisticated intelligence network and were well informed about the movements of enemies and neutrals in their areas of operation. Second, following years of poor training and inadequate attention to professionalism by the military and civilian leadership, the national army was weak. Moreover, many suspected that disenchanted elements within the SLA were actually doubling as rebel fighters in the dark hours. Before long, SLA troops were collectively branded "Sobels" (soldiers by day, rebels by night), a label that caused significant disaffection among soldiers who felt they had given their all for the defense of the country. The army's lack of capacity to defend its people and country caused civil militias, most notably the Kamajors, a traditional hunting militia of the Mende group, to become a mainstay of Sierra Leone's defense.

In the spring of 1995, the Strasser-led government engaged the services of Executive Outcomes, a South African–registered security firm, to counter the RUF insurgency, which was advancing on the capital.[10] By the end of the year, Executive Outcomes had expanded its operations into rural areas, where it cooperated with the Kamajors, providing training and logistical support to the civil militia. In return for its services, Executive Outcomes was paid in cash and kind, with diamond-mining concessions. The role of mercenaries and private armies in armed conflicts subsequently became a hotly debated issue within the international community. The government of Sierra Leone argued for the country's right to self-defense, and few could challenge this. Yet the arrangement drew attention to an emerging practice in Africa: for governments—and not simply insurgency groups—to employ the services of mercenaries, in this case on a large scale.[11]

Formed by Eeben Barlow and other veterans of the apartheid-era South African Defense Force (SADF), Executive Outcomes had first drawn public attention in 1992 with its role in Angola's civil war. In Sierra Leone, with helicopter gunships, Executive Outcomes assumed command of the air, shelling rebel strongholds in thick-forested areas and providing support to the SLA and the civil militias on the ground as they tried to comb through rebel-held areas. Progovernment forces, now made up of mercenaries, the national army, and civil militias, quickly regained control over the area around Freetown and key diamond-mining districts. By early 1996, they had successfully destroyed the RUF stronghold in the Kangari Hills in central Sierra Leone. The RUF was driven as far back as the Liberian border, though government forces were unable to capture RUF headquarters in Kailahun.

Two children enrolled with Sierra Leonean troops get ready to fight on the front line near Masiaka, May 2000.

Jean-Philippe Ksiazek/AFP/Getty Images

Despite the obvious successes, total victory proved elusive. Sierra Leone was learning the same lessons of guerrilla warfare that many other countries had previously learned. The RUF's hit-and-run tactics, mobility, and ambushes in the heavily forested countryside, where it had superior knowledge of the territory, created insurmountable problems for all progovernment forces. A crude and unspoken division soon emerged, with the progovernment forces controlling the major towns and cities, while the RUF operated on smaller linkage roads and back roads, which became death traps for unsuspecting travelers.

The war in Sierra Leone slowly emerged as a conflict to be reckoned with, as its horrors spread across the country. The RUF, like its Liberian counterpart the NPFL, launched a massive recruitment drive, coaxing, compelling, or abducting children and youths in village after village, town after town. Once on the RUF side, a young person was never the same again. The RUF committed gruesome atrocities through systematic violence against civilians. It later emerged that the SLA was also responsible for abuse against civilians and also used child soldiers, through either coercion or manipulation.[12] But the crimes of the SLA were largely under-reported during the early stages of the war, perhaps because it was not in the government's interest to reveal them. With such brutality on both sides,

Sierra Leone faced a desperately long and lonely road to rehabilitation, and the world very gradually began to take notice.

∎ Elections Before Peace

While government forces continued to counter the RUF insurgency, Sierra Leone began a process of transition from military to civilian rule. In August 1991, President Momoh had passed the multiparty constitution, several months before he was overthrown. Nearly four years later, and in response to increasing pressure from civil society and the international community, Strasser's NPRC government established the Interim National Electoral Commission (INEC) to manage the transition to a multiparty system. The INEC fought tooth and nail to set the process in motion after fending off resistance from within the NPRC itself.

The INEC, under the leadership of James Jonah, who had retired as Undersecretary-General for Political Affairs at the United Nations, organized a conference at Bintumani Hotel in Freetown in August 1995, where political leaders and civil society representatives hotly debated whether a peace settlement should come before elections, or vice versa. The vast majority of those present argued for early elections while pursuing a peace settlement at the same time. They won their argument, and elections were planned for 26 February 1996. The RUF, which was invited to the conference but did not send a representative, was opposed to elections taking place without a settlement.

Strasser had been nursing ambitions of transforming himself into a civilian president by running as an NPRC candidate in the forthcoming election, even though he clearly did not meet the constitutional criteria, the most relevant in his case being the age qualification of forty years. Waning support among his colleagues, as well as division within the NPRC on political strategy, contributed to Strasser's overthrow. On 16 January 1996, he was unseated by his deputy, Brigadier-General Julius Maada Bio. Maada Bio promised to hand over power to an elected government, but he seemed more inclined to postpone elections; in an effort to stall the process, he called for a second Bintumani conference in mid-February, which occurred under a strong military presence. Nevertheless, the conference constituents voted overwhelmingly to proceed with elections as scheduled.

In February 1996, Sierra Leoneans went to the polls against formidable odds. Voters turned out en masse, despite incessant rebel attacks on civilians. The RUF stood to lose as much as the NPRC from the election process and took deliberate action to prevent it, carrying out a campaign of terror from its bases in the countryside that involved the murder and torture of innocent civilians—toddlers, youths, and adults alike. Based on

President Ahmad Tejan
Kabbah, 2002.
© Wolfgang Kumm/dpa/CORBIS

witnesses' and victims' accounts of rebel atrocities, it seemed as though the RUF recruits had been trained to dedicate meticulous attention to methods of torture guaranteed to inflict maximum pain. It was during this period that the RUF became notorious for its practice of mutilating and amputating limbs, without discrimination. The massive amputations of arms and hands were cruelly symbolic, in that they were meant to sabotage the election process by rendering civilians physically incapable of voting. The campaign slogan of SLPP leader Ahmad Tejan Kabbah, which urged Sierra Leoneans to give their "hands" for peace, acquired a particularly gruesome double meaning.

In the run-off election between Kabbah and John Karefa Smart of the United National People's Party, Kabbah emerged as the winner and international observers declared the elections free and fair. The NPRC did not challenge the results and, remarkably for the region, the military peacefully handed power to the new civilian leader.

Yet the military's handover of power was not straightforward and may not have occurred under different circumstances. It took sustained pressure from civil society and the involvement of the United Kingdom and the United States to ensure the exit of the military, though it is difficult to assess their precise impact on Maada Bio in February 1996. During the two rounds of Bintumani talks, James Jonah collaborated with civil society, particularly with the women's movement. A number of people played prominent roles in the campaign to ensure that the military vacated power, including Shirley Gbujama, who chaired the Bintumani conferences, Julius Spencer, Zainab Bangura, Isha Dyfan, and Amy Smythe.[13] In addition, inducements from the United States and the United Kingdom, including UN-funded positions at institutes of higher education, provided the military leader with an alternative career path.[14]

Just before the February election, Maada Bio, who was by then in search of a legacy, made spirited efforts to negotiate a settlement with Sankoh. Some progress was realized. The conversation between Bio and Sankoh, which started through radio communication, eventually produced a face-to-face meeting in Yamoussoukro in March 1996, facilitated by Côte d'Ivoire's foreign minister, Amara Essy, and attended by representatives from the UN, the OAU, and the Commonwealth of Nations. It was logical that Kabbah's new government would continue these talks. But complications arose because, curiously, Bio had at some point assured Sankoh that he would be deputy chair of the NPRC if it remained in power, or that he might be able to persuade an elected government to make Sankoh vice president.[15] This revelation raised questions about Bio's real intentions and overinflated Sankoh's expectations, undermining the possibility of a deal.

In the absence of a lasting settlement to the conflict, Kabbah's newly elected government faced a difficult time ahead. As the war in southern and eastern Sierra Leone intensified, the government increasingly relied on the Kamajors, under the leadership of Chief Sam Hinga Norman, who was well respected among the Mende group. Following the appointment of Norman as deputy defense minister in 1996, the Kamajors were systematically organized into a powerful civil militia force. The combination of the Kamajors and Executive Outcomes presented a credible opposition to the RUF, but no doubt bred ill-feeling among the SLA officer corps, highlighting the mutual distrust between the government and the army. In September 1996, following rumors of a coup plot, Kabbah's government forced the retirement of over 20 senior officers and over 150 noncommissioned officers from the armed forces, including the last two heads of state, Valentine Strasser and Maada Bio.

■ The United Nations Inches In

Until the elections, Sierra Leone plodded along largely on its own. The UN system of funds, programs, and agencies was present in a development and

Sam Hinga Norman with members of the Kamajor militia in Freetown, February 1999.

© Patrick Robert/Sygma/CORBIS

humanitarian capacity, through the activities of the Food and Agriculture Organization (FAO) and the United Nations Development Programme (UNDP). But the UN was not engaged politically until February 1995, when a Special Envoy, Berhanu Dinka of Ethiopia, was appointed by then–Secretary-General Boutros Boutros-Ghali. His appointment followed a UN exploratory mission that had visited Sierra Leone in December 1994, after the Secretary-General had received a letter from Strasser, the previous month, requesting his good offices to facilitate negotiations with the RUF.[16]

Dinka had served in Ethiopia's foreign service, as ambassador to Djibouti and Canada, and as Permanent Representative to the UN. He had later joined the UN Secretariat, working in missions in Somalia, South Africa, and Cambodia, and for brief stints as a consultant for the UN Economic Commission for Africa and the UNDP. He arrived on the scene with just one assistant, Kathryn Jones, from the Secretariat's Department of Political Affairs in New York.

When Dinka became Special Envoy in Sierra Leone, the legitimacy of the RUF as a conflicting party was not seriously in dispute. Dinka represented the UN at the first face-to-face meeting between the organization and the RUF, in December 1995. He then assisted in negotiating the

Abidjan Peace Agreement between Kabbah's government and the RUF in November 1996. Alongside the Commonwealth, the OAU, and the government of Côte d'Ivoire, the UN was a moral guarantor of that agreement. Under the Abidjan Agreement, the SLPP and the RUF agreed to a cessation of hostilities; the disarmament of the RUF; the creation of a new, unified military force—to which former RUF combatants were invited to enlist; the deployment of a neutral monitoring group; the departure of all mercenaries; and the transformation of the RUF into a political party.[17]

Yet the semblance of stability in Sierra Leone was soon lost. Under the Abidjan Agreement, Executive Outcomes was to be withdrawn five weeks after the neutral monitoring group would have been deployed to oversee the cease-fire. However, unable to meet the rising costs of Executive Outcomes and under severe pressure from donor partners to reduce public spending, Kabbah asked Executive Outcomes to leave Sierra Leone even earlier, in January 1997. Without a monitoring force in place to oversee compliance with the Abidjan Agreement, the rebels were again unrestrained and the government side weakened.

By January 1997, communication between Sankoh and Kabbah had broken down irretrievably and the Abidjan Agreement had died a sure death. Sankoh pursued what many suspected was his main objective all along, the rearming of the RUF. In March 1997, he was arrested in Nigeria after being found in possession of ammunition and kept under protective custody at Kabbah's request until he was sent back to Sierra Leone in July 1998 to face trial for treason.

In May 1997, while Sankoh was still in Nigerian custody, the army colluded with the RUF and unseated President Kabbah in a military coup, forcing him into exile in Conakry, Guinea. Major Johnny Paul Koroma, who had previously commanded government forces fighting against the RUF, assumed power as leader of the Armed Forces Revolutionary Council and invited the leadership of the RUF to join the AFRC. If there were ever any doubts in some quarters about disaffection within a segment of the army, the coup quelled them, as the country watched the national army abdicate its responsibility for the defense of Sierra Leone to fight alongside a declared enemy of the state.

The coup attracted international condemnation, including in three Security Council presidential statements, in May, July, and August 1997.[18] Nigeria used ground troops based in Sierra Leone and then a naval bombardment of Freetown to try to reverse it.[19] The OAU expressed support for ECOWAS efforts to restore President Kabbah. In July 1997, the Commonwealth Ministerial Action Group suspended Sierra Leone's AFRC-led government from Commonwealth meetings. Meanwhile, representatives of the international community—including Francis G. Okelo of

Major Johnny Paul Koroma, leader of the AFRC, speaks at a press conference in Freetown, June 1997.

Corinne Dufka © Reuters/CORBIS

Uganda, who replaced Dinka as Special Envoy in September after Dinka's style had aroused RUF suspicions of partiality toward Kabbah's government—tried to persuade the junta to step down.

Meanwhile, Sierra Leonean civil society mustered a will of steel, mounting a mass resistance to the coup and embarking on civil disobedience. The women's movement, which had been prominent in the effort to ensure the exit of military rule during the Bintumani talks, remained active. Many civil servants, office workers, and shopkeepers complied, for months, with "stay at home" requests from union leaders. Quite often in the past, West African populations had resigned themselves to life under a dictatorship within days of a military coup. But to the junta's surprise, this case was different, and in the face of such opposition it soon lost any claim to legitimacy.

The determination of Sierra Leonean civil society was perhaps one of the principal factors that endeared some key international actors, not least Tony Blair's newly elected government in the UK, to Sierra Leone.[20] Because Sierra Leone was a former British colony, it had long been perceived by the United States and Europe as a British interest. Now the UK appeared to have a newfound desire to exercise its potential leadership role. It took active steps to join international efforts to remove the AFRC government and reinstate Kabbah, appointing Ambassador John Flynn, in January 1998, to cooperate with the UN and ECOWAS in this regard. It also helped galvanize the UN Security Council, on which it enjoyed permanent membership.

On 8 October 1997, the Security Council adopted its first resolution on the situation, demonstrating its increased alertness to the plight of the country. Resolution 1132, for which the UK was lead drafter and facilitator, gave unequivocal support to the ECOWAS effort to reverse the coup, and imposed sanctions on the military junta, including a travel ban and an embargo on arms and petroleum products, except petroleum products imported for use by the elected government of Sierra Leone, other governments, and ECOMOG, and for use by UN agencies for "verified humanitarian purposes."[21]

Within ECOWAS itself, opinion was divided about the right approach. Nigeria tried to pass off its initial attempts to reverse the coup as ECOWAS action, but others were quick to point out that these were unilateral Nigerian actions involving no prior ECOWAS consultation. Such efforts acquired more legitimacy later when they were processed through ECOWAS mediation committees. But while Nigeria preferred military action against the rebels, Côte d'Ivoire and Ghana preferred to embark on negotiations. ECOWAS imposed an embargo against Sierra Leone through a naval blockade and deployment of troops in Lungi, but the option of dialogue still prevailed. President Alpha Konaré of Mali also played an active role, demonstrating his commitment to stamping out the phenomenon of mobile dissident forces in the subregion, an understandable concern for a landlocked country like Mali.

Also in October 1997, an ECOWAS committee negotiated a peace plan in Conakry with representatives of the junta.[22] Among other things, the junta agreed to a cease-fire, ECOMOG's monitoring of the cease-fire, and possible deployment of UN observers. A plan for eventual withdrawal of the junta within a period of six months was also hatched. Although President Kabbah issued a statement agreeing to these terms, the junta raised complaints and reneged on the plan before the ink on the paper was dry. The junta had all the leverage and was not going to relinquish power unless compelled to do so. From his exile in Conakry, Kabbah enlisted support on all fronts, including from mercenaries. In December 1997, Kabbah reportedly contracted Sandline International to assist in the effort to have himself reinstated to power.

In February 1998, following ongoing fighting between ECOMOG and the AFRC/RUF, ECOMOG took advantage of what it called an "unprovoked attack" to launch an offensive on Freetown, overwhelming forces loyal to the junta and expelling them from the capital.[23] This paved the way for the return of Kabbah's regime, who were restored to office on 10 March in a ceremony attended by several West African leaders. A message from the UN Secretary-General was delivered by Ibrahima Fall, Assistant Secretary-General for Political Affairs.[24] Kabbah's reinstatement was well received by the international community; the Security Council responded with Resolution 1156, welcoming the "return to Sierra Leone of its democratically elected President."[25]

Yet the restoration of democracy in Freetown occurred amid widespread violence. Immediately following ECOMOG's victory in February, civilians took revenge on the junta and its supporters through practices such as "necklace burnings," whereby car tires were placed around the necks of offenders, coated with petroleum, and set ablaze.[26] This kind of mob justice reflected the level of bitterness against the rebels within society at large.[27] Kabbah's government decided to pursue justice in its own way. Alleged collaborators of the AFRC were charged with treason, Sierra Leone's former president Joseph Momoh among them. Twenty-four SLA military officers were sentenced to death and executed by firing squad in October 1998, despite pleas for clemency from the international community, including the UK government. Kabbah increasingly put his confidence in the Kamajors and other civil militias acting under Chief Sam Hinga Norman, the deputy minister of defense, and formalized them into the Civil Defense Forces (CDF) under Norman's leadership.

Meanwhile, more trouble was brewing at home and abroad. The Sandline affair hit the media in April 1998. The arms embargo imposed by the UN the previous year had been contravened by Sandline's exportation of arms for ECOMOG's use in the reinstatement of President Kabbah's government. The UK's foreign service was implicated when Sandline's chief executive, Tim Spicer, claimed he had informed UK officials, including the High Commissioner in Sierra Leone, Peter Penfold, of the arrangement. The report of the UK investigation into the Sandline affair did not entirely clear Penfold, who was thought to have been too lenient in his interpretation of the arms embargo contained in Resolution 1132, which he had interpreted as applying only to the AFRC/RUF junta, but not to ECOMOG or Kabbah's government in exile.[28] Penfold was forced to resign over the controversy.

■ The Mission Begins Small and Unarmed

In July 1998, the UN Security Council decided to establish the United Nations Observer Mission in Sierra Leone (UNOMSIL).[29] Less than thirty unarmed UN military observers under the protection of ECOMOG were initially deployed to monitor and assist efforts to disarm fighters and document human rights violations.[30] Special Envoy Francis Okelo became a Special Representative of the Secretary-General (SRSG) and chief of the mission. He had experience in UN peace operations, having previously served in Afghanistan as deputy head of the UN's special mission there, and also having worked for the UN in Haiti and Namibia.

The decision to establish UNOMSIL was influenced by several factors, not least the crisis of May 1997, the international outcry against the coup, and increased international support for the people of Sierra Leone. The UK government seemed committed, and Africans close to the UN system, among them James Jonah, lobbied actively for greater UN involvement. President Kabbah's reinstatement also provided momentum for renewed and increased engagement. The UN was slowly emerging as a visible player in Sierra Leone.

But although UNOMSIL marked an increase in the UN's engagement since the beginning of the war, there was no denying it was a small force. To the UN, it seemed neither necessary nor prudent to send a large UN presence. First, regional actors seemed to be taking the lead. Following Charles Taylor's election as Liberian president in August 1997, ECOWAS had concluded its operation in Liberia, allowing it to deploy additional troops to reinforce ECOMOG in Sierra Leone, which in turn contributed to President Kabbah's reinstatement in March 1998. There was a widespread belief in the international community that regional peacekeeping was the way forward; the surge in UN peacekeeping would not begin until the next year. Second, the tokenism of UNOMSIL suited the mood of the international community, whose attention was still primarily focused on other parts of the world such as Kosovo. There was a need to satisfy international public opinion, while keeping the costs of the Sierra Leone mission at a level acceptable to the member states responsible for paying for it.

It was not the first time that the UN would send in a meager presence—unarmed military observers—to cooperate with a more substantial regional force and depend on that regional force for security and protection. The first such instance was in 1993 in neighboring Liberia, where the United Nations Observer Mission in Liberia (UNOMIL), consisting at first of 303 military observers, was deployed alongside an 8,000-strong ECOMOG force.[31] Likewise in Sierra Leone, the UN had now joined the interesting mix of actors on the ground, but it was watching from the sidelines as regional troops, remnants of the Sierra Leone Army, and civil militias battled it out with the rebel alliance—RUF and AFRC fighters—in different locations in the hinterland.

▌ Notes

1. The Ghanaian contingent was small—a squadron of forty-two air force personnel.

2. See Yusuf Bangura, "Understanding the Political and Cultural Dynamics of the Sierra Leone War: A Critique of Paul Richards Fighting for the Rain Forest," *Africa Development* 22, nos. 3–4 (1997): 131.

3. John L. Hirsch, *Sierra Leone: Diamonds and the Struggle for Democracy.* International Peace Academy Occasional Paper series (Boulder: Lynne Rienner, 2001), p. 29.

4. It is claimed that Jamil Sahid Mohammed, an Afro-Lebanese national and close personal friend of former head of state Siaka Stevens, controlled the country's mineral resources, symbolizing the extreme state of corruption in Sierra Leone. See Ismail Rashid, "Special Issue: Youth Culture and Political Violence: The Sierra Leone Civil War," *Africa Development* 22, nos. 2–3 (1997): 26.

5. See, for example, Mark Huband, "Doe's Last Stand," *Africa Report* 35, no. 3 (July 1990): 47; and *Africa Research Bulletin*, 5 February 1990, p. 9557. Developments in the unfolding crisis in Liberia were widely reported in West African news magazines.

6. See Hirsch, *Sierra Leone*, p. 30.

7. Rashid, *Africa Development*, p. 23.

8. Ibid.

9. See Lansana Gberie, *A Dirty War in West Africa: The RUF and the Destruction of Sierra Leone* (London: Hurst, 2005), pp. 15–16.

10. The arrival of Executive Outcomes was predated by a lower-scale involvement of another private security force, the Ghurka Security Group, a contingent of Nepalese Ghurka who provided training to the SLA from 1993 to 1994, but who were forced to retreat in early 1995 after their US commander was killed by RUF forces.

11. See Abdel-Fatau Musah and J. 'Kayode Fayemi, eds., *Mercenaries: An African Security Dilemma* (London: Pluto, 2000), esp. chaps. 2–3.

12. See David Keen, *Conflict and Collusion in Sierra Leone* (Oxford: Currey, 2005), pp. 97–100, 102–105; Amnesty International, *Human Rights Abuses in a War Against Civilians*, 13 September 1995, Amnesty International Index: AFR 51/05/95; and Amnesty International, *Sierra Leone: Towards a Future Founded on Human Rights*, 25 September 1996, Amnesty International Index: 51/05/96.

13. Shirley Gbujama later became one of the longest-serving ministers in Kabbah's government, serving first as minister of foreign affairs and later as minister of social welfare, gender, and children's affairs. Julius Spencer was later actively involved in the launching of Radio Democracy and served as minister of information under Kabbah. Zainab Bangura later founded the Campaign for Good Governance and became the first woman presidential candidate in Sierra Leone when she contested the 2002 elections. Amy Smythe later became the first minister of gender and children's affairs.

14. This was confirmed in an interview with John Hirsch in Nairobi on 30 April 2006. Hirsch was the US ambassador in Sierra Leone from 1995 to 1998. See also Hirsch, *Sierra Leone*, p. 56.

15. See Hirsch, *Sierra Leone*, pp. 42–43.

16. UN Doc. S/1995/120, 7 February 1995.

17. See United Nations, *Peace Agreement Between the Government of the Republic of Sierra Leone and the Revolutionary United Front of Sierra Leone*, UN Doc. S/1996/1034, 30 November 1996.

18. See "Statements by the President of the Security Council": UN Doc. S/PRST/1997/29, 27 May 1997; UN Doc. S/PRST/1997/36, 11 July 1997; and UN Doc. S/PRST/1997/42, 6 August 1997.

19. Some observers challenged the legality of Nigeria's intervention, arguing that the status-of-forces agreement excluded the use of force in support of the regime and that the terms of the agreement were stretched beyond the breaking point to accommodate Nigeria's actions in May 1997. See, for example, Yusuf Bangura, "Security in ECOWAS," and Abass Bundu, "The Case Against Intervention," both in *West Africa*, 30 June–7 July 1997, pp. 1039–1040.

20. The date of the UK general election was 1 May 1997.

21. See *UN Security Council Resolution 1132*, UN Doc. S/RES/1132, 8 October 1997.

22. The ECOWAS Committee of Four, which initially consisted of the foreign ministers of Nigeria, Côte d'Ivoire, Ghana, and Guinea, was later expanded to the Committee of Five, to include Liberia, following Charles Taylor's assumption of power in August 1997.

23. On 9 February, ECOMOG chief of staff Brigadier-General Abdul-Ome Mohammed cited an incident in Kissy that had occurred a few days prior, in which an ECOMOG patrol vehicle, after hitting a landmine, endured "concentrated fire" from junta forces. He called it an "unprovoked attack" and promised "utter retaliation" from ECOMOG. See Sierra Leone News Archive, 9 February 1998, http://www.sierra-leone.org/slnews0298.html.

24. Beatrice Grabish, "Peacewatch: Return of President Ahmad Tejan Ahmad Kabbah to Power," *UN Chronicle*, Summer 1998.

25. See *UN Security Council Resolution 1156*, UN Doc. S/RES/1156, 16 March 1998.

26. See Conciliation Resources, *Implementing the Lomé Peace Agreement* (London: CR, September 2000).

27. Among the rebels, infighting occurred between AFRC and RUF fighters as they retreated from Freetown. Following a clash with the RUF in Makeni, one faction of AFRC fighters retreated to the Occra Hills, where they became known as the West Side Boys. See Keen, *Conflict and Collusion in Sierra Leone*, p. 222.

28. Sir Thomas Legg and Sir Robin Ibbs, *Report of the Sierra Leone Arms Investigation* (London: Stationery Office, 27 July 1998).

29. See UN Security Council Resolution 1181, UN Doc. S/RES/1181, 13 July 1998 (see text of Resolution 1181 in this volume).

30. *UN Security Council Resolution 1181* authorized up to seventy UN military observers, but only forty in the first phase, to be deployed as security conditions permitted.

31. See Abiodun Alao, John Mackinlay, and 'Funmi Olonisakin, *Peacekeepers, Politicians, and Warlords* (Tokyo: United Nations University Press, 1999), pp. 93–94.

2 | Stepping Up UN Engagement

SIERRA LEONE'S FATE hung in the balance in 1998, the token UN presence paling in comparison to the country's recent history of flagrant abuse of the innocent. But then, a series of events altered the regional context of the Sierra Leone conflict: a sudden change in Nigeria's domestic politics meant that steady support from Nigeria could no longer be guaranteed. The RUF and AFRC were able to take advantage of the apparent vacuum, and from late 1998 the security situation deteriorated rapidly, unleashing a degree of human rights violations not previously witnessed in the country. This situation generated an unprecedented level of international attention and forced a reevaluation within the UN.

This chapter traces the events that compelled the UN to play a greater role in Sierra Leone and how the decision to scale up its engagement in Sierra Leone impacted the situation on the ground. What made the UN sit up and take action? How would that action be framed by regional dynamics? Would the Lomé Agreement offer a real chance for the UN to make a difference? And what would be the impact of Security Council decisions on the UN staff on the ground?

■ The Changing Regional Tide

As the dominant regional power, Nigeria has always been critical to the maintenance of peace and security in West Africa. Observers of West African politics agree that the prospect of an unmanaged crisis in Nigeria would pose a real danger for the entire subregion, as Karl Maier captured in his book *This House Has Fallen: Midnight in Nigeria*: "Designed by alien occupiers and abused by army rule for three quarters of its brief life

29

span, the Nigerian state is like a battered and bruised elephant staggering toward the abyss with the ground crumbling under its feet. Should it fall, the impact will shake the rest of West Africa."[1] In the late 1990s, Nigeria's unstable political environment thus had real crisis potential. In 1998, domestic politics in Nigeria entered a period of uncertainty with the sudden death of Nigeria's strongman General Sani Abacha in June,[2] and one month later, that of Moshood Abiola, the presumed winner of the June 1993 presidential election.

Nigeria had been steadily inching toward crisis and instability since 12 June 1993, when President Ibrahim Babangida annulled the results of presidential elections deemed to have been won by Abiola. In the face of civil unrest, Babangida resigned and handed over power to an interim government in August, which was edged out of power three months later in a quiet military takeover by Abacha. A day before the first anniversary of the annulled elections, Abiola made claims that he was cheated of his rightful place as elected president of Nigeria, which led to his arrest on 23 June 1994. He was scheduled to be released within days of his unexpected death on 7 July 1998.[3]

Under Abacha's leadership from 1993 to 1998, Nigeria continued to support the ECOMOG operations in Liberia and Sierra Leone, gaining international legitimacy for the regime even as human rights abuses continued to be committed in Nigeria itself. While the Liberia mission was inherited from his predecessor, General Babangida, Abacha made Sierra Leone his pet project. Indeed, Nigeria single-handedly bankrolled the Liberia and Sierra Leone operations, with the exception of a short stint of external support for the so-called "extended ECOMOG," which included one battalion each from Uganda and Tanzania between 1993 and 1994.

During this period, the irony of a military dictator in Nigeria championing the cause of democracy in Sierra Leone was clear for all to see. Yet it seemed acceptable to the world community that Abacha was prepared to commit human and financial resources to a noble cause, whatever his real motives. Leaders of democratic states could not embark on intervention in Sierra Leone, for fear of having to justify "body bags" to their electorates. In contrast, the military regime in Nigeria was prepared for such eventualities and offered Nigerians no explanation or justification for the thousands of Nigerian soldiers sacrificed in Liberia and Sierra Leone. Thus a pariah government could be a hero abroad.

Hence, the deaths of Abacha and Abiola not only created panic and a vacuum in Nigerian politics, but also altered the political rhythm in the subregion. While Nigerians at home and abroad rejoiced at the news of Abacha's sudden death, Sierra Leone was the only country where his death was publicly mourned. Many Sierra Leoneans wept for him, and today a street in Freetown immortalizes his name.

As feared, in 1998 the military operation in Sierra Leone no longer occupied pride of place in the considerations of a new Nigerian leadership seeking to avert a national crisis. An interim military government under Abdusalam Abubakar was unable to commit the same level of support to Sierra Leone. From here, things would go downhill for the ECOMOG mission in the country, as the force, which had already weathered many storms, began to show even more strain. The extent of the crisis was not apparent to all, however. Ahmad Tejan Kabbah's government continued to cling to every promise made by ECOMOG commanders, even as the tide was clearly changing.

◾ A Downward Spiral of Horror

As the rebels continued to operate in the countryside in 1998, Sierra Leoneans remained confident that ECOMOG would eventually crush them. In May, one month before Abacha's death, Maxwell Khobe, the brigadier-general and defense chief who had headed the ECOMOG task force during the recapture of Freetown in February, was likewise optimistic, expecting that additional troops would soon be deployed by Nigeria in order to maintain the momentum. During an ECOWAS regional forum in Ouagadougou, he said:

> We envisage to conclude the war soon despite the difficulties
> of terrain and logistics that we are faced with. Presently, we
> have been able to restore peace, law and order in more than 80
> percent of the country. The remnants of AFRC/RUF regime
> are still taking advantage of the unfavourable terrain and its
> imposed delay on our advance to inflict unimaginable cruelty
> on innocent civilian populations. But time and international
> opinion are against them. We have taken the war to their last
> frontier and will soon bring them to justice.[4]

General Khobe had requested two additional battalions following the defeat of the junta in Freetown. But this request was not honored during his tenure as commander of the ECOMOG task force. By this point, the Nigerian public was appalled by the resources expended on war in Sierra Leone, and previously in Liberia, when millions of Nigerians did not have access to clean water and endured nights of darkness for months at a time for lack of state capacity to generate electricity efficiently. ECOMOG's commanders could no longer rely on an ever-flowing supply of funds from home.

By December 1998, there were rumors that the rebel alliance was regrouping and heading for Freetown. Wary not to increase public anxiety, all key actors—the UN, ECOMOG, and the government alike—dispelled these rumors. A press release on 26 December by the Sierra Leone Ministry of Information stated:

> Government wishes to reiterate that the security situation in the country is firmly under the control of ECOMOG and the other security forces. As far as Government is concerned, we remain faithful to the position adopted by the United Nations Security Council with respect to the conflict in Sierra Leone, which is to simultaneously pursue the military option and dialogue. . . . Contrary to reports by the BBC, RFI and other media institutions, Makeni town is in the hands of ECOMOG, although there are continuing rebel attacks on the township. . . . Government also would like to express its grave concern at the manner in which the crisis in Sierra Leone is being aggravated by inaccurate reporting of the events taking place by some international media houses. It is unfortunate that some of them are allowing themselves to be used as tools in the propaganda machinery of the rebels.[5]

The government had little choice but to remain optimistic about ECOMOG. Meanwhile, UNOMSIL took steps to exit quietly. As rumors of advancing rebels were publicly discounted, the UN made the necessary arrangements to take staff and military observers from Bo and Kenema and to relocate them closer to Lungi and Freetown. Then, on 24 December 1998, UNOMSIL began making plans to evacuate nonessential staff from Sierra Leone. The same day, a BBC radio broadcast stated that UNOMSIL had pulled out entirely. UNOMSIL responded with a press release denying that this was the case, but the movement of nonessential staff was a clear sign that security was indeed deteriorating.

In January 1999, the Sierra Leone conflict reached a new level of infamy, alongside the conflicts in Liberia, Somalia, and Rwanda. The rumors of a rebel advance were confirmed by the brutal entry of AFRC and RUF fighters into Freetown on 6 January. There was pandemonium in the capital as the rebels overwhelmed the city and the ECOMOG force.

Within days, rebels had killed hundreds of West African troops, most of them Nigerian. The Nigerian press was full of stories about body bags being flown home, with at least 700 killed in January alone.[6] The most barbaric methods of killing were flaunted. The rebels displayed the body parts of Nigerian soldiers at road blocks, in some cases using victims' intestines as demarcation lines.[7] Innocent Sierra Leoneans were raped, molested, and mutilated during the war's most intense period of human rights abuses, and more than 2,500 children were abducted from Freetown and taken hostage in RUF bases in the countryside.[8] One of the youngest victims of the rebel atrocity, Abu Sesay, was two months old when his mother fled to escape a rebel soldier. Unable to catch his mother, the soldier returned to the crying child and chopped off his left foot.[9] Termed "Operation No Living Thing" by the rebels, the offensive in January left 5,000 dead in its wake.

Especially with the interim government in Nigeria preoccupied with elections to usher in a new civilian regime, ECOMOG could not save the day. It was suffering from what General Khobe diplomatically referred to as a "command structure problem,"[10] involving a leadership split that undermined serious preparations for the rebel advance. ECOMOG had six battalions on the ground in January 1999, but they were not judiciously employed. Troops were placed on the outskirts of Freetown, in Lungi, Jui, and Allen Town, rather than in the city itself, and when the crisis loomed, they were sent even farther out, to Hastings and Waterloo. The commanders in these different places were not all aware of each other's presence, resulting in a lack of communication.

In the end, the bulk of the ECOMOG troops were bypassed by the rebels as they advanced on Freetown, and the rest were encircled. Meanwhile, many of the AFRC and RUF members had been spotted in the city days before the attack. They were mingling casually among the people, having hidden their weapons on the outskirts of the city. It was only a matter of time before they would regroup and wreak maximum havoc on Freetown.

President Kabbah's government again went into hiding as the rebels unleashed their brutal attack. The UN also departed from the scene; most of the UN's military observers were evacuated, and a small number moved to Guinea with SRSG Okelo, who was in regular touch with Kabbah's government in exile. But Sierra Leone's civil society once again rose to the occasion. ECOMOG began to fight back, relying on civil society groups and activists to provide much-needed intelligence on the identity and location of known rebel members. Those present in Freetown during that period recounted how ordinary Sierra Leoneans offered assistance to ECOMOG, showing them routes and known rebel hideouts.

When ECOMOG began its counteroffensive, it did so with a mercilessness that at times matched that of the rebels. The rebels had killed and mutilated many of their comrades with fervor, and now they retaliated, smoking rebels out of their hideouts with a sense of purpose. Suspected rebels were tortured and summarily executed. The Civil Defense Forces and the Sierra Leone Police were likewise accused of such grave violations of human rights.[11] In one incident on 13 January, ECOMOG and the CDF summarily executed twenty-two suspected rebels, and disposed of their bodies by tossing them off Aberdeen Bridge in Freetown.[12]

As ECOMOG and the CDF pursued the rebels, innocent civilians were affected. ECOMOG's method of warfare—including the use of jet fighters and cluster bombs within city limits—resulted in significant civilian casualties and destruction of property, generating great agitation within the humanitarian community. Yet there was sympathy for such tactics in some quarters of the population and government, and even in UN circles the behavior of ECOMOG and the CDF was largely blamed on RUF provocation. Nonetheless, UNOMSIL made inquiries and ECOMOG reported that many of the accused soldiers had been disciplined.

■ The Road to Lomé

In the aftermath of January 1999, it was clear that the UN's token presence had been too little to make a difference. Dependence on regional troops for the protection of UN military observers had left UNOMSIL with little choice but to evacuate its observers and staff to Conakry. Given the changed political climate, it also seemed unrealistic to expect a Nigerian-led ECOMOG to deliver a military victory against the RUF and the AFRC in the future, since this would require a military and logistical capability that ECOMOG lacked. Before the January crisis, ECOWAS had been by far the most prominent external actor in Sierra Leone. Now it was obvious that the United Nations would have to step up its role.

The UN Security Council issued a presidential statement on 7 January 1999, condemning the attacks that began in Freetown the previous day.[13] On 12 January, the Council adopted Resolution 1220, extending the mandate of UNOMSIL until 13 March 1999. The number of military observers in UNOMSIL was reduced, as they could not conceivably operate in Sierra Leone at the time, but a small number were retained in Conakry with the aim of redeploying to Sierra Leone when the security conditions were right.[14] By March 1999, plans had been made to reestablish UNOMSIL in Freetown.[15]

Meanwhile, pressure mounted on Kabbah from all sides to negotiate with the rebels. ECOMOG troop contributors, including Ghana and Guinea, could no longer sustain the campaign against the rebels, and urged the president to pursue dialogue. In Nigeria, newly elected president Olusegun Obasanjo was under considerable domestic pressure and warned that failure to make a deal would lead to Nigerian withdrawal. Likewise, the United Kingdom and the United States, as permanent members of the Security Council and supporters of the government and ECOMOG, were embarrassed by the events of 6 January,[16] and a dialogue with the rebels seemed the best option to them. Finally, many Sierra Leoneans also urged dialogue, whether or not they were rebel sympathizers.

Such pressure was indicative of the impact of the January 1999 attack. Ordinary Sierra Leoneans were demoralized and wanted an end to the war, as did the states that were committing soldiers and money to Sierra Leone's defense, with no end in sight. There could have been only one result. Kabbah's government bowed to the pressures and found its way to the negotiating table with the RUF. But in order to retain some leverage over the rebels, Kabbah needed to ensure that he still had a military option to use against them. He proposed a dual-track approach, involving on the one hand strengthening ECOMOG to counter rebel threats and on the other hand pursuing a dialogue with the RUF and the AFRC.

Following a diplomatic tour by Kabbah in West Africa, during which he tested the pulse of regional leaders and sought their continued support, a cease-fire agreement between Kabbah and Sankoh was signed on 18 May 1999 in Lomé, Togo, facilitated by SRSG Okelo. The cease-fire opened the way for a full dialogue between Kabbah's government and the rebels, and Okelo, in consultation with West African leaders, began talks with a view to establishing this dialogue. Although the UN was only one of many actors, it played a role in both the intra-RUF dialogue and the government-RUF dialogue that followed. In addition to the SRSG's diplomatic role, the mission provided valuable logistical support, transporting Sankoh from Sierra Leone to Lomé on 18 April, and fourteen other members of the RUF to Lomé via Liberia. The UN would later be saddled with the hotel bills incurred by RUF members present in Togo for the peace talks; ironically, an organization able to finance a war was not able to pay the relatively meager costs of peace.

The Lomé peace talks took place between 25 May and 7 July 1999, hosted by ECOWAS chairman and Togolese president Gnassingbe Eyadema. The negotiating process was directed by a facilitation committee under the chairmanship of Togolese foreign minister Joseph Koffigoh, who was assisted by Okelo, and comprising representatives of the OAU, the UN, ECOWAS, and the Commonwealth of Nations.[17] The Sierra Leone parliament and civil society groups also participated actively in the process. The Inter-Religious Council of Sierra Leone was included in a "Council of Elders and Religious Leaders" charged with the task of mediating any "conflicting differences of interpretation" between the RUF and the Sierra Leone government in the future.[18] The council had played a prominent role previously, making spirited efforts to bring the parties together.

On 29 May 1999, the government of Sierra Leone and the RUF reached an agreement about the status of Foday Sankoh, who was in the middle of his appeal against a death sentence for treason. Under the arrangement, Sankoh was granted an absolute and free pardon and "judicial leave" to proceed to Lomé, in return for which he agreed for his delegation to proceed with the dialogue. On 2 June, in line with the cease-fire agreement, Kabbah's government and the RUF sought UNOMSIL assistance to establish a committee chaired by the UN's chief military observer, to ensure the release of prisoners of war and noncombatants.[19] As well as ensuring the development of a distinct role for the UN, this signified that talks were well and truly under way.

The RUF's own internal consultation process, between 26 April and 10 May 1999, resulted in a position paper in which several key requests were made. The RUF demanded blanket amnesty for the organizers of the May 1997 coup, a four-year transitional government that would oversee the drafting of a new constitution, restructuring of the security institutions, supervision of a disarmament and demobilization program, and preparation for elections. For its part, the RUF would transform itself into a political party. The government saw the demand for a transitional government as unconstitutional, but seemed ready to consider the call for amnesty and welcomed the proposal to transform the RUF.[20]

The RUF also requested a neutral force to monitor the peace, and through this an end to the presence of all foreign troops and mercenaries. In particular, this would entail the termination of the status-of-forces agreement between the governments of Sierra Leone and Nigeria.[21] Nigeria's presence, often synonymous with ECOMOG, had twice prevented the rebels from gaining and holding on to power, and the rebels had a healthy fear of Nigerian soldiers, a fact that was not lost on the UN and the rest of the international community.

Indeed, the peace negotiations in Lomé owed much to ECOMOG's continued containment of the rebels in the months leading up to the signing of the peace agreement. After January 1999, the rebels remained present in virtually all of Sierra Leone except Freetown, with the result that humanitarian agencies had no access to much of the country. When Major-General Felix Mujakperuo assumed command of ECOMOG in March 1999, the force launched an offensive aimed at providing greater security cover for Freetown and Lungi. As a result, some major roads and supply routes became accessible, opening up connections all the way to Port Loko and Kambia. Likewise, the clearing of a secondary road from Freetown to Moyamba and Bo opened

ECOMOG units patrol streets devastated by civil war and riots in Freetown, February 1999.
© Patrick Robert/Sygma/CORBIS

up access and supply lines for Bo and Kenema.[22] Each success meant access to communities in need of humanitarian assistance.

The odds of an accord being signed in Lomé were favorable. With neither side ensured a military victory, both were willing to make concessions. The RUF and the AFRC knew that with ECOMOG weakened, they had their best shot at a favorable political deal. Negotiating peace was also the best option for those awaiting execution in jail. Meanwhile, for Kabbah and his government, there was no guarantee that the rebels could ever be defeated on the battlefield, meaning possibly years of stalemate. The government, having essentially no presence or authority in the countryside, where the rebels continued to roam, needed significant help to pacify Sierra Leone. But with ECOMOG severely weakened and powerful states such as the United Kingdom and the United States not willing to fight a war of attrition on Sierra Leone's behalf, the government had little option but to negotiate.

▌ Stoking the Fire from Liberia

At the same time that diplomatic efforts were being sought for ending the Sierra Leone war, Taylor's support for the RUF from across the border continued, with a steady flow of arms from Liberia and Burkina Faso to the RUF. ECOMOG's Force Commander, Major-General Mujakperuo, confirmed reports that the governments of Liberia and Burkina Faso were involved in the shipment of arms to the rebels,[23] and threatened to launch air strikes into both countries if they did not stop the flow.[24] As the government kept to its dual-track approach of strengthening ECOMOG while pursuing negotiations, external support for the rebels from Liberia did not quite stop.

The continued supply of arms strengthened the position of the RUF and the AFRC, creating more difficulties for ECOMOG. Rebels maintained control over the Northern and Eastern provinces and moved freely through much of the Western Area and the Southern province, retaining the ability to restrict ECOMOG's lines of communication. The rebels also controlled the mining areas in Kono, and the arms supplies and technical support provided from outside greatly strengthened their antiaircraft capabilities. Even after the signing of the cease-fire, violations occurred on both sides. Rebel raids continued, albeit with less frequency. Remnants of the former SLA congregated between Occra Hills and Port Loko, where they posed a threat to the route from Port Loko to Rogberi to Lungi.[25]

The UN Secretary-General, on instruction from the Security Council, consulted ECOWAS about the possibility of deploying ECOMOG troops along the border between Sierra Leone and Liberia, to reduce the tensions brewing as a result of the arms supply allegations. But while ECOWAS troop-contributing countries welcomed the proposal, they requested logistical support from the UN, including equipment, helicopters, communications equipment, and ground transportation, given the difficult terrain. This process stalled and was later overshadowed by the Lomé Agreement.[26]

Meanwhile, the period after the 6 January 1999 rebel incursion saw increased international condemnation of Taylor's role, as his assistance to the RUF became an irritation for even his supporters in the United States. Taylor's connections in the Congressional Black Caucus in the United States were utilized to full effect in the effort to obtain US backing for negotiations with the RUF. Yet the Bill Clinton administration could not turn a blind eye to reports of Taylor's obstruction of the Sierra Leone peace process, as credible evidence of his support for the RUF surfaced. In 1999, both the United States and the United Kingdom became more vocal in criticizing Taylor's actions.

■ Lomé: The United Nations Prepares for Center Stage

In June 1999, the Secretary-General made known his intentions to propose an expanded role for UNOMSIL if negotiations between the Sierra Leone government and the rebels in Lomé were successful.[27] In Resolution 1245 of 11 June, the Security Council encouraged the peacemaking process and acknowledged the possibility of an expanded role in the event of such an outcome.[28] Supporting the reconciliation process now gave the UN a meaningful role in Sierra Leone.

In line with the Secretary-General's intentions, a military and planning assessment team was sent to Sierra Leone as early as May 1999 to "develop a revised concept of operations for a possible enlargement" of UNOMSIL.[29] Although the negotiations were still ongoing, it was already envisaged that an expanded UNOMSIL would need to provide active support in the implementation of any peace plan concluded in Lomé. The UN would be expected to provide security for vital areas of Sierra Leone, and for this it would need more than unarmed military observers; the force would need to be armed.

As expected, a peace agreement was signed in Lomé on 7 July 1999 and became the basis for an expanded UN presence. It was the first comprehensive agreement on Sierra Leone, even if it was an uncomfortable deal for many, including Kabbah's government, its defenders in ECOMOG, and much of the Sierra Leonean population. The Lomé Agreement offered to pardon Sankoh and top RUF leaders of previous sins, and it brought them into the heart of government in a power-sharing arrangement. Sankoh was made chairman of the Strategic Mineral Resources Commission and accorded the status of vice president, a decision described by one observer of the peace agreement as "putting the fox in charge of a chicken coop,"[30] and by another as "asking a hyena to guard a slaughter house."[31] The AFRC was initially excluded from the agreement as well as negotiations, and disturbances by the junta group continued in the aftermath. Largely in response to the AFRC's demands for inclusion, Koroma was drafted into a power-sharing arrangement in October and made chairman of the Commission for the Consolidation of Peace,[32] which was established under the Abidjan Agreement in 1996.

Although peace was welcomed, many Sierra Leoneans saw the power-sharing agreement as a setback, if not a humiliation, for the government, and chastised Kabbah for succumbing to the wishes of the rebels. They accused the UN of brokering a deal with Sierra Leone's worst enemies and felt that Kabbah had been stampeded by some of his supposed friends and allies into signing the Lomé Agreement. In his book *Conflict and Collusion in Sierra Leone*, David Keen aptly captures the tying of Kabbah's hands by his friends in the international community, citing a Sierra Leonean journalist's account of the moments leading up to Lomé: "Kabbah went to Accra for a meeting of the Afro-American group. US Ambassador Melrose, Okelo, Jesse Jackson were all there. Jackson and

Melrose said 'Come, let's go and talk to Sankoh.' I like to say they 'kidnapped Kabbah.' They took him to Sankoh's hotel in Lomé, and made him sign. There was no threat to Freetown at that time."[33]

Many Sierra Leoneans were also angered by the actions of Jesse Jackson, the US presidential envoy in Sierra Leone, who made controversial comments on 12 May 2000 comparing the RUF to Nelson Mandela's African National Congress (ANC). Given Jackson's long-standing relationship with Charles Taylor, his remarks were particularly ill-advised and caused widespread condemnation among West African leaders.[34] Although Okelo fared slightly better, active members of civil society tended to recall in private conversation that he helped to deliver them to the RUF.

For the UN, one part of the Lomé Agreement that was difficult to accept was the amnesty clause. The fight against impunity, as reflected in the International Criminal Tribunals for the former Yugoslavia and Rwanda, had become a pattern of UN response. In addition, the organization could not ignore pressure from human rights organizations such as Human Rights Watch and Amnesty International. But SRSG Okelo was forced to concede to decisions made collectively. In addition to President Kabbah and Foday Sankoh, Okelo was only one of ten other signatories to the Lomé Agreement, and the UN could not obstruct the only real hope for a peace that had so many stakeholders.[35]

However, it was important for the UN that its position on the amnesty be made clear. On instructions from New York, SRSG Okelo attached a handwritten note to the Lomé Agreement stating that crimes against humanity, acts of genocide, war crimes, and other grave violations of human rights were excluded from the amnesty, in the UN's understanding. Secretary-General Kofi Annan reported back to the Security Council that the agreement had only been signed by Okelo with this "explicit proviso."[36] The handwritten note is not included in official publications of the agreement. But its inclusion effectively untied the hands of the international community, leaving the door wide open for international actors to wield a big stick should the rebels go back on their word. It turned out to be a saving grace and enabled the establishment of a Special Court in the years ahead.[37]

In this atmosphere of divided views and uncertain hopes, the job of implementing the Lomé Agreement began in earnest, with the UN emerging at center stage. The text of the agreement implied that external support would be required in order to facilitate its implementation. It made provision for adjustments to the mandates of both UNOMSIL and ECOMOG in order to provide security and to support the disarmament, demobilization, and reintegration (DDR) of former combatants. Within several months, the

UN mission would expand rapidly, from a meager twenty-four military observers, twenty-nine international staff, and twenty-four national staff in June 1999,[38] to more than six infantry battalions, a total of 6,000 troops.

■ Stepping Up the Game

Following the signing of the Lomé Agreement, the first step toward scaling up UN peacekeeping efforts in Sierra Leone came in Security Council Resolution 1260 of 20 August 1999, which authorized the expansion of UNOMSIL to include up to 210 military observers and the strengthening of the political, information, civil affairs, human rights, and child protection functions of the mission.[39] Then, on 22 October, the Security Council decided, in Resolution 1270, to establish a peacekeeping mission, the United Nations Mission in Sierra Leone (UNAMSIL), while terminating UNOMSIL and subsuming its observer functions within the new mandate.[40]

Unlike its predecessor, UNAMSIL was to comprise armed troops, to be deployed to locations throughout the country. As a peacekeeping force, rather than an observer mission, its mandate was much broader and included, among other things, the following specific tasks:

(a) To cooperate with the Government of Sierra Leone and the other parties to the Peace Agreement in the implementation of the Agreement; (b) to assist the Government of Sierra Leone in the implementation of the disarmament, demobilization and reintegration plan; (c) to that end, to establish a presence at key locations throughout the territory of Sierra Leone, including at disarmament/reception centers and demobilization centers; (d) to ensure the security and freedom of movement of United Nations personnel; (e) to monitor adherence to the cease-fire in accordance with the cease-fire agreement of 18 May 1999 (S/1999/585, annex) through the structures provided for therein; (f) to encourage the parties to create confidence-building mechanisms and support their functioning; (g) to facilitate the delivery of humanitarian assistance; (h) to support the operations of United Nations civilian officials, including the Special Representative of the Secretary-General and his staff, human rights officers and civil affairs officers; (i) to provide support, as requested, to the elections, which are to be held in accordance with the present constitution of Sierra Leone.[41]

The resolution envisaged that the force would coexist with ECOMOG, which was providing security for the Western area, particularly Freetown and Lungi, but was not deployed in rebel-controlled territories. The resolution was based on what was thought to be an established understanding between the UN and ECOMOG, with the Security Council commending what it saw as ECOMOG's readiness to "continue to provide security for the areas where it is currently located, in particular around Freetown and Lungi, to provide protection for the Government of Sierra Leone, to conduct other operations in accordance with their mandate to ensure the implementation of the Peace Agreement, and to initiate and proceed with disarmament and demobilization in conjunction and full coordination with UNAMSIL."[42] The Council stressed the need for "close cooperation and coordination between ECOMOG and UNAMSIL in carrying out their respective tasks" including through the "establishment of joint operations centers at headquarters and, if necessary, also at subordinate levels in the field."[43]

With the level of collaboration envisaged between UNAMSIL and ECOMOG, the latter of which already had approximately 13,000 troops in Sierra Leone,[44] the Council's authorization of not more than 6,000 military personnel, including 260 military observers, seemed appropriate.[45] After all, UNAMSIL's mandate was based entirely on a comprehensive agreement that outlined the process leading to lasting peace. It seemed reasonable to expect a smoothly running operation, conducted under relatively peaceful conditions, notwithstanding occasional violations of the cease-fire.

But UNAMSIL was authorized to use deadly force if needed. A distinction is often drawn between consent-based "peacekeeping missions" established under Chapter VI of the UN Charter and coercive "peace enforcement" missions under Chapter VII, the latter involving the robust use of force as an integral part of the mission. The distinction is slightly misleading because there is little doubt, for example, that missions operating under Chapter VI have the right to use force in self-defense, including defense of the mission. However, Resolution 1270 clearly equipped UNAMSIL with Chapter VII powers, recognizing that even in seemingly benign environments, the UN must have a robust mandate to tackle potential spoilers. In addition, UNAMSIL was authorized to use force not only for the protection of UN personnel but also "to afford protection to civilians under imminent threat of physical violence."[46] It thereby became the first UN force to have the protection of civilians explicitly included in its mandate.

▇ The United Nations Alone

But even before the Security Council's adoption of Resolution 1270, there were signs that ECOMOG would not remain in Sierra Leone for long. In

Nigerian president
Olusegun Obasanjo at
UN headquarters, 2003.
UN Photo/Evan Schneider

preparing for an expanded role for UNOMSIL, Secretary-General Kofi Annan wrote to President Obasanjo in August 1999, proposing a division of labor between ECOMOG and the UN. He suggested that UNOMSIL would include infantry battalions and provide security for its areas just as ECOMOG was doing. In his response, President Obasanjo notified the Secretary-General of his intentions to withdraw 2,000 Nigerian troops each month from the end of August 1999, with the last batch leaving at the end of December.[47] This effectively meant the full withdrawal of ECOMOG, given that Nigeria contributed more than 90 percent of the force.[48]

Why did Nigeria decide to withdraw its troops so suddenly when ECOMOG's mandate had just been revised and renewed in the Lomé Agreement a month before?[49] The fact is that the decision by the UN to deploy infantry battalions in Sierra Leone was not well received by West African leaders, particularly in Nigeria. It was interpreted as signaling a lack of appreciation for the role played by ECOWAS and particularly Nigeria. In addition, the proposal for an expanded UN role provided President Obasanjo with a way out, since he had made an election promise to withdraw Nigerian troops. Nonetheless, following several conversations with the UN Secretariat, Nigeria was persuaded to hold off on the withdrawal, and this was the basis upon which the Secretary-General proceeded to propose the concept of operations for an expanded UN force.

Recognizing the central role of Nigeria in the subregion, the UN Secretariat appointed a Nigerian, Oluyemi Adeniji, as SRSG and head of UNAMSIL, in November 1999.[50] As well as placating Nigeria, the appointment replaced Okelo, whose position had become compromised by the perception in Sierra Leone that he had helped to orchestrate Kabbah's signing of the Lomé Agreement. Adeniji was a retired diplomat who had most recently been SRSG in the United Nations Mission in the Central African Republic (MINUCA). Some of those who worked with him there remember him as charming and talented; others remember him as aloof and quietly resolute, to the point of intransigence.

Meanwhile, there was some hope that the continued presence of Nigerian troops in Sierra Leone could be justified to the Nigerian public if the bulk of ECOMOG costs could be transferred to the UN or external donors. The support from Canada, the Netherlands, the United Kingdom, and the United States was meager in comparison to support from Nigeria, which had spent in excess of US$4 billion on operations in Liberia and Sierra Leone, and was reportedly spending US$1 million per day in Sierra Leone. Nigeria did request that the UN take over the cost of ECOMOG troops and, until December 1999, held out hope that either the United Nations or the United States might foot the bill. Obasanjo also expressed concern to the UN about the possibility of two sharply contrasting standards in Sierra Leone: a well-funded, well-equipped, and well-paid UN force operating alongside a poorly equipped and underfunded regional force.[51]

But Obasanjo's expectation did not take into consideration the US domestic environment at the time, which was hardly favorable to UN peacekeeping. A dramatic change of policy in the United States toward UN peacekeeping would later occur during Richard Holbrooke's term as US Permanent Representative to the United Nations, yielding handsome dividends for the UN in Sierra Leone. But it did not happen soon enough for Nigeria. Following a visit to Nigeria by Madeleine Albright in December 1999, it became clear that the United States was not going to pay for Nigerian troops. The only realistic option for Nigeria was to withdraw its troops, which it announced in December 1999. This had major repercussions for the UN, where, following the Security Council's authorization of UNAMSIL in October, preparations were already under way for a mission that would deploy alongside ECOMOG.

Despite this blow, a UN takeover of the peacekeeping effort in Sierra Leone actually seemed the best option to many. First, any objective observer would admit that ECOMOG, especially its Nigerian contingents, was exhausted. Many soldiers had been on the Liberia and Sierra Leone peacekeeping and enforcement circuit since the Liberia mission began in 1990; and due to a lack of resources, they enjoyed only brief periods of respite at home. Certain problems inherent to the mission, particularly logistical difficulties, also had a huge impact. It was no wonder these frustrated soldiers had mood swings at checkpoints.

Second, the lack of rotation meant that many soldiers had seen friends and comrades mercilessly killed by rebel soldiers in January 1999. Asking these same soldiers to assume a conciliatory mood toward the former rebels, and a friendly posture while implementing the Lomé Agreement, may have been asking for the impossible. As a Nigerian battalion commander who was serving with ECOMOG remarked: "A human being is not a machine to switch automatically from peace enforcement to peacekeeping. The element of aggression lingers on for sometime. Reflex action too continues to make soldiers overreact. Human defensive nature keeps soldiers on the path of war even in a peacekeeping role."[52] A UN deployment without an ECOMOG presence would mean fresh troops who did not regard the rebels as old enemies and who would therefore aggravate them less. There was a potential downside, however; as Targema Takema, a Nigerian diplomat in Liberia, once said: "those who did not participate in winning the peace are likely to be reckless with it."[53]

The third reason a UN takeover was attractive concerned the image and credibility of the UN itself. Whereas in 1998, UN member states hoped to rely on regional peacekeeping, by 1999, regional actors were taking far bolder steps than the UN and exposing the international community's lack of political will. With the exception of East Timor, Bosnia, and Kosovo, the UN was deploying only small observer forces to the world's conflict hotspots, and even in Kosovo and Bosnia it was perceived to be the junior partner, compared to NATO's more robust stance. In Liberia, ECOMOG had conducted a seemingly successful mission (although the peace of 1993 had eventually unraveled), whereas the UN had only established an observer mission. Resolution 1270 offered a hope of reversing that trend.

In the calculations of UN planners, the agreement signed in Lomé offered a real opportunity to preside over a stable peace. The RUF-AFRC alliance seemed reasonably satisfied, even if a little too triumphant, with the power-sharing agreement and the prospect of a neutral monitoring force. Surely then, the rebels would abide by the terms of the Lomé Agreement. And even if ECOMOG had traditionally brought a more forceful approach, the Security Council had empowered UNAMSIL to use force if and when it became necessary. All the UN needed was sufficient time to deploy troops to take over from ECOMOG.

In the end, negotiations with Nigeria resulted in the retention of two Nigerian battalions in Sierra Leone, to be "rehatted" as part of the new UNAMSIL mission. Some Nigerians recall, however, that the UN agreed to this with some reluctance. While some argued that the involvement of troops from the region would bring in much-needed institutional memory and a healthy dose of fear, there were fears that Nigerian troops carried "baggage." UNAMSIL's Force Commander, Major-General Vijay Jetley, expressed concern that some of these troops had not been rotated for more than two years, and that the involvement of ECOMOG troops risked giving Sierra Leoneans the impression that nothing had changed.

In addition, the inclusion of troops from the region was seen as problematic within parts of the international community. UN rules precluded the use of troops from neighboring countries; this was deeply problematic for Guinea, which was part of ECOMOG but wanted its troops rehatted into UNAMSIL. Disappointed, Guinea sent a high-level delegation to New York to lobby. It was offered the opportunity to deploy a company-sized force, and later, following negotiations with Nigeria, a battalion-sized force, as part of UNAMSIL.

■ Realities on the Ground

The UN's optimism that it could manage without ECOMOG was not shared by those who understood the character of West African rebel groups. Not only would the UN have to maintain security in the areas currently under ECOMOG control, but it would also have to move troops into rebel strongholds in the Northern and Eastern provinces. Liberia had aptly demonstrated that rebels could seize every opportunity to test the resolve and commitment of peacekeepers to the limit. As General Maxwell Khobe said of his experiences there: "Rebels will ever be rebels. Even though they sign documents one hundred times, they can always renege on such accords."[54]

For this reason, ECOMOG commanders like Khobe often argued for robust mandates regardless of the comprehensiveness of a peace agreement and for a force of significant size.[55] UNAMSIL did not lack a robust mandate, but the plan for equipping the force also envisaged the necessary support to back up this mandate, including provision for attack helicopters and a mobile support unit. Unfortunately, negotiations with the countries that would provide this support stalled, and so the necessary equipment was not on the ground when UNAMSIL was deployed. Moreover, whereas ECOMOG troop strength once stood at 13,000, only 6,000 UN troops were deployed at the start.

On the ground in Sierra Leone, Nigerians seemed perturbed by the arrival of armed troops under a UN mandate alongside the regional force. Quite apart from the political discussions happening behind the scenes, certain psychological effects could be seen among the ECOMOG soldiers in the field. They were used to assuming full command of the terrain under their control, but things would be different now. The UN military observers and civilian staff could now rely on their own troops to protect them, such that ECOMOG soldiers were no longer "kings of the road."

Added to this, UN soldiers were arriving with better payment arrangements compared to the meager allowances of ECOMOG. More important, the countries contributing troops to UNAMSIL were seen to be getting a better deal under the UN's "wet lease" arrangement, under which troop-contributing countries were supposed to provide self-sustaining battalions and were reimbursed by the UN for both the troops and logistical support. African countries tend to sign "wet lease" agreements because the level of reimbursement is higher than for "dry lease" agreements, under which the UN provides logistical support. But in many cases, troop-contributing countries have been unable to provide the level of logistical support committed to. When troops in Sierra Leone started to complain about the level of support they had in the field, the UN had to remind the troop-contributing countries of their responsibility.

Meanwhile, ECOMOG's impending withdrawal led to a sense of panic within Sierra Leone's government and civil society alike. They were sure that the RUF would test UNAMSIL to its limits, and did not trust that the mission would be able to maintain security. Sierra Leoneans did not necessarily understand that Resolution 1270 provided Chapter VII coverage for the use of force against the rebels if the situation called for it, and only remembered times when the UN had evacuated its personnel at the first, slightest sign of escalating crisis or violence. The arrangement by which some ECOMOG troops were "rehatted" was not particularly reassuring for Sierra Leoneans, though it was better than nothing.

UNAMSIL began the first troop deployment (of 130 Kenyan troops) in late November 1999, just one month after the Security Council authorized it.[56] For many soldiers and civilians alike, this was their first UN mission, and more than this, their first time in such treacherous terrain. The rebels' reputation, established by international media reports of their campaign of terror, preceded them. Many would-be UNAMSIL peacekeepers, especially civilians, were inevitably apprehensive.

For Sheila Dallas, who was recruited to UNAMSIL, her first UN mission, to oversee radio programming for the mission's Public Information section, her first day on the job still stood out the most after six years in UNAMSIL, and was indicative of the environment at the time:

> I came in from Guinea Conakry on the WFP helicopter on 1 December 1999. There were soldiers on the ground. They were UN soldiers. As I came off the helicopter, someone shouted "run!" I started running through the bush, thinking about snakes as I tried to flee from danger. One of the soldiers ran after me. It took a while for me to realize that he was trying to get me to come back. When he yelled run, he was simply asking me to run in order to move away from the helicopter propeller!
>
> As we approached town, people's faces told the story. I never saw such despondency and poverty. People's faces showed toil and desperation.
>
> The following day, we went to the office. There were only two international staff in Public Information section. I came in to do Radio but there was no equipment yet. A new SRSG was coming in and Okelo was leaving. The offices at Pademba Road were containers. I had lunch at Crown Bakery on Pademba Road. Then suddenly, there were kids running and there was shooting. We were warned to stay indoors. The terrain was rough on top of which one had to contend with mosquitoes.[57]

Clearly, Freetown had no air of security to it. UNAMSIL personnel reporting for duty must have been keenly aware of the uncertainty and relative instability of the terrain in which they would be operating.

The way that UNAMSIL personnel, both civilian and military, trickled into Sierra Leone after the authorization of the mission was characteristic of most UN operations. The 6,000 approved troops arrived slowly, hampered as in other cases by the challenge of securing the necessary contribution commitments and support from UN member states. In February 2000, the Security Council augmented troop size to 11,100, to compensate for the now clearly envisioned departure of ECOMOG.[58] At the time of the final ECOMOG withdrawal, at the beginning of May 2000, UNAMSIL deployment had not reached this target number, though by then it was quite close. By 19 May, UNAMSIL had deployed 9,495 personnel in total.[59]

On the civilian side, only a handful of staff reported initially, serving as an advance party, coping with inadequate logistical support, and filling in the gaps until the full staffing complement was reached. But by April

2000, the mission had set up a more secure and spacious headquarters in the Mammy Yoko, a modestly renovated hotel in the Aberdeen area of Freetown. UNAMSIL occupied the top four floors, together with cabins constructed in the hotel compound, while the ground floor was still used as a hotel.

The UN had awoken to the need for deeper engagement in Sierra Leone. But its calculations were based on two key assumptions that would soon be tested. The first was that the RUF and the AFRC would abide by the terms of the Lomé Agreement and not unleash chaos. The second was that ECOMOG would be there to deal with potential challenges or, as its withdrawal became clearer, that the UN could address the situation on its own. By initially deploying less than half the number of troops that ECOMOG had on the ground, and slowly, the UN only exacerbated the mood of apprehension surrounding ECOMOG's departure. But inside the UN, few staffers anticipated the humiliation and rapid capitulation of UN troops that would result from these decisions, or the repercussions that would follow.

▌ Notes

1. See Karl Maier, *This House Has Fallen: Midnight in Nigeria* (New York: PublicAffairs, July 2000), p. 4.

2. Abacha allegedly died of a heart attack on the morning of 8 June 1998. However, the lack of an autopsy and conflicting reports of the details surrounding his death led some to suspect foul play. See "Abacha: He May Have Been Murdered," *The Observer*, 14 June 1998, p. 8; and Hirsch, *Sierra Leone*, p. 75.

3. Shortly after assuming power as head of the interim government, Abdusalam Abubakar promised the release of many of Nigeria's political prisoners. Though autopsy reports confirmed that Abiola had died of a heart attack, his family and others suspected that he had been poisoned. Extensive medical examinations by an international team of experts later ruled out any foul play, though supporters still held the military regime responsible, maintaining that Abiola's ill treatment in prison was to blame for his rapid decline. See "Abiola's Death Not Suspicious," *BBC World News*, August 12, 1998.

4. Interview with Brigadier-General Maxwell Khobe in London, January 2000. In April 1998, Kabbah appointed him Sierra Leone's defense chief and began facilitating the restructuring of the Sierra Leone Armed Forces. However, Khobe died suddenly in 2000.

5. Sierra Leone Ministry of Information, Communication, Tourism, and Culture, "Press Release," 26 December 1998, http://www.sierra-leone .org/gosl122698.html.

6. See "Nigeria: Denial Even in Death," *Africa News*, 27 January 1999; Tokunbo Fakeye, "Nigeria: Man Collapses Finding Son Among Dead," *Africa News*, 3 February 1999; and "Nigeria's Military Leader Expresses Hope of Peace in Sierra Leone," *Associated Press*, 6 February 1999.

7. See Tim Sullivan, "Nigeria's Painful War in Sierra Leone Becomes an Election Issue," *Associated Press*, 25 February 1999.

8. See Marcus Mabry, "War with No Rules," *Newsweek*, 29 March 1999, p. 44.

9. Account by Abu Sesay's mother during a meeting with civil society groups conducted by Olara Otunu, UN Special Representative of the Secretary-General for Children and Armed Conflict, in Sierra Leone, September 1999.

10. "Sierra Leone: 'Massive Recruitment' Under Way, Army Chief Says," *IRIN News*, 4 February 1999.

11. See Human Rights Watch, *Sierra Leone: Getting Away with Murder, Mutilation, Rape* (New York, July 1999).

12. Amnesty International, "Press Release," 25 January 1999, Amnesty International Index: AFR 51/03/99.

13. See "Statement by the President of the Security Council," UN Doc. S/PRST/1999/1, 7 January 1999.

14. See *UN Security Council Resolution 1220*, UN Doc. S/RES/1220, 12 January 1999.

15. See *UN Security Council Resolution 1231*, UN Doc. S/RES/1231, 11 March 1999.

16. See David Keen, *Conflict and Collusion in Sierra Leone* (Oxford: Currey, 2005), pp. 248–250.

17. See *Seventh Report of the Secretary-General on the United Nations Observer Mission in Sierra Leone*, UN Doc. S/1999/836, 30 July 1999.

18. *Lomé Peace Agreement*, art. VIII, sec. 1, UN Doc. S/1999/777, 7 July 1999 (see text of the Lomé Agreement in this volume).

19. See *Sixth Report of the Secretary-General on the United Nations Observer Mission in Sierra Leone*, UN Doc. S/1999/645, 4 June 1999.

20. Ibid.

21. Ibid.

22. Ibid.

23. Ibid.

24. See David Pratt, "Sierra Leone: The Forgotten Crisis," report to the Canadian minister of foreign affairs, 23 April 1999, http://www.sierra-leone.org/pratt042399.html.

25. Ibid.

26. Ibid.

27. Ibid.

28. See *UN Security Council Resolution 1245*, UN Doc. S/RES/1245, 11 June 1999.

29. See *Sixth Report of the Secretary-General on the United Nations Observer Mission in Sierra Leone*, UN Doc. S/1999/645, 4 June 1999.

30. Quotation from Lomé observer paraphrased in John L. Hirsch, "Sierra Leone," in David M. Malone, ed., *The UN Security Council: From Cold War to the 21st Century* (Boulder: Lynne Rienner, 2004), p. 527.

31. Focus-group discussion conducted by the author in Sierra Leone in 2003.

32. Keen, *Conflict and Collusion in Sierra Leone*, p. 256.

33. Ibid., p. 251.

34. Jackson's comments were made to reporters in Washington in anticipation of a crisis mission to West Africa to help secure the release of UN peacekeepers held hostage by the RUF. Specifically, he compared the RUF to the ANC during

its transition into peaceful politics, speaking positively of Foday Sankoh and suggesting that foreign aid to the RUF would help legitimize the rebel group as a
political party. Though he clarified his remarks on 16 May in a strong condemnation of Sankoh, Sierra Leonean outrage was still so prevalent that Jackson chose
to skip a stopover to the country during his visit to the region. See Osman Benk
Sankoh, "Sierra Leone; Jesse Jackson Says: RUF Is Like ANC," Africa News, 14
May 2000; and "Sierra Leone; Full Text of Jesse Jackson's Statement on Sierra
Leone," *Africa News*, 16 May 2000.

35. The additional nine signatories included the presidents of Togo, Burkina
Faso, Liberia, and Nigeria; high-level representatives of Ghana, Côte d'Ivoire,
ECOWAS, the OAU, and the Commonwealth of Nations.

36. See *Seventh Report of the Secretary-General.*

37. See *Fifth Report of the Secretary-General on the United Nations Mission
in Sierra Leone*, UN Doc. S/2000/751, 31 July 2000, p. 2; and *UN Security
Council Resolution 1315*, UN Doc. S/RES/1315, 14 August 2000 (see text of
Resolution 1315 in this volume).

38. Ibid.

39. See *UN Security Council Resolution 1260*, UN Doc. S/RES/1260, 20
August 1999.

40. See *UN Security Council Resolution 1270*, UN Doc. S/RES/1270, 22
October 1999 (see text of Resolution 1270 in this volume).

41. Ibid.

42. Ibid.

43. Ibid.

44. Figures provided to the author by ECOMOG headquarters in Freetown in
May 1999 put troops from Nigeria at 11,191, troops from Ghana, Guinea, and Mali
at 680, 600, and 427, respectively, and troops from Benin and Niger at one platoon
each.

45. This was to be subject to a periodic review of the situation on the ground
and the level of progress achieved in implementing the peace plan.

46. See *UN Security Council Resolution 1270.*

47. See *Eighth Report of the Secretary-General of the United Nations
Observer Mission in Sierra Leone*, UN Doc. S/1999/1003, 28 September 1999.

48. See Adekeye Adebajo, *Building Peace in West Africa: Liberia, Sierra
Leone, and Guinea-Bissau* (Boulder: Lynne Rienner, 2002).

49. See *Lomé Peace Agreement*, art. XIII.

50. See "Oluyemi Adeniji Appointed Secretary-General's Special
Representative for Sierra Leone," press release, UN Doc. SG/A/713, 19 November
1999.

51. Interview with a senior UN official in New York, March 2006.

52. Interview in Liberia, 1994. See also, 'Funmi Olonisakin, *Reinventing
Peacekeeping in Africa: Conceptual and Legal Issues in ECOMOG Operations*
(The Hague: Kluwer Law International, 2000), p. 163.

53. Interview with Targema Takema at the Nigerian embassy in Monrovia, July
1994.

54. Interview with Maxwell Khobe in Monrovia, Liberia, July 1994.

55. Ibid.

56. See *First Report of the United Nations Mission in Sierra Leone*, UN Doc.
S/1999/1223, 6 December 1999.

57. Interview with Sheila Dallas at UNAMSIL headquarters in Freetown, December 2005.

58. See *UN Security Council Resolution 1289*, UN Doc. S/RES/1289, 7 February 2000 (see text of Resolution 1289 in this volume).

59. See *Fourth Report of the Secretary-General on the United Nations Mission in Sierra Leone*, UN Doc. S/2000/455, 19 May 2000.

3 | UNAMSIL's Midnight Hour

FEW COULD HAVE IMAGINED the depths to which UNAM-SIL would sink upon ECOMOG's departure in May 2000, when nearly 500 UN peacekeepers were captured by the RUF, stripped of their weapons, and shown to be mere sitting ducks. The UN, whose very emblem once commanded respect among warlords, heroes, and villains alike, became the focus of their violence and the target of bitter anger and ridicule among the local population.

Sierra Leone was not the first conflict situation in which UN troops were severely tested. The telltale signs had been evident in Somalia nearly a decade earlier, and later in Cambodia and Rwanda. In several instances, similar accusations—weak mandate and poor troop strength—were leveled against the UN and seen to indicate its lack of willingness to take action against the tormentors of innocent populations.

This chapter recounts the events surrounding UNAMSIL's darkest days in April and May 2000, which called into question the integrity of the mission and threatened its collapse. Why had the UN so badly misread both the RUF and its own capacities? What would this mean for the credibility of the UN? And how could it recover its tarnished image?

Ironically, the scene that unfolded in Sierra Leone during May 2000 is seen by many within UN circles as a "necessary evil" that spurred the UN to do some serious soul-searching and to reinvent itself. It is, they argue, the single most important factor behind the upturn in UNAMSIL's fortunes and the resurgence of UN peacekeeping in the country, one whose implications far transcend the boundaries of Sierra Leone.

■ The RUF Undermines UNAMSIL

It was as though the rebels had carefully choreographed their actions. ECOMOG had barely departed the scene—the last of its troops left on 2

May 2000—when the rebels began to exhibit the very tendency that many had feared. Prior to this, several incidents had led to a gradual buildup of tensions, primarily involving not the RUF but former AFRC soldiers. On 28 April, there was a confrontation in Freetown between some former AFRC soldiers and ECOMOG troops from NiBatt-35 (a Nigerian battalion) over a stolen vehicle that belonged to ECOMOG but was in the possession of the renegade soldiers. When the ECOMOG soldiers attempted to recover the vehicle, a scuffle ensued that resulted in the death of one AFRC soldier.

The tension in Freetown that resulted from this incident indicated how fragile the security situation was. News of the scuffle traveled rapidly through the city, and for a few days the main story in the newspapers was ECOMOG's shooting of a former AFRC soldier. It was the sort of news that, if not carefully managed, could whip up sentiments against both ECOMOG and UNAMSIL, as confirmed by demonstrations in central Freetown by several former AFRC soldiers. But UNAMSIL managed to bring the situation under control before it escalated into a larger crisis, immediately deploying troops from another Nigerian battalion in UNAMSIL and a quick-reaction company.

Within days, the differences between the roles of the AFRC and the RUF would become clearer, the former characterized by the provocation of sporadic incidents and the latter seemingly more systematic in its destabilization campaign.[1] On 30 April 2000, two days after the incident in Freetown, UNAMSIL soldiers from NiBatt-2 were deployed to deal with armed banditry by AFRC soldiers along the road from Port Loko to Rogberi. They were rounded up and disarmed by rebels; the patrol's sergeant sustained serious injuries after being shot in the chest and the leg. On 1 May, one day before the ECOMOG High Command bid farewell to its Sierra Leonean counterparts and government officials, the RUF moved to the center of the anti-UNAMSIL campaign and attacks on UNAMSIL personnel intensified and steadily gained momentum.

Earlier, there had been worrying signs as the establishment of DDR camps, as per the Lomé Agreement, forced the RUF to show its hand. The DDR process, which involves the peaceful disarmament of ex-combatants, the demobilization of armed groups, and the reintegration of ex-combatants into civil society, is a standard component of UN peacekeeping operations. Since mid-April 2000, when DDR camps were made ready at Makeni, Magburaka, Bo, and Moyamba, the RUF had found ways to obstruct the process. The first attempt was seen in a confrontation with UNAMSIL troops at Magburaka on 22 April, shortly after the opening of the DDR camp there. Following a fight between armed RUF troops and KenBatt (a Kenyan Battalion) guarding the camp, it was temporarily closed down.

Despite the RUF's effort to prevent its soldiers from disarming, persistent persuasive efforts by KenBatt and UN military observers yielded some positive results in late April, when ten RUF soldiers presented themselves for disarmament at the DDR reception center in Makeni. They were registered and discharged at their own request, after paying for their own traveling allowances, on 1 May. However, later that afternoon, RUF commanders arrived at the DDR camp and forcefully dismantled it. At the same time, RUF troops surrounded the camp in Magburaka. By the end of that day, seven UNAMSIL personnel had been detained by the RUF, including the KenBatt commander with three peacekeepers and three UN military observers. On 2 May, both DDR camps, at Makeni and Magburaka, were destroyed.[2]

The security situation in Makeni and Magburaka rapidly deteriorated. On 2 May 2000, following RUF attempts to disarm UNAMSIL troops at Magburaka, fighting broke out, followed by an exchange of fire between UNAMSIL and the RUF in Makeni. The disruptions quickly spread into RUF strongholds where UNAMSIL was deployed. The same day, in the Kailahun area, the RUF took thirty UNAMSIL personnel hostage, as well as the crew and passengers of a UNAMSIL helicopter.[3] This development was a vindication for those who had argued all along that the RUF could not be trusted and that it was simply biding its time, waiting for ECOMOG troops to depart.

Yet despite the appearance of a systematic campaign, it is not in fact clear that Sankoh had full control of the RUF troops on the ground; by mid-May, nearly 5,000 RUF combatants had been disarmed, indicating that Sankoh's control was slipping.[4] Moreover, it is not clear that the obstruction of the peace process was part of a carefully designed plan. Instead, the turn of events suggests that Sankoh and the RUF simply took advantage of local dynamics as they unfolded. The initial disruption created by AFRC soldiers had already indicated the volatility of the situation. Then, as RUF troops in the field saw how small the UNAMSIL contingents outside Freetown were, they tested the resolve of these troops in typical rebel fashion.

In contrast, the AFRC's Johnny Paul Koroma seemed to be more cooperative and actively engaged in the work of the Commission for the Consolidation of Peace, which he chaired. In late April 2000, "Johnny Paul," as he was commonly referred to, gave his own opinion of the RUF commitment to peace during a meeting with Olara Otunnu, who was at that time the UN Secretary-General's Special Representative for Children and Armed Conflict. He said that many RUF members insisted that Sankoh had not given them the "code" to disarm. It was clear that Sankoh often made commitments at meetings that he did not intend to honor. But

Koroma was of the opinion that Liberia's president, Charles Taylor, could be approached to prevail upon Sankoh.[5]

Koroma felt that a compromise with Sankoh was the best way forward. He argued that it was important to acknowledge and address some of Sankoh's grievances, particularly his irritation at the focus of the government and the international community on the implementation of the military, rather than political, aspects of the Lomé Agreement. He wanted the RUF to be given diplomatic positions and control of key government agencies, such as those that managed natural resources, though the government pointed out that the RUF was still in control of the mining areas.

Johnny Paul was proven correct in his assessment of the RUF attitude toward disarmament. In private conversations and interviews during the same period, Foday Sankoh complained about the lack of government commitment to the political terms of the Lomé Agreement compared to its interest in disarming the RUF:

> We will disarm when the Lomé structures are in place. We are not represented in Ambassadors [diplomatic appointments]. RUF is not represented even in parastatals. Since Lomé, the president has appointed two ambassadors but none from RUF. The commission I am to lead is not even in place. Lomé has no trust fund to implement it unless donors give us money. You can't use miracles to implement peace accord. The basic needs of our men, we must provide ourselves. We have to work hard to get two meals for our boys. The basic needs of the men are not met.[6]

Referring to the presence and relevance of the UN mission, he continued:

> The peacekeepers are a waste of money. Money should be spent on more meaningful things. . . . We are the peacemakers; we are the warriors, only we can bring peace. No one can threaten us by bringing thousands of troops. Leave us to disarm. Give us what is due us in the accord. In the DDR meetings, people don't want to listen. They do not respect the leadership of the RUF. Without us there will be no peace in this country. If you want to help us, do so and do not threaten us. We were not being provoked in 1991. We planned and organized it [the war]. All their intelligence network was nil.
>
> I think we are doing something great. My mere presence in Freetown itself is an indication of RUF's commitment to

peace and development. They care more about their positions. The structures called for in the Lomé peace accord are not in place and they refuse to complete it. All they care about is disarming the RUF. They can shoot any former combatants in the street. Your UN peacekeeping force shot people on the streets in violation of the peace accord [referring to the incident on Friday, 28 April 2000]. Tell the UN Secretary-General we are committed to peace but we are being marginalised.[7]

■ The Situation Worsens

RUF hostility toward UNAMSIL intensified and escalated rapidly, as the events of 1–2 May 2000 seemed to have a cascading effect almost everywhere. By May 3, the RUF had abducted at least forty-nine UNAMSIL peacekeepers. A UN military observer team and some members of the Indian battalion were detained in Kailahun, and four soldiers from the Kenyan battalion were reportedly killed following fierce fighting in Makeni.[8] A Zambian battalion, newly deployed to UNAMSIL, was dispatched to reinforce Kenyan troops in Makeni, and a 100-man unit of the Indian quick-reaction company was sent from Hastings to Magburaka for the same purpose.[9]

Meanwhile, the RUF played games with the international community, giving the impression that it was responding to pressure from the region while continuing with its obstruction of the peace process. Regional players, including Nigeria, Mali, and Libya, dispatched special envoys to Freetown to put pressure on Sankoh to return to the peace implementation plan. Following a meeting on 3 May with General Aliyu Mohammed, who was Nigerian president Obasanjo's special envoy and national security adviser, Sankoh signed an agreement, which was read over state radio and television, to release any UNAMSIL personnel being held hostage, to halt further attacks on UN peacekeepers, and to grant freedom of movement to UNAMSIL personnel as well as the personnel of humanitarian organizations. On 4 May, over 100 NiBatt-2 officers and soldiers held in Kambia (including two Indian soldiers) were released, but without their uniforms and some of their weapons.[10]

Yet what Sankoh gave with one hand, he seemed to take away with another. On 5 May 2000, the day after the Nigerian contingent in Kambia was released, Fred Eckhard, spokesman for the UN Secretary-General, announced that the RUF had forcibly disarmed and detained approximately 208 troops of the Zambian battalion on the way to Makeni. The total number of UNAMSIL personnel held by the RUF was estimated at 318.[11] The situation of the Zambians infuriated their home government, as it was claimed the battalion had not been prepared before being sent to the heart of the crisis area. The troops had been deployed immediately upon their arrival in Sierra Leone, with no orientation, no maps, and therefore no knowledge of the terrain. Others argued that, given only one major road connecting Freetown to Makeni, the lack of maps was not the major problem. In less than a week, the number of UNAMSIL peacekeepers held hostage by the RUF rose to 498.[12]

It was very clear that Sankoh was not supportive of UNAMSIL and hated its presence in Freetown. At every given opportunity, he blamed UNAMSIL for the crisis. In a press conference on 1 May, for example, he erroneously attributed the incident of 28 April—the shooting of an AFRC solider by ECOMOG troops—to UNAMSIL.[13] Perhaps he saw all armed troops (including ECOMOG and UNAMSIL troops) as the same, or perhaps he was simply uncomfortable with the UN presence. Yet it was he who had demanded a neutral monitoring force during the Lomé talks.

The contradictions in Sankoh's actions and statements led to widespread disquiet about his state of mind, with some concluding that he was mentally imbalanced. He seemed impossible to satisfy, and seemed obsessed with his personal status, frequently stating that he did not get the material and social trappings of office. It was said that he fell asleep intermittently at meetings and was seemingly paranoid and delusional.

But the air of uncertainty was not created by Sankoh alone. A generalized confusion surrounded the May crisis, with contradictory information and actions by all concerned. On 3 May 2000, reports circulated that Sankoh had been placed under house arrest. During his meeting with General Aliyu, Sankoh reacted angrily to these rumors, and later that day he drove around Freetown in the company of some of his supporters, as if to demonstrate that he could move freely.

Then on 4 May, at the same time as a diplomatic solution was being pursued through dialogue with Sankoh, members of the Sierra Leonean parliament called for his arrest, amid rumors that the RUF was advancing toward Freetown. In a radio address on 7 May, Johnny Paul Koroma called on Sierra Leonean soldiers, both enlisted and retired, to join him and the Civil Defense Forces to fight the RUF and prevent Sankoh from derailing the peace process, adding to the already confused situation.

■ The View from the United Nations

Despite widespread disquiet within Sierra Leone, there was no indication in the period before the crisis began that the UN expected mischief of a significant degree from the RUF. It was business as usual at UN headquar-

ters in New York, and the communications between Freetown and headquarters focused on deployments and the need for troops outside Freetown
so that DDR could begin in earnest.

However, with rumors of an RUF advance on Freetown so widespread, UN headquarters sought confirmation. SRSG Adeniji was away
from Freetown, busy negotiating for the release of UN hostages, leaving
UNAMSIL's Force Commander, General Vijay Jetley of India, in control.
Yet Jetley was unable to confirm any of the reports before an aerial reconnaissance had been conducted. And by then the spokesman for the UN
Secretary-General had been authorized to make a statement that the RUF
was indeed marching on Freetown and the Americans began evacuating
people. In UNAMSIL's headquarters inside Mammy Yoko Hotel, civilian
staff were handed evacuation instructions to be followed should the situation escalate, and some were later evacuated to Banjul. When Jetley per-
sonally conducted the aerial reconnaissance, he found no evidence of RUF
movement. But the damage had already been done.

The events of May 2000 were a source of great distress to ardent supporters of the UN and its ideals. Regardless of its many acknowledged

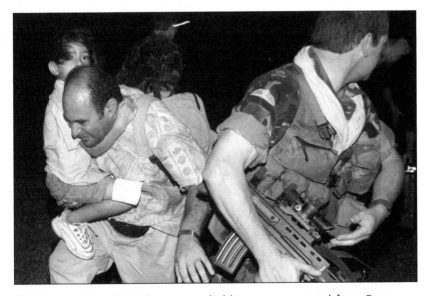

UN personnel and British passport holders are evacuated from Freetown,
9 May 2000.

Dylan Martinez © Reuters/CORBIS

faults, the UN had previously enjoyed a reasonable measure of respect among populations in countries like Sierra Leone. Its practical effect was often felt through the work of its funds, programs, and agencies, such as the UNDP, the United Nations Children's Fund (UNICEF), and the World Health Organization (WHO). But peacekeeping, considered by many as the "bread and butter" of the UN, gave it political stature and visibility and spoke to the very reason for the UN's existence: the maintenance of international peace and security. When states, gangs, warlords, and organized groups clashed, the UN was supposed to remain an impartial mediator whose authority was not to be breached. May 2000 saw these credentials slipping away.

Even Ahmad Tejan Kabbah's government, about the only friend UNAMSIL had, was very concerned about the situation on the ground. On 6 May 2000, a delegation led by Sierra Leonean vice president Joe Demby visited SRSG Adeniji to express concern about the security of Freetown and the ease with which UN troops were being disarmed. Adeniji assured the delegation that UNAMSIL would not abdicate its responsibility.

On 6 May, with the security situation deteriorating, Freetown was geared for a large demonstration against Foday Sankoh. SRSG Adeniji warned against the demonstration, given the potential for an escalation of the crisis, urging President Kabbah to dissuade civil society leaders from the possibility of a march to Sankoh's residence. But the demonstration took place anyway and ended in bloodshed. On 8 May, some 30,000 people participated in a protest at Sankoh's house on Spur Road, calling for the release of the UN peacekeepers. UNAMSIL troops were stationed at Sankoh's house, but could not control the situation. Foday Sankoh's bodyguards fired into the crowd, killing some twenty people and injuring dozens more, while Sankoh managed to escape. Although he was apprehended and arrested on 17 May in Freetown, UNAMSIL by now faced a hostile Sierra Leonean press and local community.

Meanwhile, regional leaders were also deeply concerned about the rapid deterioration in Sierra Leone. On 9 May 2000, an emergency "mini-summit" of ECOWAS was called in Abuja, Nigeria, to discuss the situation. It was attended by members of the Joint Implementation Committee for the Lomé Peace Agreement, which comprised representatives from Burkina Faso, Côte d'Ivoire, Ghana, Guinea, Liberia, Mali, Nigeria, and Togo, with representatives from Sierra Leone in attendance as nonmembers and Adeniji as an observer.[14] ECOWAS member states argued that the previous year's proposal for ECOMOG troops to remain in Sierra Leone, with financial and logistical support from the UN or other external backers, was a missed chance. The troops deployed by UNAMSIL, by comparison, were insufficiently committed and had inferior knowledge of the terrain.

ECOWAS leaders felt that UNAMSIL could guarantee a turnaround in its fate only if it had more latitude to use force against the rebels. In the absence of an amendment from the Security Council authorizing such force, the best bet, they argued, was to redeploy ECOMOG to Sierra Leone with a mandate to enforce peace, backed by logistical and financial support from the international community. They were determined to prevent a takeover of power by force in Sierra Leone, which they believed was about to occur. In a strongly worded communiqué issued after the meeting, ECOWAS threatened to revoke the blanket amnesty granted to the RUF in the Lomé Agreement and requested the UN Executive Secretary Lansana Kouyate to convene a meeting of ECOWAS ministers of defense and chiefs of staff to discuss the modalities for ECOMOG involvement.[15]

■ Explaining the Crisis

In hindsight, the two key assumptions of UNAMSIL's planners discussed in Chapter 2—that the RUF would abide by the terms of the Lomé Agreement, and that the UN force could cope with challenges after ECOMOG's withdrawal—proved disastrously wrong. Regarding the first, the RUF was heavily armed even in the aftermath of Lomé, and its military structure was intact. Added to this, it was in control of much of the countryside, not least the diamond- and gold-mining areas, and felt threatened by the plan to deploy UNAMSIL to those areas. The struggle for Magburaka and Makeni was telling in this respect; both places were strategically important to the RUF, because they were the major routes to the diamond-rich area of Koidu. Sankoh probably overestimated the threat that UNAMSIL posed to his agenda. But he was eager to preserve the status quo, whereby armed groups and the peacekeeping forces shared control, the latter hardly venturing beyond Freetown and the Western area.

Second, UNAMSIL proved unable to tackle threats to the fragile peace once ECOMOG was withdrawn. Clearly, the RUF had attacked UNAMSIL at its weakest points: remote areas outside Freetown to which the UN had been under pressure to deploy but lacked significant strength to accommodate. But the RUF may itself have been surprised by how relatively easy it was to break UNAMSIL defenses and destabilize the already precarious security situation.

Whether or not more West African troops should have been included in UNAMSIL (an issue on which there remain contending views), the mission was considered weak. Its troop strength was limited to 6,000 when it was established in October 1999, and it was not until February 2000 that an increase to 11,100 was approved. It took several months to put this increase into full effect, by which time the ECOMOG withdrawal was already at an advanced stage. From the outset, Sierra Leoneans continuously questioned the decision to send in a limited number of fighting forces, all the more important because Sierra Leone essentially did not have a fighting force. The new Sierra Leone Army was being trained, first by the Nigerians under General Khobe, and subsequently by the British, but it would not be properly combat-ready for some time.

As with other peace operations, the number of troops for UNAMSIL was decided by the Security Council on the basis of proposals made by the Secretariat's Department of Peacekeeping Operations (DPKO). There was no mathematical formula for determining the number; instead, proposals had to be based on an assessment of the financial and troop burdens that key member states and their domestic publics could accept. With the exception of the UK, Sierra Leone still remained low on the priority list of key actors in 1999, and the DPKO's proposal on troop strength accurately reflected that mood: 6,000 troops was all that the paymasters—particularly the United States, which was responsible for over a quarter of the peacekeeping budget—were likely to fund.

The feeling among the Security Council membership was that the RUF was sufficiently pacified, and the terrain less belligerent, after the deal struck in Lomé, and that ECOMOG would be at hand to do the murkier job should the need arise. But whether UNAMSIL's planners in the Secretariat were also convinced of this, or merely realistic as to what the membership would accept, is unclear. Certainly, Nigeria's chief of army staff at the time, General Malu, warned against deploying such a small force. But one can only wonder whether a correct reading of the post-ECOMOG environment by the DPKO might have generated a different decision from the Council.

In addition to the troop numbers, UNAMSIL was considered weak because of its mandate. Resolution 1270 clearly spelled out that UNAMSIL could take necessary action under Chapter VII to protect its personnel and civilians facing threat of violence. Yet this did not create confidence in the force; some expected tougher language to send a clear message that UNAMSIL would crush the rebels should they test the peacekeepers' resolve.

However, UN staff argue that the real challenge was not the mandate itself but its interpretation by troop-contributing states and their troops on the ground. The mandate was sufficiently robust to allow for forceful action by UNAMSIL troops to defend themselves when they faced rebel attack. The UN had even provided a document to all troop-contributing countries prior to deployment, highlighting the rules of engagement for the mission. Yet it later emerged that whereas some contingents had been ready to use force, notably the Nigerians, others had understood their role in Chapter VI "peacekeeping" terms. Some had been briefed by their governments on this basis, with instructions that casualties would not be tolerated back home. Compounded in some cases by a lack of logistical support, the troops did not turn their mind-set to enforcement even when the threat posed by the RUF became obvious.

The issue of contingents taking orders directly from their home capitals is a serious problem that has plagued many other peacekeeping missions; UNAMSIL was not the first, and will probably not be the last. The problem is often particularly acute when a mission moves from a traditional peacekeeping mode to a more robust approach. The United States was considered to have set a bad precedent in Somalia during the operations against Mohammad Farah Aideed, where the Special Representative of the Secretary-General (an American) was totally sidelined. The practice of communicating with and taking orders directly from home governments tends to be more rampant in dangerous missions or during crises within missions, as occurred in UNAMSIL in 2000.

Interestingly, it was the UN as a whole, and not the troop-contributing states and their troops, that was the focus of criticism at the time. However, some contingents were singled out later for failure to protect civilians and their own colleagues. UN headquarters would later institute regular consultations with the defense chiefs of troop-contributing countries in an attempt to bridge the gap between mandates and their application, and ensure that, for all UN missions, troops would deploy at full capacity as agreed under "wet lease" arrangements.

The United Kingdom's Role and Its Unintended Consequences

In the midst of the May 2000 crisis, the UK government intervened by sending troops, at their high point numbering 1,200. Their role was initially to evacuate UK and other European nationals from Sierra Leone, but later also to assist UNAMSIL and stabilize the situation. The presence of the force around Lungi airport, and in Aberdeen near the UNAMSIL helipad, lifted the spirits of Sierra Leoneans. It also gave UNAMSIL much-needed support and allowed it to redeploy to other parts of the capital where security was urgently needed.

The British launched a number of operations intended to show the strength of their forces. A series of offshore firepower demonstrations—the "over-the-horizon" force—were the most highly visible. The "over-the-horizon" concept was not new, having been used by NATO in the for-

British Royal Marines prepare to move ashore at Aberdeen beach in Freetown, November 2000.

Bob Bishop/AFP/Getty Images

mer Yugoslavia and by the UN in East Timor.[16] Now, in Sierra Leone, the "over-the-horizon" displays left no doubt that the British were prepared to unleash maximum damage should the rebels test their resolve. British military operations continued in Sierra Leone years after the May 2000 crisis.

This did not do much for UNAMSIL's reputation, however. The more power the British projected through displays of military strength, the more useless UNAMSIL seemed in the eyes of Sierra Leonean citizens and observers alike. The UN Secretary-General's statement in his 19 May 2000 report to the Security Council captured the timeliness of the British arrival and its stabilizing role, but also conveyed the neediness of UNAMSIL:

> A pivotal factor in restoring stability was the arrival of the United Kingdom troops on 7 May and of a substantial British Naval presence offshore a week later. The deployment of British troops at Lungi and in the Western part of Freetown had as its objective the safe evacuation of nationals of the United Kingdom and others for whom it was responsible. Nevertheless, this presence boosted the confidence of the Sierra Leoneans and enabled UNAMSIL to redeploy much-needed troops to areas east of Freetown. It is hoped that that the United Kingdom will be able to maintain a military pres-

ence in the country until UNAMSIL has received necessary reinforcements.[17]

For this reason, the United Kingdom's role tends to be an emotive subject among former UNAMSIL staff. The more objective among them agree that the UK intervention was crucial and was a key factor in halting the rebel advance and stabilizing the situation. Even if its greatest impact was psychological, they recognize the value of that impact. But some UN staff dwell angrily on the negative publicity suffered by UNAMSIL as a result of the United Kingdom's role. Their irritation toward the UK is derived less from UNAMSIL's position of helplessness than from an apparent exaggeration of the United Kingdom's role and its visible reveling in the media attention generated. While UNAMSIL was acquiring all the negative nicknames that Sierra Leoneans cared to confer on it, UK troops were treated like heroes who had come to rescue them from the RUF and to clean up the UNAMSIL mess.

Anti-UNAMSIL and anti-UN opinion went beyond Sierra Leone to conference and seminar rooms in Europe and North America, where UN staff had to tolerate harsh criticisms from cynics and hard questions from UN optimists. According to some reports, the UK had rejected pleas from the Sierra Leone government to commit troops to UNAMSIL,[18] instead sending troops under its own command. How could it be that even the UK, one of the five permanent members of the Security Council, had so lacked confidence in the UN that it chose to deploy separately?

The view of a former UNAMSIL staff member, expressed five years after the May 2000 crisis, reflects the continuing sensitivity of the issue:

> In actual fact, the UK role was not substantive but dramatic. The use of the "over-the-horizon" forces had an impact. It had a dramatic aspect. The testing of fire along the coastal line played a hugely important role. The negative role of the UK presence however, was that it assumed credit for all the success of that period. They used this to the extent of undermining the mission.[19]

Another former UNAMSIL staff member said:

> The British role should not be trivialized. It was a major role. The mission was initiated to evacuate Europeans. They did not come with the intention of rescuing people. But their mere presence kept rebels out of Freetown. UNAMSIL was already

pulling troops from Hastings. Had the UK not arrived, we would have seen an evacuation of UNAMSIL and entry of rebels into Freetown. When the UK saw that their presence had a positive impact, the "over-the-horizon" mission was borne out of this. Its presence, even if it did nothing, had an impact. The problem was the trend in the British press to downgrade what the UN had done and play up the British role.[20]

To worsen matters, the UNAMSIL leadership and the UK had opposing viewpoints on the required stance toward the RUF. As if to rub salt in UNAMSIL's wounds, the leadership of the UK presence in Sierra Leone argued that UNAMSIL ought to be employing maximum force against the rebels. In the absence of that use of force, the government of Sierra Leone was encouraged to deploy the newly trained battalions from the armed forces, working with the Civil Defense Forces, against the rebels. This was in sharp opposition to Adeniji's view that the most viable option was to salvage the Lomé Agreement by reengaging the RUF. Adeniji knew that UNAMSIL did not have the capacity to win a war against the RUF, whereas one UNAMSIL staffer said of the British:

> They at times created the impression that UNAMSIL had the capacity but did not want to deploy the troops. The British were carried away with successes from targeted military operations and gave the Government the impression that if only UNAMSIL had been deployed, the RUF rascals would have succumbed. The Brits emboldened the government to put pressure on RSLAF [Republic of Sierra Leone Armed Forces] to deploy in Kambia. They said the new army was capable of deploying in Kambia with Guinea.[21]

■ UNAMSIL's Image Problems

Some of the differences in approach between the UK leadership and the UNAMSIL leadership were due to a difference in orientation. Officers of the International Military Advisory and Training Team (IMATT), a British force that was primarily providing training for the national army, tended to see the UN mission as unduly large administratively and possessing a huge support base, but weak on military substance. In contrast, IMATT was relatively small, in both troop strength and support staff, but its visibility around the capital and ability to put on a show of force instilled confidence among the local population. As one UK lieutenant-colonel serving in

Oluyemi Adeniji, SRSG
and head of UNAMSIL, at
UN headquarters, 2003.

UN photo/Mark Garten

IMATT put it, "perception management is the biggest thing."[22] This was where the UK succeeded and UNAMSIL failed in May 2000.[23]

In contrast to the UK, UNAMSIL's public image sank as a result of its humiliation at the hands of the RUF. It was the butt of negative remarks in the media—radio, newspapers, and television—and was accused of military incompetence, or worse, of protecting the RUF and making it impossible for victims of RUF atrocities to seek retribution. In the press, unfortunate acronyms like "U-NASTY" became common, while on the streets of Freetown, children called the mission "UNAMSILLY." At the height of the UNAMSIL-bashing, on 10 May 2000, SRSG Adeniji went on national television in Sierra Leone to respond to the accusations and defend the mission, but this had little effect.

Sierra Leoneans expressed strong views about several key issues. One was security and, relatedly, the mandate and posture of UNAMSIL. A second was the UN's treatment of the government and the rebels as conflicting parties with equal standing. Some deemed this stance unhelpful, though others stuck to the view of the government as a party to the conflict whose role and methods were at the root of the crisis.

Within the domestic defense community of Sierra Leone were more specific complaints. First, there was a strong impression that the troops

SLA soldiers in Benguema training camp, outside Freetown, June 2000.
Nikola Solic © Reuters/CORBIS

being contributed to UNAMSIL were improperly equipped and improperly trained by their home countries for the terrain in which they were being deployed.[24] Instances of UNAMSIL soldiers fleeing when RUF troops attacked only enhanced the perception that troop-contributing countries placed greater premium on the benefits received than the ability to perform, a problem the DPKO was dealing with on a daily basis.

Second, there was a sense among loyal Sierra Leonean soldiers retained within the new army that ECOMOG had been sidelined by the UN and had not received the recognition it deserved. According to one Sierra Leonean colonel, without ECOMOG "there would have been no UNAMSIL and no IMATT."[25] While these Sierra Leoneans openly acknowledged the reported human rights violations by ECOMOG and other acts of indiscipline, their preference for ECOMOG's operational methods was glaring.

Third, officers in the new Sierra Leone army who remained loyal to the government and continued to serve felt that it was a mistake to ignore the standing army, no matter how weak. Though battered and divided, the standing army still had an operational core and continued to operate in the countryside, particularly following initial reconstructing efforts and training. With their superior knowledge of the territory, army commanders felt that UNAMSIL should have utilized them during the May 2000 crisis.

A Sierra Leonean brigadier-general who was a commanding officer during the May crisis recounted an incident during which UNAMSIL troops from Kenya came under attack from rebels and failed to realize, due to a total lack of communication, that Sierra Leone's national army was in a position to assist. With a common enemy in their midst, either side could have been the victim of friendly fire; the Sierra Leoneans did indeed fire in the direction of the Kenyan battalion, not certain whether they were RUF. But UNAMSIL justified its lack of communication with the Sierra Leone Army in terms of its neutral position between conflicting parties and its concerns about RUF sympathizers within the army's ranks.

Regardless, espousing a litany of complaints against UNAMSIL, the Sierra Leonean public was not on the side of the UN in May 2000. It would take a lot to turn the situation around. But securing the release of all UNAMSIL troops held by the RUF was the first order of business.

▌ Notes

1. This reflected a marked change from the offensive on Freetown in January 1999, when the AFRC was largely responsible for atrocities perpetrated against civilians, which were carried out in a highly systematic manner.   ·

2. See *Fourth Report of the Secretary-General on the United Nations Mission in Sierra Leone*, UN Doc. S/2000/455, 19 May 2000.

3. Ibid.

4. Ibid.

5. Meeting between Olara Otunnu, Special Representative of the Secretary-General for Children and Armed Conflict, and Johnny Paul Koroma, Chair of the Commission for the Consolidation of Peace and former leader of the AFRC, Freetown, 29 April 2000, at which I was present.

6. Meeting between Sankoh, Olara Otunnu, and Lloyd Axworthy (the latter was Canada's foreign minister at the time), at Sankoh's residence in Freetown, 30 April 2000, at which I was present; citations are based on my notes.

7. Ibid.

8. See "Daily Press Briefing of Office of Spokesman for Secretary-General," 3–4 May 2000, http://www.un.org/news/briefings/docs/2000/20000503.db050300 .doc.html, and http://www.un.org/news/briefings/docs/2000/20000504.db050400 .doc.html.

9. See *Fourth Report of the Secretary-General*.

10. Ibid., and "Daily Press Briefing of the Office of Spokesman for Secretary-General," 5 May 2005, http://www.un.org/news/briefings/docs/2000/20000505 .db050500.doc.html.

11. Ibid.

12. See Chris McGreal, "Panic Usurps Peace As Rebels Close In," *The Guardian*, 11 May 2000, p. 4.

13. See *Fourth Report of the Secretary-General*.

14. The Joint Implementation Committee was established under the Lomé Peace Agreement to oversee the peace process in Sierra Leone, under the chair-

manship of ECOWAS. The committee was mandated to meet once every three months to monitor the implementation of the agreement. See *Lomé Peace Agreement*, art. XXXII, UN Doc. S/1999/777, 7 July 1999 (see text of the Lomé Agreement in this volume).

15. See *Fourth Report of the Secretary-General*.

16. Telephone interview with Adriaan Verhuel, former staff member of the UN Department of Peacekeeping Operations in charge of the Sierra Leone Desk in 2000.

17. See *Fourth Report of the Secretary-General*.

18. See Richard Norton-Taylor and Chris McGreal, "Britain Rejects Call to Join UN Peacekeepers in Sierra Leone," *The Guardian*, 11 May 2000, p. 1.

19. Interview with a former UNAMSIL staff member, New York, November 2005.

20. Interview with a former UNAMSIL staff member, New York, December 2005.

21. Interview with UNAMSIL officer, Freetown, November 2005. The SLA was renamed the RSLAF in January 2002.

22. Interview with IMATT officer, Freetown, November 2005.

23. Several years later the UK began to de-emphasize the "over-the-horizon" force concept in a bid to reduce local expectations and counter the tendency for UNAMSIL to rely on the UK presence in its own planning. By 2005, the British had become increasingly keen to point out that IMATT was a training team and not a rescue force, a bilateral arrangement that should not been seen as part of the UN effort.

24. Focus-group discussion, Sierra Leone Ministry of Defense, Freetown, November 2005.

25. Ibid.

4 | Tangoing with Taylor

IN THE CONFUSED DAYS of the May 2000 crisis, the one person who seemed able to influence Foday Sankoh was Liberia s Charles Taylor. Taylor had been a factor in the Sierra Leone conflict from the start in many ways the fourth party alongside the RUF, the AFRC, and the Sierra Leone government. A mentor to Sankoh and a godfather figure to the RUF, he had exploited his RUF connection to maximum personal, political, and financial advantage. In 2000, he represented the single most persistent source of external threat to the Sierra Leone peace process, but also the greatest source of opportunity, positioned at the intersection of political influence and political mischief.

The May crisis forced the UN to realize that resolving the conflict in Sierra Leone required dealing with the regional dynamics in the Mano River area. By then, however, the UN found itself not only dancing with Taylor on the political stage, but also dancing to a tune dictated by him. The main external obstacle to the attainment of peace had suddenly become the figure upon whom the UN would rely to preserve it. As regional and UN actors scrambled to regain control over the peace process, Taylor dictated the pace as go-between with Sankoh and guarantor of the RUF s promise to release the UNAMSIL troops it held hostage. Through Foday Sankoh, Taylor was on the way to realizing his dream of a greater Mano River region dominance.

This chapter traces Taylor s involvement in the conflict in Sierra Leone and the immediate region, examining the initial delay in responding to the Taylor challenge, the UN s resultant dependence on him after May 2000, and the subsequent efforts of the international community to restrict Taylor s involvement in Sierra Leone. What were the dynamics behind UN decisions in relation to Taylor? What would these decisions mean for the region, for peace in Sierra Leone, and for justice?

■ The Taylor-Sankoh Alliance

Taylor and Sankoh, and by extension the RUF, had a shared history as dissidents roaming West Africa, backed by Libyan leader Muammar Qaddafi.[1] Taylor and Sankoh first met in 1987 in Ghana, home to various West African exiles in the mid-1980s, and they received training at the Benghazi camps in Libya at about the same time, in 1987 and 1988.[2] They had a common sense of purpose: to remove their respective governments from power and, to this end, exploit all opportunities along the way. But the rapport between them was not necessarily an instant one. There is no indication that Taylor gave much consideration to a partnership with Sankoh during this initial meeting, or that he considered Sankoh an equal.

Although Sankoh had a certain charisma of his own, Taylor was outwardly more magnetic and more elegant. UN officials recalled SRSG Oluyemi Adeniji s discussions with Taylor, in which he admitted that Sankoh was his friend but always hastened to add that comparing Sankoh to himself was an insult.[3] It is not clear whether the perceived difference had to do with the conduct, educational achievements, or personal styles of the men. Taylor, a university graduate schooled in economics, considered himself part of the Liberian elite and certainly felt superior to Sankoh, who had received only primary school education and worked in the postal service before joining the Sierra Leone Army.

Taylor and Sankoh s paths crossed in the course of two very different careers. Taylor, who was the director of the Liberian General Services Agency under Samuel Doe s regime, had fled to the United States in 1983 following allegations of embezzlement. He was arrested there in 1984, but escaped in 1985 from a prison in Plymouth, Massachusetts, where he was awaiting extradition.[4] He later reappeared in Ghana, and then in Burkina Faso, where his insurgency plans began to take shape. It is reported that he was introduced to Qaddafi by Blaise Compaor , who would become president of Burkina Faso in 1987 following a bloody coup that ousted Thomas Sankara.[5] Having allegedly assisted his friend to the seat of power in Burkina Faso, Taylor could be assured of high-level support for his rebellion against the Doe regime.[6]

Sankoh s route to war was rockier. Born and raised in poverty, with limited opportunities beyond his primary education, he was far from the corridors of power. He joined the Sierra Leone Armed Forces   in the 1950s and 1960s seen as a destination for school dropouts and thugs   rising only to the rank of corporal. However, his army training equipped him with skills in communications relevant to radio and television, allowing him to work in the Sierra Leone Broadcasting Service (SLBS) and then to pursue a career in photography.[7]

The closest Sankoh came to the elite and the center of power was through his claimed involvement in the 1968 coup that restored Siaka Stevens s APC government to power. He would later turn against Stevens and the APC government by participating in an unsuccessful coup attempt led by Brigadier John Bangura in March 1971. His support for the coup, and his enthusiasm in broadcasting the events of this coup at the SLBS, landed him at Pademba Road Prison for the next several years.[8]

Sankoh s release from prison in 1978 coincided with a wave of student unrest and activism that had been sparked the previous year by a brutal government response to a series of student demonstrations.[9] This provided Sankoh with a perfect opportunity to take up his grievances against the APC government. His association with members of the Pan African Union (PANAFU), an organization that emerged from the radical student and youth movements of the time, provided Sankoh with a platform through which to pursue his ambitions. He was able to connect with other radical groups, mingling with angry youth and students, some of whom were expelled from university and later left with him for Ghana and then for training in Libya under Qaddafi.[10]

Both Taylor and Sankoh shared ambitions of overthrowing their governments and saw the benefit of allying in order to realize these goals. But Taylor s aspirations transcended Liberia; those who knew him well suggest that he had always envisioned a greater Mano River region over which Liberia would dominate. His overarching goal was to be the leading statesman of this neighborhood, commanding respect from all its leaders. If Sankoh attained power in Sierra Leone, Taylor would be halfway toward the realization of this ambition.

The invasion of Sierra Leone in 1991 by Sierra Leonean dissidents and Taylor s National Patriotic Front suited the agendas of both Taylor and Sankoh. Launching the RUF rebellion at that time provided them with much-needed access to valuable natural resources to fund their wars, because Sierra Leone, like Liberia, was a land flowing with bloody milk and honey. The Taylor-Sankoh alliance was fundamentally an economic partnership, with Sierra Leone diamonds at its core.

Throughout the war, diamonds flowed from Sierra Leone into Liberia, from which they were transported to destinations within and outside Africa. They returned to Sierra Leone in the form of weapons, therefore enabling the continuing recalcitrance of the RUF and, in the lead-up to Lom , strengthening Sankoh s position. From across the border, Taylor sustained the RUF lifeline by keeping the flow of arms constant. Burkina Faso also channeled arms and resources to the RUF, largely under the influence of Taylor, who had a well-cultivated relationship with

Compaor , as well as ties established through C te d Ivoire s first president, F lix Houphou t-Boigny.

▌ Taylor the Peace Broker

The UN was blind to these regional dimensions for several years. The embargo following the May 1997 coup applied only to the junta and the RUF, although it rhetorically placed responsibility on regional actors to prevent importation of weapons to these groups. Initial reports on Taylor s interference did not receive attention until 1999, when the international community slowly began to increase its engagement with Sierra Leone, and when Taylor s obstruction of the peace process became a major irritant. It was only in July 2000   after Taylor s role was made crystal clear during the May crisis   that the UN Security Council took action on the question of sanctions violations.[11]

In May 2000, however, the UN and regional actors were at the mercy of Taylor. West African leaders and the UN, as well as observers within Sierra Leone, saw Taylor as the best channel through which Sankoh and the RUF could be persuaded to release the 498 UNAMSIL peacekeepers in RUF custody. Taylor finally assumed his desired place at the center of West African politics and relished his role as the man of the moment.

Commenting to the press on 4 May 2000, UN Secretary-General Kofi Annan said: My latest discussion this afternoon was with President Taylor of Liberia, who has been on the phone several times with Foday Sankoh and has sent an envoy there. He has been given an assurance that the helicopter crew will be allowed to return tomorrow morning. We will see; he got it from Foday Sankoh himself. We hope to see, we wait to see if this happens. [12] The following morning, the RUF released the helicopter crew and its passengers. If there was any doubt about Taylor s influence on Sankoh, the release of the helicopter crew dispelled it. Annan was keen to highlight that leaders in the region, including those from Nigeria, Mali, Burkina Faso, and Libya, had dispatched Special Envoys to Freetown to put pressure on Sankoh.[13] But Taylor seemed to be the only person able to promise and then produce a specific result. There was no doubt who was in the driver s seat.

Observers could only wonder what games Taylor would decide to play with the issue of hostage release. In the face of the UN s powerlessness, Taylor could have chosen to drag out the situation, milking it for full political advantage while helping Sankoh gain political leverage. A slow process would have enabled Taylor to demonstrate just how much power and influence he had over the RUF and, by extension, the Sierra Leone peace process. But instead, Taylor succeeded in integrating himself into

Charles Taylor in Monrovia, 2003.

© Nic Bothma/epa/CORBIS

the West African political process, and aimed himself at addressing the Sierra Leone crisis. ECOWAS leaders relied on Taylor as a major channel for effecting the release of UN peacekeepers and returning Sankoh to the Lom process. At the ECOWAS minisummit in Abuja on 9 May 2000, Taylor was assigned the task of contacting Sankoh and relaying the demands of regional leaders.

Taylor was instrumental in negotiating the release of 139 UNAMSIL peacekeepers on 15 May 2000, following the third meeting of the Joint Implementation Committee for the Lom Peace Agreement in Freetown on 13 May.[14] At the meeting, Adeniji called on the committee to support President Taylor s efforts to secure the unconditional release of all UNAMSIL personnel and equipment. Liberia s foreign minister, Monie Captan, presented Taylor s plan for the peacekeepers release, involving direct consultations between Taylor and the RUF leadership and the establishment of a committee to propose strategies for restoring the peace process. Taylor seemed confident that the consultations would soon yield positive results, and when the prisoners were released two days later, he secured maximum mileage.

There was no doubt that Taylor exploited the hostage situation for his own personal political advantage. The day after the Joint Implementation

UN peacekeepers return to Lungi airport following their release by the RUF, 28 May 2000.

British Army/Jim Elmer © Reuters/CORBIS

Committee meeting, Adeniji met with Taylor in Monrovia. Taylor was quick to reiterate an earlier request for material support, while indicating that his emissary might return to Liberia on that same day with some hostages in a chartered helicopter (which he would need the UN to provide). Taylor said that he would arrange to receive the hostages at the airport and that his government would provide them with basic items such as toiletries and clothing. When Adeniji suggested an alternative arrangement whereby the UN helicopter would transport the hostages directly to Lungi airport, where they would be welcomed by their colleagues, Taylor insisted on having the hostages transported to Monrovia and did not hide his desire for Liberia to receive full credit for their release. Adeniji told UN headquarters in New York that he had no choice but to go along with Taylor s plan, and arranged to send a UN MI-26 helicopter to Monrovia the following day. On 15 May, 139 peacekeepers, all from the Zambian battalion, were released from the RUF and flown to Liberia   to Monrovia and the border town of Foya   with plans to be transported from there to Freetown.[15]

Taylor s influence with the RUF went beyond Sankoh. After Sankoh s arrest on 17 May 2000, Taylor was able to continue consultations with other RUF commanders to secure the release of the remainder of the kidnapped UNAMSIL troops. By the end of May, most UNAMSIL personnel held hostage had been released through Monrovia.

Next, UNAMSIL and regional leaders turned to Taylor to help solve the issue of RUF leadership. At ECOWAS consultations in Liberia on 26 July 2000, it was agreed that the RUF should nominate a new leader, because as long as Foday Sankoh remained the nominal head, the commanders would be reluctant to participate in the peace process.[16] Taylor brokered this process, and was responsible for transmitting this message to the RUF commanders in the field, who responded by appointing Brigadier-General Issa Sesay as interim leader in August. Presidents Alpha Konar of Mali and Olusegun Obasanjo of Nigeria traveled to Lungi airport in Sierra Leone, where Sankoh was flown from prison to meet them. The presidents delivered a letter from RUF commanders appointing Issa Sesay as their leader, and Sankoh gave his consent to the appointment, thereby legitimizing the new leader to the rank and file of the RUF.

During this period, the UN was happy to allow regional political leaders and ECOWAS to take the lead in brokering some of the more sensitive political arrangements, a job to which regional players were better suited by virtue of their connections and influence. For their part, regional leaders did not see a big role for the UN; at the ECOWAS minisummit in May, for example, SRSG Adeniji was only allowed to be present as an observer.

▌ From Courted Peace Broker to Indicted War Criminal

Taylor perhaps thought that he had done enough to earn the legitimacy he sought and the status that he craved within the regional political scene and at the UN. In West Africa, it was not unthinkable that he would be given pride of place as one of the key facilitators of the Sierra Leone peace process. After all, Houphou t-Boigny, who was once seen as an obstacle to peace in Liberia, was later accorded the role of lead peacemaker. But Boigny s case was very different from Taylor s. Houphou t-Boigny had earned his place in West African postcolonial history and, unlike Taylor, did not have a reputation for waging war in the region and committing heinous atrocities against innocent people. Houphou t-Boigny had been a force to be reckoned with, but not one requiring special rehabilitation into the regional political scene.

Even if West African leaders had been ready to rehabilitate Taylor, the rest of the international community was not prepared to let him off so easily, especially because he continued to pose a threat to Sierra Leone and the Mano River region as a whole. In the midst of the May crisis, several members of the Security Council treated the issue of Taylor s role as go-between with the RUF with caution and raised concerns about his complicity in the provision of external support to the RUF. Opinions varied as to how to deal with Taylor. While some expressed a preference for containing him through diplomatic steps by African leaders, others wanted to seek accountability for Liberia s role in supporting the RUF and supporting the trade in diamonds. Taylor s prominence in regional politics would be short-lived. He gradually became the focus of international attention and condemnation as the UN became more determined to turn things around in Sierra Leone.

After May 2000, proof of Charles Taylor s role in diamond sales and the supply of arms increasingly emerged. The floodgate was opened with Ian Smillie, Lansana Gberie, and Ralph Hazelton s publication *The Heart of the Matter: Sierra Leone, Diamonds, and Human Security*, which became a major advocacy tool used by the nongovernmental organization (NGO) Global Witness.[17] In July 2000, the Security Council adopted Resolution 1306, which was proposed by the UK and US ambassadors to the UN and received active support from other members. The resolution banned importation of rough diamonds from Sierra Leone and established a Panel of Experts to report on the sanctions, focusing specifically on the linkage between the trade in diamonds and the transfer of arms into Sierra Leone.[18] One day later, a BBC news report provided details of secret documents, obtained directly from Sierra Leone Police files, that exposed the extent of Taylor s involvement in gun running and diamond smuggling in collusion with rebels in Sierra Leone.[19]

The report submitted by the Panel of Experts on Sierra Leone in December 2000 recommended, among other things, imposition of sanctions on Liberia.[20] As a result, the Security Council passed Resolution 1343 in May 2001 to impose sanctions on Liberia, banning Liberian diamond exports, imposing a travel ban on key regime members, and strengthening the arms embargo.[21] As Alex Vines, a member of the Panel of Experts, has noted, Resolution 1343 marked the first time the Security Council had imposed sanctions on one country for its refusal to comply with the sanctions on another, indicating how decisive the UN Security Council could be when its most powerful members were in agreement.[22] This was followed by the creation of a Panel of Experts on Liberia, whose reports resulted in other resolutions.[23]

Ironically, by proving so publicly that he had influence over RUF operatives in May 2000, Taylor provided evidence that would later be used by the Special Court to indict him on charges of war crimes and crimes against humanity. He also galvanized the Security Council to assume a regional framework in its response to Sierra Leone and to focus on arms and diamonds, addressing for the first time the key factors sustaining the RUF and the conflict. Although so much damage had already been done, it was not too late for the UN to make a difference in Sierra Leone, which now became a regular feature on the Security Council s agenda.

▮ Notes

1. See for example, Stephen Ellis, *The Mask of Anarchy: The Destruction of Liberia and the Religious Dimension of an African Civil War* (London: Hurst, 1999); and Lansana Gberie, *A Dirty War in West Africa: The RUF and the Destruction of Sierra Leone* (London: Hurst, 2005).

2. Gberie, *A Dirty War in West Africa*, p. 52.

3. Interview with former UNAMSIL official, New York, March 2006.

4. Taylor s background and the circumstances leading to his launch of the Liberian war were first widely reported in *Africa Research Bulletin*, 15 February 1990, p. 9557, and 15 April 1990, p. 9633.

5. Gberie, *A Dirty War in West Africa*, p. 53.

6. See Ellis, *The Mask of Anarchy*, for a detailed discussion of the evolution of the Taylor rebellion.

7. Gberie, *A Dirty War in West Africa*, pp. 39–41.

8. Ibid., p. 42.

9. For a discussion of the student and youth radicalization in Sierra Leone during this period, see Ismail Rashid, Student Radicals, Lumpen Youth, and the Origins of the Revolutionary Groups in Sierra Leone, 1977–1996, in Ibrahim Abdullah, ed., *Between Democracy and Terror: The Sierra Leone Civil War* (Dakar: CODESRIA, 2003). See also Ibrahim Abdullah and Patrick Muana, The Revolutionary United Front of Sierra Leone: A Revolt of the Lumpenproletariat, in Christopher Clapham, ed., *African Guerrillas* (Bloomington: Indiana University Press, 1998).

10. For a detailed account of the origins of Sankoh and the RUF, see Ibrahim Abdullah, Bush Path to Destruction: The Origin and Character of the Revolutionary United Front (RUF/SL), in Abdullah, *Between Democracy and Terror*. See also Abdullah s article of the same name in *Africa Development* 22, nos. 3–4 (1997): 45–76.

11. See *UN Security Council Resolution 1306*, UN Doc. S/RES/1306, 5 July 2000 (see text of Resolution 1306 in this volume).

12. Comments by the Secretary-General following the Security Council meeting on Sierra Leone, 4 May 2000, http://www.un.org/news/ossg/sgcu0500.htm. The Security Council issued a presidential statement after this meeting, condemning the RUF attacks on UNAMSIL forces and arguing that Sankoh must be held accountable alongside other perpetrators. See Statement by the President of the Security Council, UN Doc. S/PRST/2000/14, 4 May 2000.

13. Comments by the Secretary-General, ibid.

14. See *Fourth Report of the Secretary-General on the United Nations Mission in Sierra Leone*, UN Doc. S/2000/455, 19 May 2000.

15. Ibid.

16. Some suggest that in the period 1999–2000, Taylor s approach to the RUF was increasingly one of divide and rule in an attempt to solidify his control of the diamond industry. See David Keen, *Conflict and Collusion in Sierra Leone* (Oxford: Currey, 2005), pp. 253–254.

17. See Ian Smillie, Lansana Gberie, and Ralph Hazleton, *The Heart of the Matter: Sierra Leone, Diamonds, and Human Security* (Ottawa: Partnership Africa Canada, 2000).

18. See *UN Security Council Resolution 1306.*

19. Liberia Selling Arms for Diamonds,   *World: Africa,* BBC News Online, 6 July 2000, http://news.bbc.co.uk/1/low/world/Africa/839206.stm.

20. See *Report of the Panel of Experts Appointed Pursuant to Security Council Resolution 1306 (2000), Paragraph 19, Concerning Sierra Leone,* UN Doc. S/2000/1195, 20 December 2000.

21. See *UN Security Council Resolution 1343,* UN Doc. S/RES/1343, 7 March 2001.

22. Alex Vines, Combating Light Weapons Proliferation in West Africa, *International Affairs* 81, no. 2 (2005): 349.

23. See, for example, *Report of the Panel of Experts Pursuant to Security Council Resolution 1395 (2002), Paragraph 4, Concerning Liberia,* UN Doc. S/2002/470, 19 April 2002; and *Report of the Panel of Experts Appointed Pursuant to Security Council Resolution 1408 (2002), Paragraph 16, Concerning Liberia,* UN Doc. S/2002/1115, 25 October 2002.

5 | A House Divided

THE WEAKNESS OF UNAMSIL had been exposed by the events of May 2000 and further underlined by the role of the UK and then the UN's dependence on Taylor to resolve the hostage issue. As if things were not bad enough, UNAMSIL then became riddled by internal divisions and by contradictions across the UN as a whole. The exit of UNAMSIL's Force Commander, Major-General Vijay Kumar Jetley, and the abrupt withdrawal of the Indian contingent, in what became known as the Jetley affair, visibly demonstrated the internal fragility of the mission at a particularly critical moment.

This chapter looks at the key issues that caused the internal disharmony within UNAMSIL following the May crisis and the impact these had on the mission. What were the international and interpersonal dynamics that gave rise to the crisis? What were the constraints in resolving it? And how did the issue affect the mission staff and the credibility of UNAMSIL in Sierra Leone?

■ Echoes of the Rehatting of ECOMOG

As discussed in Chapter 2, the rehatting of ECOMOG troops had been a difficult process, and the UNAMSIL force that took over from ECOMOG was a compromise arrangement that created a force composed of troops from many different countries. West African troops rehatted into UNAMSIL included contingents from Nigeria, Ghana, and Guinea, alongside those from other African regions, including troops from Kenya and Zambia. The non-African components of UNAMSIL consisted of troops from seasoned peacekeeping nations: India (and later Pakistan), Bangladesh, and Jordan. India sent a Ghurka battalion that had just seen

81

two years of hard fighting in Kashmir, whose members were described as tough professionals and battle-hardened troops. The different national contingents and their leaderships also had various impressions and interpretations of the events of the preceding months.

The senior leadership of the mission reflected the diversity of the troops, with a Nigerian, SRSG Oluyemi Adeniji, alongside an Indian, Force Commander Major-General Jetley. Jetley was highly regarded as a competent and professional officer and Adeniji an able diplomat; the combination was considered a potential winner for UNAMSIL.

But the choice was politically sensitive. When consulted by the UN on deployment planning for UNAMSIL in September 1999, President Ahmad Tejan Kabbah had expressed concern that the Force Commander be someone who understood the regional dynamics in West Africa and be capable of dealing with Nigeria. Special Representative Okelo had also echoed this view in one of his communications with New York. In the field, some of the Nigerian commanders were openly critical of the Force Commander decision, in addition to other decisions made at UN headquarters. They argued that since Nigeria was providing the largest number of troops, the Force Commander should be Nigerian, or at least West African. But as Nigeria's Major-General Martin Agwai said, it was surely asking too much for Nigeria to expect both the Force Commander position and the SRSG position.[1] Instead, a Nigerian, Brigadier-General Mohammed Garba, was appointed to serve under Jetley as Deputy Force Commander.

Although not openly admitted by the Nigerian officers, the issue was partly one of remuneration. The Force Commander was paid according to UN pay scale, while the Deputy Force Commander was seconded by his country and retained on regular salary (though his country was reimbursed by the UN under the "wet lease" arrangement). This only added to the resentment of senior Nigerian commanders over what they felt was a lack of appreciation for Nigerian and West African sacrifices in Sierra Leone. Under these circumstances, General Jetley, or indeed a Force Commander from any country other than Nigeria, was bound to face a difficult time.

■ Personality Matters

This unfortunate political dynamic required the UN to tread carefully in structuring the day-to-day organization of the mission. But unfortunately, the mix of personalities and leadership styles that were brought to bear on UNAMSIL only worsened the situation. In an environment where the West Africans already felt marginalized, Jetley was seen to have surrounded himself with mostly Indian staff officers, as one Nigerian officer described: "All key principal officers were Indian, both allocated and unallocated. Nigeria and India were par in troop strength. But if you checked the key positions, how many Nigerians were there?"[2] In addition, Jetley was allegedly suspicious of what seemed to be an unusually keen interest in border patrols by Nigerian troops; he sent Indian troops to the border instead.

Meanwhile, General Garba, the Nigerian Deputy Force Commander, though remembered by some with fondness, was also described as outspoken, gregarious, and lacking in sophistication. He was the most outspoken embodiment of the Nigerian position, and there were tensions in his relationship with General Jetley almost from the start. Garba's style contributed to escalating his differences with Jetley into a division between Nigeria and India. Some officers recall that Garba sometimes behaved as if he did not have to report to a Force Commander, preferring instead to report directly to the Special Representative, also a Nigerian.

■ The Jetley Report

These internal divisions came to a head with one particular incident, now commonly known as the Jetley affair. In an internal report written in May 2000, Jetley leveled a number of accusations against Nigerian troops. He claimed that Nigerians were engaged in illegal diamond mining and were being paid handsomely by the RUF for turning a blind eye to rebel operations in the diamond-mining areas. He also claimed that Sankoh had wanted a Nigerian to be appointed as UNAMSIL Force Commander, implying that this accounted for Sankoh's intransigence. The report was leaked in September 2000, when it promptly made the rounds on the Internet and was widely circulated among those interested in UN affairs and Sierra Leone.

Jetley correctly located the origin of the internal crisis in the issue of ECOMOG's rehatting. Having expected that ECOMOG soldiers would constitute the bulk of the neutral force implementing the Lomé Peace Agreement, the Nigerians, Jetley said, were disappointed to learn that this would not be the case:

When [former ECOMOG commander] Gen. Kpamber went to UN HQ New York, he was very disappointed to learn that he was not going to be the Force Commander of UNAMSIL and that Nigeria would have three bns [battalions] as part of UNAMSIL, out of this they had to concede one battalion to the Guineans. The Nigerians therefore felt that they were not getting a fair deal in the Peace Process in Sierra Leone despite the sacrifices they had made to pave the way for the peace process. This to a very large extent is the genesis of the present crisis.[3]

But Jetley also suggested that ECOMOG's relationship with the RUF was such that the RUF stood to benefit from the Nigerian position:

After the initial fighting between ECOMOG and RUF, the relationship had thawed when a stalemate had been reached militarily. It is understood that a tacit understanding was reached between the RUF and ECOMOG of non-interference in each other's activities, the total absence of ECOMOG deployment in RUF held areas is indicative of this. I believe that the RUF leader Foday Sankoh was also under the impression that the UN Peace Keeping Force agreed to in Lomé was primarily a rehatted ECOMOG with Maj Gen Kpamber as its boss. The dply [deployment] of a neutral peacekeeping force (UNAMSIL) under an Indian General, keen to implement the Peace Accord in letter and spirit was not what Sankoh had bargained for. He viewed UNAMSIL as a big obstacle in his ambition of becoming the next President of Sierra Leone.[4]

Although there was no evidence for Jetley's claims that senior staff carried over from ECOMOG were systematically looting Sierra Leone's diamonds, there was evidence to support some of his other allegations. The UN's Panel of Experts on Sierra Leone later obtained anecdotal evidence that former ECOMOG troops bought diamonds from the RUF or traded weapons with the RUF in exchange for diamonds, cash, and other goods.[5]

The allegations of complicity with the RUF were reminiscent of a pattern from ECOMOG's earlier operation in Liberia, where, after years of fighting with heavy losses, ECOMOG was accused of looking the other way when arms flowed freely to anti-Taylor factions.[6] It is not inconceivable that this scenario was being played out in Sierra Leone after ECOMOG's losses to the RUF in January 1999. Nigeria was clearly tired of supporting the Sierra Leone operation, no longer a priority for the new leadership, and Nigerian soldiers were tired of doing a thankless job. Sankoh was ready to manipulate any situation to his advantage and, regardless of his initial animosity toward ECOMOG, he knew that a tired Nigeria-led force was preferable to a fresh, committed, and neutral UN force.

All of this coincided with the appointment of Adeniji, a Nigerian SRSG who believed that a military campaign against the RUF would not succeed,

UNAMSIL Force Commander
Major-General Vijay Jetley,
May 2000.

© Patrick Robert/Sygma/CORBIS

and that peace depended upon bringing the rebel group back into the peace process. With limited knowledge of the recent history and West African dynamics, and partly as a result of his poisoned relationship with his deputy, General Garba, Jetley read the situation inaccurately, seeing the Nigerian leadership as actively complicit in the RUF's agenda. Moreover, in his most explosive claim, he alleged that the supposedly subversive actions of the SRSG and Deputy Force Commander were orchestrated by Nigeria:

> The SRSG and DFC [Deputy Force Commander] had instruc-
> tions from Nigeria to pursue the agenda for which they had
> been sent by him. Keeping the Nigerian interests was para-
> mount even if it meant scuttling the Peace Process and this
> also implied that UNAMSIL was expendable. To this end the
> SRSG and DFC cultivated RUF leadership especially Foday
> Sankoh behind my back.[7]

Had this claim been made during Abacha's brutal military dictatorship in Nigeria, some might have been inclined to agree with Jetley's analysis. However, with a democratically elected President Olusegun Obasanjo recently at the helm, this accusation was easily dismissed by analysts. UN staffers also rejected the claims, and one former staff member recalled that "Jetley was an extremely talented military officer but had no political bone in his body."[8]

The strongest objections came from Nigeria, which demanded Jetley's exit from UNAMSIL. Nigeria's army chief, Major-General Victor Malu, himself a former ECOMOG commander in Liberia, publicly denounced UNAMSIL's management of the military operation in Sierra Leone and called for Jetley's removal. In the ensuing controversy, President Kabbah backed the Nigerians. ECOMOG's shortcomings notwithstanding, the force had historically done enough to earn the sympathy of Sierra Leoneans. In the end, the West Africans and other African contingents in UNAMSIL closed ranks on Jetley and the Indians, not as a complete rejection of the validity of his claims, but rather because of regional ties that compelled them to align against the outsider.

General Jetley claimed that his leaked May 2000 report had been stolen from his computer, though others said it had been discovered on a shared computer drive by a Nigerian staff officer. Some close to the mission have claimed that the author was not actually Jetley, but one of his staff officers.[9] Though the UN did not conclude its investigations into the matter, its support for General Jetley was difficult to maintain, not least because he refused to withdraw the statements he had made in the report. As it became clear that Jetley could no longer serve as UNAMSIL's Force Commander, the Indian government, also now embroiled in the situation, followed through on its threat to withdraw its contingent from the mission.

The UN considered starting afresh with an entirely new team to lead UNAMSIL. But the UN's hand was forced when, in a phone call to the Secretary-General, President Obasanjo threatened to withdraw Nigerian troops if Adeniji was removed. Adeniji remained as Special Representative, with the compromise being that Garba was removed as Deputy Force Commander, though his replacement, Major-General Martin Agwai, was also Nigerian. In November, Jetley was replaced by Lieutenant-General Daniel Ishmael Opande of Kenya.

The departure of the Indian contingent opened the way for Pakistan, another seasoned peacekeeping nation that was also keen to participate in the mission. Privately, however, UN staff have admitted that losing the Indian contingent was a blow, because the Indian troops were perceived to be the best in the mission.

■ Command and Control

The Jetley affair demonstrated how seemingly perfect matches for mission leadership can unravel. What seemed a "dream team" on paper—a talented diplomat and a battle-tested general—was difficult to realize in practice. More dramatically, the crisis highlighted the differences in orientation and approach by troops from two different regions. Reports of indiscipline among ECOMOG troops, particularly Nigerian soldiers, were not new. Long-term military rule had impacted the Nigerian officer corps, creating a wide gulf between professional officers and corrupt ones. Efforts by the professional officers to have their counterparts disciplined fell on deaf ears in Abuja, and after years of regional operations, other West Africans had come to accept the good with the bad when it came to Nigeria's role in regional security.

The real lesson for the UN was that regional or lead-nation actors supporting peace efforts should not be left to go it alone for long periods of time without a credible degree of burden sharing. Nigeria and ECOMOG were left to dominate the Sierra Leone scene for a long period with little or no attention from the international community. When the UN was eventually ready to engage more actively, these regional actors felt they were being dispossessed of their rightful role in a situation where they had for so long borne the costs.

But with the constraints of the time, there were few options open to the mission planners, even if they had clearly predicted the regional and interpersonal dynamics leading up to the crisis. Acquiescence to Nigerian demands for the Force Commander position would have reduced UN control over the mission. Yet excluding Nigeria altogether from the peacekeeping force would have been difficult, if not impossible. Even if other countries had been queuing to send troops to Sierra Leone (which they were not), the political consequences of excluding Nigeria from the peace process in Sierra Leone would have been dire.

Interestingly, the Jetley affair generated more interest from the international community than within Sierra Leone. The population was less interested in tales of internal wrangling within UNAMSIL than in whether the mission was improving their security, and it was the May crisis that therefore stuck in their minds. It is also reasonable to suggest that the Jetley affair might not have become serious had the May crisis not occurred. The kidnapping of UNAMSIL personnel put everyone under pressure, widened cracks that already existed in the mission, and exposed the fact that UNAMSIL did not have the managerial or coordination capacity to deal with the situation.

UNAMSIL'S command and control problems were created partly by different interpretations of the mission's mandate, as discussed in Chapter 3, but also by technical weaknesses. Many contingents lacked adequate orientation and had no maps of the terrain for which they would be responsible; some were not even aware of UNAMSIL's rules of engagement and standard operating procedures. The rehatting of some ECOMOG contingents into UNAMSIL had been expected to produce a certain level of troop readiness and institutional memory. But some of these battalions did not have the requisite logistical support agreed upon with the UN, and many lacked the right communications equipment. All of this left UNAMSIL in an extremely vulnerable position. With a total lack of communication between force headquarters and the field, there was an absence of coordination at all levels—strategic, operational, and tactical.

Ironically, these command and control issues were highlighted in the Jetley report, but were completely overshadowed by the report's allegations against the Nigerians. In a section titled "Other Constraints in My Functioning," Jetley had much to say about poor communications with troops in the field:

> Even after months, since the establishment of peace keeping mission, I cannot talk directly to any battalion commander. There are severe shortages of communication equipment in a number of units which have not been made up despite several reminders to the adm [administrative] staff. Some battalions have only one radio set in the company available with them. Most battalions have no Fax facilities to fwd [forward] sitreps [situation reports] or reports and returns. . . . Most units under my command other than India, Kenya and Guinea have very little or no equipment with them. They have not been properly brief [sic] in their country about the application of chapter VII in this mission for certain contingencies.[10]

Accounts in the international media confirmed the rumors floating around Freetown that UNAMSIL was suffering from major internal contradictions. On 1 September 2000, a damning report appeared in *The Guardian* suggesting that the Jordanian contingent had undermined the safety of ordinary Sierra Leoneans and their own colleagues by failing to act when the dreaded West Side Boys harassed innocent civilians at checkpoints. The Jordanians were even accused of looking away while people were held at gunpoint.[11]

■ Coordination in the UN Family

The military component was not the only aspect of UN operations in Sierra Leone that suffered from a lack of coordination. As is often the case within the UN family, in Sierra Leone the peacekeeping mission and the

Country Team were poles apart. The UN agencies, funds, and programs that composed the latter dealt largely with humanitarian and development issues, under the leadership of the Resident Coordinator, and had been on the ground in Sierra Leone long before the arrival of UNAMSIL. From the beginning, then, the relationship was uneasy, as actors like FAO and the UNDP feared that their mandate would be compromised by close association with a security force.

In September 2000, the UN presence in Sierra Leone was not only divided, but also terribly dysfunctional. Information was not systematically shared, and the Country Team considered UNAMSIL to lack transparency in its planning. The SRSG was perceived as aloof, operating only at a very high political level, and as disinterested in humanitarian and development concerns. The mission and UN agencies pursued largely independent agendas and had radically different understandings of the UN's purpose in Sierra Leone. Similarly, development actors from civil society did not find UNAMSIL accessible. Although they valued the political role of the SRSG, they craved some kind of interaction on development and humanitarian initiatives.

It was clear that across all aspects of the mission, much had to be done to turn things around if the UN was to become relevant to the effort to bring peace to Sierra Leone. The existence of multiple viewpoints between the Security Council, the Country Team, and the military contingents had given rise to unhappy compromises and dysfunctional arrangements, strangling the UN's ability to act for clearly defined goals and seriously undermining its credibility. As the dust settled following all the turmoil of 2000, it was clear that the task of renewing UNAMSIL would require change at all levels, from the Security Council all the way down to the field.

◼ Notes

1. Interview with General Martin Agwai, London, March 2006. General Agwai was appointed Deputy Force Commander for UNAMSIL to replace General Mohammed Garba in early November 2000, a week after Lieutenant-General Daniel Opande of Kenya was appointed Force Commander to replace Major-General Vijay Jetley.

2. Interview with a former UNAMSIL officer, New York, December 2005.

3. See Vijay Jetley, "Report on the Crisis in Sierra Leone," http://www.sierra-leone.org/jetley0500.html.

4. Ibid.

5. David Keen, *Conflict and Collusion in Sierra Leone* (Oxford: Currey, 2005), p. 266.

6. During the Liberian civil war in the early 1990s, ECOMOG unofficially

supported the Armed Forces of Liberia (AFL) and the United Liberation Movement for Democracy in Liberia (ULIMO), both of which were fighting against Taylor's NPFL, which was simultaneously supporting the RUF in Sierra Leone.

7. Ibid. See also Dena Montague, "The Business of War and the Prospect of Peace in Sierra Leone," *Brown Journal of World Affairs* 9, no. 1 (Spring 2002): 236.

8. Interviews with a UN staff member, New York, December 2005.

9. Ibid.

10. See Jetley, "Report on the Crisis in Sierra Leone."

11. Chris McGreal, "UN Troops 'Collaborate' with West Siders: Peacekeepers Seen Standing By As Renegades Rob at Checkpoints," *The Guardian*, 1 September 2000, p. 12.

6 | Fighting Back

BY MID-2000, many observers were expecting a Somalia-type retreat from Sierra Leone that would bring shame on UNAMSIL. Yet in this instance, the UN chose precisely the opposite path. After spending much of the month of May reacting to the RUF attacks, the task of transforming UNAMSIL into a credible mission began in earnest in June 2000. The journey back from May 2000 would require commitment from the highest levels in New York, a clear strategy, and brave leadership in the field to implement it without wavering.

Sierra Leone benefited from a variety of factors that came together in the second half of 2000, notably a determination within the Security Council to regain the UN's credibility, and a period of introspection within the UN peacekeeping community that produced new momentum. Although there were many competing priorities, there was a degree of clarity at the highest levels about what needed to be done.

This chapter looks at the dynamics that enabled UNAMSIL's return from the brink. How did the UN take stock of what had gone wrong? What made the Security Council so determined to address the situation? What was the impact of leadership and personality? And what risks were taken to put Sierra Leone back on the path to peace?

■ Taking Stock

In the aftermath of the May crisis, there was no shortage of analysis of what had gone wrong. One of the UN Secretariat's initial responses was to send German general Manfred Eisele, a former UN Assistant Secretary-General for Peacekeeping, to Sierra Leone in June 2000 to lead a comprehensive assessment of UNAMSIL's organization, operation, and resources.

The final report found "a serious lack of cohesion within the Mission," due to a lack of understanding of UNAMSIL's mandate and rules of operation, as well as a lack of communication, coordination, and military training and equipment.[1] Allegedly the original version, which was never made public, went further, and was very critical of several key actors.[2] Its recommendations were the basis of discussions between the Secretary-General and member states, and informed various decisions to reorganize UNAMSIL, revise the rules of engagement, and strengthen command and control.

Meanwhile, SRSG Oluyemi Adeniji assessed three possible options in responding to the May 2000 crisis. One, a nonoption really, was to maintain the status quo and keep the mandate set out in Resolutions 1270 and 1289. Another was to rely on action by a regional group, such as ECOWAS or a coalition of willing states. But Adeniji was skeptical that ECOWAS, without significant financial and material support, would be able to return to Sierra Leone so soon after having left. Similarly, there did not seem to be any group of states willing to carry out an "Operation Desert Storm" in Sierra Leone.

A third option was to amend UNAMSIL's mandate and concept of operations. Adeniji argued that Resolutions 1270 and 1289 needed to be enhanced, and urged UN headquarters in New York to facilitate a new concept of operations and mandate for UNAMSIL. His analysis was not dissimilar to General Vijay Jetley's. There were not enough troops on the ground, and those who were deployed were not adequately equipped or trained and were not exploiting the mandate's robustness. The approved troop strength of 11,100 was inadequate to meet the tasks that UNAMSIL was supposed to perform.

The situation in Sierra Leone was indicative of a broader crisis in UN peacekeeping, one that by 2000 had led to a period of serious soul-searching. In March 2000, Secretary-General Kofi Annan had convened a panel on UN peace operations, headed by UN veteran Lakhdar Brahimi. UNAMSIL was omnipresent in the Brahimi Report, as it became known; on its first page, the report claimed that the need for change had been "rendered even more urgent by recent events in Sierra Leone."[3] Moreover, Sierra Leone and UNAMSIL were cited countless times in reference to the typical problems confronting the UN, such as low troop numbers, overstretched support from headquarters, problems of command and control, the existence of "spoilers,"[4] and the ease with which UN troops were being attacked. Fortunately for Sierra Leone, it would also become the testing ground for some of the report's recommendations.

The Brahimi Report paved the way for significant changes at multiple levels of UN peacekeeping, but an overarching theme was that if UN peacekeeping was to succeed in creating the space for peace agreements to take hold, good intentions could not substitute for the fundamental ability of the UN to project credible force. Though impartiality was often core to UN missions, the report argued, when one party to a peace agreement clearly and incontrovertibly violated its terms, equal treatment of all parties by the United Nations could only lead to ineffectiveness, or worse, complicity. Hence, the report continued, UN troops "must be capable of defending themselves, other mission components and the mission's mandate." Furthermore, "mandates should specify an operation's authority to use force" and "not force United Nations contingents to cede the initiative to their attackers." But the UN must also have bigger and better-equipped forces and a planning process in which the Secretariat did not simply present to the Security Council "what it wants to hear."[5]

■ Security Council Activism

Thankfully, the trend in thinking about UN peace operations was already impacting the Security Council in its approach to Sierra Leone. In February 2000, when it was clear that the ECOMOG force would be withdrawn, the Council had taken steps in Resolution 1289 to increase UNAMSIL's troop strength from the initial 6,000 to 11,100.[6] Amid the deteriorating situation in May 2000, Resolution 1299 approved another increase in UNAMSIL troop strength, to 13,000.[7] From a force of 9,495 in May 2000, UNAMSIL had increased to 12,455 by December 2000.[8] In March 2001, in Resolution 1346, the Council approved another increase in UNAMSIL troop strength to 17,500.[9] Resolution 1346 also welcomed a revised concept of operations for UNAMSIL, as set out in the Secretary-General's report, that envisaged the successive deployment of a more robust, better-trained, and better-equipped force into all RUF-controlled areas. The goal was to assist the Sierra Leone government in consolidating state authority and stabilizing the country, in order to create conditions conducive to a comprehensive disarmament and the holding of free and fair elections.[10] The Secretary-General's report also stressed the uniform understanding and application of the mission's rules of engagement, which "allow it to respond robustly to any attack or threat of attack, including, if necessary, in a pre-emptive manner."[11]

The increase in numbers helped give UNAMSIL a newfound confidence, as demonstrated through the success of operations like "Khukri," an offensive military operation under the UN flag in July 2000. Despite poor weather conditions, the operation led to the rescue of more than 200 UN troops held in Kailahun and inflicted massive losses on the RUF while suffering only one UN fatality. As this operation occurred prior to the withdrawal of the Indian contingent, the majority of the troops involved were Indian (and the planning and execution were effectively led by Jetley, shortly before his departure from UNAMSIL), with vital support units provided by Ghana and Nigeria and logistical support provided by the UK. Previously, the absence of logistical capacity to support the mandate had been a major gap. Now, MI-35 and upgraded MI-8 helicopters sent in by India, alongside the Chinook helicopters provided by the UK, made all the difference.

The rapid reinforcement of UNAMSIL troops after May 2000 could not have occurred without the dedication of logistical staff members at headquarters in New York, who arranged for overhead clearances and landing rights for troop deployment. In the period after May 2000, they worked extremely long hours to ensure the rapid reinforcement. It was a nervous period. During Operation Khukri, Adriaan Verhuel, who was Desk Officer for Sierra Leone at the time, took his seat in the DPKO's situation room early each morning, waiting to draft a report to Assistant Secretary-General Hedi Annabi in the event that things went wrong. Happily, the operation's success showed that UNAMSIL was capable of meeting threats and challenges posed by the RUF with the robustness that they deserved.

Some argued that Khukri was a demonstration that the UNAMSIL mandate had been strong enough all along. But in August 2000, the same month that the Brahimi Report was released, UNAMSIL's mandate was made more robust by Security Council Resolution 1313, which called for UNAMSIL to "deter and, where necessary, decisively counter the threat of RUF attack by responding robustly to any hostile actions or threat of imminent and direct use of force."[12] In his report to the Security Council in September 2000, the Secretary-General claimed that the new approach to UNAMSIL was "an important first test of our joint responsibility to implement the practical recommendations made by the Panel [on United Nations Peace Operations], with a view to making the United Nations truly credible as a force for peace."[13] There was a nod of approval from all quarters in Sierra Leone.

Key to the Security Council activism of the time was the leadership eventually provided by the UK on the Council under Ambassador Sir Jeremy Greenstock. The UK was by now prepared to assume a higher political stake in Sierra Leone and would invest a considerable amount in the country. Its interest galvanized action among a host of players who might otherwise not have considered Sierra Leone a priority. As a result of pressure from the UK and in response to the May 2000 crisis, the United

States, whose interest in Africa in the late 1990s had centered on Liberia, became much more active in Sierra Leone.[14] The new and more engaged US policy in 2000 was also facilitated by US Permanent Representative to the UN Richard Holbrooke, who had arrived the previous summer.[15] Whereas in 1999 the United States had played an active role in limiting UNAMSIL's troop strength, now it worked with the United Kingdom to mobilize Council support and encourage contributing states to provide more troops. As one UN staff member put it, "We understood there was a new Sheriff in town."[16]

Holbrooke also played an important role in forging a bipartisan compromise with a key skeptic of the US policy toward Sierra Leone, and releasing US funding for UNAMSIL. Senator Judd Gregg, a New Hampshire Republican and chairman of the Senate appropriations subcommittee that controlled the State Department's budget, had been so disgusted by the concessions offered the RUF in the Lomé Agreement that he blocked the transfer of close to US$400 million in funding for four UN peacekeeping operations, UNAMSIL among them. Despite protracted discussions with the Clinton administration, it took a letter from Holbrooke

Richard Holbrooke, US ambassador to the UN (right), and Sir Jeremy Greenstock, British ambassador to the UN, at a Security Council meeting, June 2000.

Mike Segar © Reuters/CORBIS

to convince Gregg that the administration was serious about defeating the RUF, addressing the role of diamonds in Sierra Leone, and holding Foday Sankoh and Charles Taylor responsible for their roles in the conflict. Holbrooke's letter convinced Gregg to release the US$50 million allocated for UNAMSIL in June 2000.[17]

The Security Council crowned its activism on Sierra Leone with a visit to the country in October 2000 led by Sir Jeremy Greenstock. Eleven of the Council's fifteen ambassadors participated, reflecting the seriousness accorded the situation. Inside Sierra Leone, this made all the difference, as the political scene buzzed with life and a sense of importance. Everyone, including civil society and government representatives, had an interest in the Council's visit and followed it keenly.

Traveling with the eleven ambassadors was a team of technical experts including Adriaan Verhuel, Secretariat Desk Officer for the DPKO; Kathryn Jones, Secretariat Desk Officer for the Department of Political Affairs (DPA); Kate Smith, from the UK mission; and Alex Laskaris, from the US mission. It was an intensive trip, as described by Verhuel: "We had breakfast with Obasanjo, lunch with Taylor, tea with Conté and dinner with Konaré and then flew to Senegal to spend the night. We had met with four Presidents in one day."[18] The UK provided the plane, which was nicknamed "Rosy Scenario" by the team of experts aboard. Believed to have been used by the British royal family, the plane was adequately equipped for extensive administrative work, including an onboard printer and photocopier so that the team could draft texts and pass them to the Council ambassadors as required.

In response to its members' observations in Sierra Leone, the Security Council endorsed several innovative steps aimed at improving coordination of the international community and removing obstacles to peace. It signaled its support for a DPKO-proposed reorganization of UNAMSIL, suggested a UN-based mechanism for overall coordination in the field, and backed efforts by ECOWAS to resume dialogue with the RUF through the Joint Implementation Committee, thereby strengthening the political links between the Security Council, the region, the troop contributors, and the government of Sierra Leone. In December 2000, it received the report of its Panel of Experts on Sierra Leone, and in March 2001 moved toward imposing sanctions against Liberia.[19]

■ The Reorganization of UNAMSIL

Inside mission headquarters in Freetown and the Secretariat headquarters in New York, much thought was being given to translating the Security Council's activism into results on the ground. At the same time that high-

UN Deputy Force Commander Martin Luther Agwai talks to Kamajor combatants about disarmament, May 2001.

Tyler Hicks/Getty Images

level political efforts in West Africa and New York began to bring the peace process back on track, UNAMSIL underwent a complete reorganization. A new Force Commander was appointed, Lieutenant-General Daniel Opande of Kenya, as was a new Deputy Force Commander, Major-General Martin Agwai of Nigeria; both were in position by November 2000. The schism between these posts was ended.

Resolving the deeper problems of coordination across the UN family also presented an enormous challenge. After May 2000, the gulf between the political/military arm of UNAMSIL and the development and humanitarian perspectives of the UN Country Team widened even further as UNAMSIL was forced into combat with the RUF in operations like Khukri. This was consistent with the concept of robust impartiality contained in the Brahimi Report, but on the ground it inevitably compromised the perception of the UN as neutral, which complicated life for humanitarian actors within the UN system. Reportedly, between May and July, not a single meeting took place between the SRSG and the UN agencies; their relationship had reached a low point.

Exacerbating the coordination problem for UNAMSIL, the post of Deputy Special Representative of the Secretary-General (DSRSG) was still unfilled due to a delay in identifying a suitable candidate. After the

May crisis, two DSRSG positions were allocated to UNAMSIL, which by late January 2001 were both filled. Behrooz Sadry of Iran, a UN veteran and experienced troubleshooter who had worked in many parts of the UN system, was named DSRSG for Political and Administrative Affairs. Alan Doss of the UK, also a UN veteran and who had previously directed the UN Development Group, was appointed DSRSG for Governance and Stabilization. Under a newly conceived mission structure, Doss served concurrently as Humanitarian Coordinator and Resident Coordinator for UNAMSIL, as well as UNDP Resident Representative. This enabled him to perform the task of ensuring better links between UN agencies and the mission. Such multiple appointments became a core component of the UN's "integrated mission" approach. This new practice of "double-hatting" was endorsed by the Brahimi Report, and was said to have been recommended for Sierra Leone by Greenstock following the Security Council trip. Verhuel, tasked with drafting Doss's terms of reference, said he had "nothing to fall back on."[20] But in years to come the practice would be emulated in other missions and would become fairly standard in UN peace operations.

With new leadership in place, the coordination problems within the military component of UNAMSIL were systematically addressed. UN-owned equipment was provided to UNAMSIL to address shortfalls, particularly among the West African contingents. Helicopter gunships (which had been planned for but never deployed) were deployed with the Council's approval. The problem of communications, demonstrated by the complete isolation of UNAMSIL headquarters from the field in May 2000, was addressed through the deployment of a full signals battalion. For reconnaissance purposes, the mission obtained detailed maps as well as satellite imagery. Partly in response to Sierra Leone, the DPKO began a practice of obtaining satellite imagery commercially to use for tracking refugee populations, displaced communities, troops, and when necessary, large numbers of hostages. Some troop-contributing countries also conducted predeployment reconnaissance visits to the mission area to improve their contingent's knowledge of the terrain and understanding of the environment.

Steps were also taken to improve the mission's capacity to conduct threat and enemy assessments, through the establishment of a Military Information Cell at UNAMSIL headquarters in Freetown. The information cell was able to develop a network of sources that included contingents, civilian personnel, military observers, and public information officers located all around the country. The gathering and processing of reliable information enhanced UNAMSIL's ability to respond better and in a timely manner. In conventional military language this function would have been described as "intelligence," but for the UN a more benign term—"military information"—was chosen, to avoid suspicion from parties to the conflict and from member states.

At headquarters level, regular contact was initiated between troop-contributing countries and the UN Secretariat in an attempt to improve coordination. A meeting on 23 August 2000 at UN headquarters between Secretary-General Kofi Annan and the chiefs of defense from UNAMSIL's troop-contributing countries was the first of its kind.[21] The issues tabled by the Secretary-General included command and control, equipment short-falls, and the mandate and rules of engagement. He stressed the initial conception of UNAMSIL as a robust mission, able to defend itself and deter attacks, and emphasized the need for all contingents to be equally willing and ready to share the risks on the ground. It has since become common UN practice to maintain regular contact between troop-contributing countries, the Security Council, and the Secretariat, principally through the DPKO.

■ The Approach to Peace

With a stronger, more modern force, new leadership, and better coordination at all levels, UNAMSIL had started down the path to recovery. But its long-term success would depend on the broader problem: whether the UN could help rejuvenate the peace process in Sierra Leone, which had unraveled in May and was still stalled in late 2000.

Between May and August, with Foday Sankoh and many RUF leaders imprisoned, there were regular skirmishes between the RUF and UNAMSIL and the humanitarian situation deteriorated. However, the appointment in August of Issa Sesay as the RUF's interim leader helped quell much of the tension. Sesay took a more diplomatic approach and was largely responsible for softening the RUF's stance toward the UN. Likewise, human rights abuses by the RUF fell sharply under his leadership. His approach was indicative of a desire to present the rebel group as a valid political movement, willing to cooperate with the peace process.[22]

Meanwhile, although Koroma had abided by the Lomé Agreement since he had been included in the power-sharing arrangement, he was not in full control of all AFRC elements. The West Side Boys, a faction of AFRC soldiers who had retreated east from Freetown to the Occra Hills in February 1998, had rearmed to counter the RUF threat in May 2000 following Koroma's call for all Sierra Leoneans to defend their country against the RUF. But Koroma was no longer able to control them, and their

Members of the West Side Boys, 2000.
David Rose/Panos Pictures

resentments were numerous. Because they were not included in the Lomé Agreement and had many criminal elements in their ranks, the West Side Boys were not able to integrate into the Sierra Leone Army and were not eligible for benefits under the DDR program.[23]

Matters were brought to a head when the West Side Boys, on 25 August 2000, captured eleven British soldiers who were part of the British effort to retrain the army. They demanded supplies, reinstatement in the national army, and the release of one of their leaders from prison. On 30 August, five of the soldiers were released. When negotiations broke down a week later, on 7 September, 150 British troops attacked two villages controlled by the West Side Boys. The remaining six hostages were airlifted to safety, several hundred West Side Boys later reported for demobilization, and Koroma declared that the AFRC was a thing of the past.[24]

As for the RUF, the question of approach for dealing with the rebel group would prove divisive. As discussed in Chapter 3, two of the most critical actors—the UK and SRSG Oluyemi Adeniji—were poles apart on this issue. The UK favored the option of using force against the RUF and tried to persuade President Ahmad Tejan Kabbah that if UNAMSIL was not prepared to do so, the newly trained Sierra Leone battalions were up to the task. They were frustrated at watching a ragtag force terrorize the population while a large and expensive international peacekeeping force stood by.

But Adeniji cautioned Kabbah's government against such an approach. He argued, first, that UNAMSIL was not in a position to launch a military campaign against the RUF, notwithstanding the success of Operation Khukri. Its troop strength, logistical capacity, and coordination had been too poor to resist RUF attacks, let alone to launch counteroffensives. Second, plunging UNAMSIL into war with the RUF would significantly reduce the mission's capacity to take on the role of a credible peacemaker. Third, Adeniji felt strongly that peace could not be achieved through the use of force against the RUF, and that the path to peace lay in diplomatic efforts toward the RUF, backed by a more robust mandate and sufficient troop strength.

Adeniji's position was not popular in the post–May 2000 environment. The British were opposed to his strategy and wanted Adeniji removed from UNAMSIL. Other commanders argued for the more direct military option. Nigerian commanders had been just as frustrated in Liberia after a surprise attack by Charles Taylor's NPFL on ECOMOG in Monrovia in 1992. In the counterattack that followed, ECOMOG overwhelmed the NPFL, pushing it back to the hinterland while seizing control of strategic locations. But then the political leaders forced the ECOMOG commanders to halt the counterattack and negotiate a cease-fire with the NPFL.

In the end, Adeniji was vindicated. UNAMSIL implemented a strategy of negotiation with the RUF and dialogue with all parties to the conflict, combined with what was later described as the "progressive demonstration of deterrence."[25] The Security Council helped to galvanize support for that policy combination, both in the region and with the troop-contributing countries. And while diplomatic channels remained open, West African leaders, not least Obasanjo, made it clear to the RUF that this was their last chance. Despite the RUF's initial hostility, UNAMSIL used "contact groups"—consisting of military and civilian representatives from UNAMSIL and representatives from the RUF—to keep open the lines of communication with the rebels.

▉ The Kambia Formula

This blend of pressure and diplomacy informed a series of negotiations held in Abuja in the fall of 2000 between the government of Sierra Leone and the RUF. In a meeting in Abuja on 10 November 2000, the government of Sierra Leone and the RUF signed a cease-fire agreement. Both parties agreed that the UN would play a monitoring role and would therefore be enabled to deploy countrywide. The RUF also agreed to grant access for all humanitarian activity and to return the weapons and equipment seized from UNAMSIL troops.[26]

The new leadership of UNAMSIL's military component was proactive in its engagement with Issa Sesay and the RUF, and several staff emphasized that the personalities and styles of Generals Opande and Agwai contributed in no small measure to improved relations with the rebels. Opande dealt with them in what was described as a masterly and fatherly way, and was in turn accorded the respect that African youth show elders in the community. Agwai reportedly moved from one RUF location to another, countrywide, talking to the RUF, securing their confidence, and encouraging them to participate in the DDR program.

In a first face-to-face meeting with General Opande and his team on 8 December 2000, a month after the Abuja cease-fire agreement, Sesay gave assurances that the RUF would cooperate with UNAMSIL. He promised that, upon UNAMSIL's deployment in RUF-controlled areas, his men would readily disarm. He also reiterated his commitment to allow access to RUF-held areas and to return UNAMSIL weapons and equipment in RUF custody, the latter of which was to happen at public events in Makeni and Magburaka on 13 December.[27]

But implementation of this first Abuja cease-fire did not progress as rapidly as expected. The RUF was not as forthcoming as initial contacts had suggested. The much-hyped ceremony to hand over weapons did not amount to much; on 13 December, the RUF returned only eleven armored vehicles, all of which had been stripped of their mounted weapons and equipment. In addition, UNAMSIL was barred from moving into RUF-controlled areas.[28] It would take many more months of continued engagement to advance the peace process.

As it turned out, the RUF could not have immersed itself in any peace process at that time, as it was heavily engaged in trouble along the border with Guinea. Since September 2000, regional tensions had been mounting, as President Charles Taylor of Liberia and President Lansana Conté of Guinea traded accusations that each was supporting rebellion in the other's territory. As with Liberia, the RUF was already neck-deep in this regional conflict, and both were attacking Guinea at the same time.

The RUF and Liberian incursions into southern and southwestern Guinea resulted in large-scale displacement of Guineans for the first time since the country had received nearly half a million Liberian and Sierra Leonean refugees. In response to this, Guinea was forced to attack the RUF on Sierra Leone territory at its base in Kambia district.[29] To prevent this situation from escalating into an uncontrollable regional crisis,

ECOWAS made plans to deploy a monitoring force along Guinea's border with Liberia. But the government of Guinea was reluctant to accept a monitoring force unless it was deployed to assist actively in the defense of its territory. The RUF's involvement in the Guinea-Liberia tensions threatened not only to complicate the peace process in Sierra Leone, but also to destabilize the entire Mano River region.

The so-called Kambia formula served as a solution to this problem and kick-started a disarmament and demobilization process that spread across Sierra Leone. There was a large concentration of RUF troops in Kambia district near Sierra Leone's border with Guinea. If they could be disarmed and demobilized, allowing for the deployment of the Sierra Leone national army at the border with Guinea, this would persuade Guinea to stop its attacks. It might also encourage the RUF to give its full attention to the peace process inside Sierra Leone, effectively cutting them off from Taylor's regional ambitions.

Although the RUF was under artillery fire from Guinea and attacks from the Civil Defense Forces, it did not offer to disarm. Instead, the RUF asked UNAMSIL for free passage to Kailahun in the east of Sierra Leone, so that its troops could join their comrades. Adeniji, aware of how weak the RUF position was, skillfully exploited the situation. Instead of free passage, he proposed that the RUF disarm simultaneously with the CDF in Kambia district. The RUF commander in Kambia district at the time cooperated with the Kambia formula, and Adeniji achieved a major breakthrough.

A joint committee consisting of UNAMSIL, the government of Sierra Leone, and ECOWAS met with the RUF in Abuja on 2 May 2001 to review the implementation of the Abuja cease-fire agreement. There, the RUF renewed its commitment to the peace plan and agreed to the formula for beginning disarmament in Kambia and Port Loko districts. A timetable was set whereby simultaneous disarmament of the RUF and CDF would begin in those two districts on 18 May and conclude by 28 May, after which the Sierra Leone Army would begin deployment to Kambia to patrol the border with Guinea.[30] UNAMSIL managed to ensure the full participation of the progovernment movement in the DDR program through contacts with Kabbah's government and the leadership of the CDF.

This plan was implemented on schedule, but not before the Nigerian factor reared its head again. Through notes and discreet conversations, RUF commanders sent messages to UNAMSIL that the RUF would only disarm in Kambia to Nigerian soldiers. As if to test the RUF's resolve, UNAMSIL deployed non-Nigerian troops anyway, but they did not last two days before being driven away by the RUF. It was only when Nigerian troops were deployed that the RUF began disarming. It is not clear whether the RUF's preference was a result of trust and respect for, or fear of, the Nigerians. It is possible that RUF commanders simply knew that their men were most likely to surrender their weapons to the contingent they feared the most.

The disarmament of the RUF in Kambia and continued engagement by UNAMSIL senior commanders, as well as facilitation by the Joint Implementation Committee, opened the floodgate to all sorts of compliance by the RUF. The DDR process was restarted as the RUF disarmed in other districts throughout Sierra Leone and began releasing some of the abducted children it held in custody. By now, the DDR process had been delayed an entire year. But this turned out to be a blessing, since it allowed time for sufficient planning and a more sound financial footing to be secured. The year before, in 1999, the international community, distracted by crises in Timor and Kosovo, had provided only scant support for the DDR process. Some even argued that the May 2000 crisis spared the government and donors "serious embarrassment" resulting from a possible collapse of the system.[31]

Other progress was made: roads previously blocked by the RUF were opened. The humanitarian community had access to populations in need of assistance throughout Sierra Leone. For the first time, it was possible to conduct accurate assessments of the population's support requirements, rather than relying on wild guesses. The RUF participated in subsequent peace meetings and began the process of transforming itself into a political group.

In the end, the combination of diplomacy and a demonstration of military capability won the peace in Sierra Leone. Even those who had argued against Adeniji's diplomatic approach could not challenge the success of the Kambia formula, which was made possible by the fact that diplomatic channels had remained open throughout. In Adeniji's own view:

> If a single measure could be considered as the crucial step which accelerated the peace process in post-May 2000, it was the Kambia Formula. Besides its importance in enabling fast implementation of the central internal issue—the DDR—it also resolved the immediate regional complication linked to the attitude of Guinea. Other regional aspects were addressed by Security Council actions in imposing sanctions on Liberia as well as on the export of Sierra Leone diamond which was known to have fuelled the conflict.[32]

Former RUF child soldiers run to a UN transport helicopter in the eastern provincial capital of Kaliahun, June 2001.

Chris Hondros/Getty Images

▌ Radio: The Mainstay of Mass Communication

Alongside the military and political crises that May 2000 gave rise to, there was an additional crisis related to the credibility of the UN in Sierra Leone. To revive the image of the mission, UNAMSIL's leadership realized that public information was key. But as long as the Sierra Leone media continued to be the gatekeeper of public information, it would not be easy to counter the UNAMSIL-bashing that was so prevalent. In May 2000, one could not listen to the radio for a few minutes without hearing anti-UNAMSIL sentiments, and the newspapers were no different. UNAMSIL was an easy target and the mission was blamed for everything. For example, when there were riots on the streets of Freetown, or when the National Commission for Disarmament, Demobilization, and Reintegration was delayed in making payments, UNAMSIL was blamed.

UNAMSIL staff were exasperated and felt that the absence of a strong public information unit was proving near fatal to the mission's credibility. The Public Information section began the process of reversing this negative publicity by airing pro-UNAMSIL jingles on Sierra Leonean radio stations. Radio Democracy played the jingles, as did the Voice of the Handicapped. But neither of these stations could broadcast much farther than Freetown, and the government stations did not play the jingles. UNAMSIL did not have its own radio station, as it was waiting for equipment from a mission winding down in Central Africa.

The May crisis brought a sense of urgency to the mission's public information efforts, and Radio UNAMSIL was set up at break-neck speed by the innovative Sheila Dallas. Fairly soon, it had developed from an initial eight hours of programming into a twenty-four-hour operation. It covered 90 percent of Sierra Leone, giving it a much needed edge over other stations, and maintained a permanent presence in all the provinces, where it employed local staff to file reports back to headquarters. And it was able to broadcast in a number of local languages, including Mende, Temne, Limba, and local Krio. Adeniji's fluency in Krio was used to maximum advantage by the station.

Radio UNAMSIL's programs combined popular music with civil affairs, news, and phone-ins. On civil affairs, it covered communities and chiefdoms and took up topical issues such as amputees and the war-wounded, which were hotly debated through phone-ins. It helped foster more moderate and objective views among Sierra Leoneans toward the

Yayando Mu'azu working as a technician at the UNAMSIL radio station, October 2005.

Fredrik Naumann/Panos Pictures

UN. Less often acknowledged, but equally important, it also helped make Sierra Leone more cohesive, by encouraging open discussion and countering some false impressions among Sierra Leoneans of what was happening in other parts of the country.

With Radio UNAMSIL as its mass communications arm, UNAMSIL began a media campaign through which it gained the upper hand in the information war. Key to this was the existence of a proactive Chief of Information, Margaret Novicki, described by her colleagues and other Sierra Leoneans as full of life and passionate about her work. As a spokesperson for UNAMSIL, Novicki dealt effectively with the press across the board, and developed a comprehensive, proactive information strategy to counter the negativity and misinformation surrounding UNAMSIL.

In the process, UNAMSIL's Public Information section provided Sierra Leone's media institutions with valuable capacity development. Several journalists were trained by the UN to work on the station. Young people were helped to broadcast their own programs through a Voice of Children radio program, run by and for children, which was established at the initiation of Olara Otunnu, then Special Representative of the Secretary-General for Children and Armed Conflict; many of these young people later became broadcasters on other radio stations. When the mission withdrew, Radio UNAMSIL was left in place for Sierra Leoneans to continue nationwide broadcasting, an important legacy of the mission.

▌ Quick-impact Projects

Another way that UNAMSIL was able to come back in the battle for "hearts and minds" was through a charm offensive by several UNAMSIL contingents. Using their own human and financial resources, some contingents—especially those from Bangladesh and Pakistan—rebuilt community infrastructure, including mosques and schools. These activities, which had become widespread by mid-2001, were later labeled quick-impact projects. Some outside observers criticized these efforts as missionary causes, concerned that the building of mosques, for example, was unduly influencing the local population to take up a particular religion. However, the locals did not tend to see things this way, as they watched schools, wells, and other projects unfold.

The proliferation of quick-impact projects was not in fact a conscious strategy designed by UNAMSIL, but rather the product of disjointedness between UNAMSIL and the humanitarian community. As UNAMSIL battalions began to deploy in Sierra Leone's hinterland, the extent of the humanitarian crisis outside Freetown became apparent. But attempts by some battalion commanders to liaise with the humanitarian agencies on the ground met with resistance. Though there was good reason to work together, the humanitarian's code of conduct, oriented around strict neutrality, did not make this possible. For example, when the Kenyan commander in Makeni called a meeting in a bid to organize humanitarian assistance for people in that community, the humanitarian agencies refused to attend because the meeting would have been held in a military compound and would have undermined their humanitarian space.

The frustration of not being able to collaborate formally with humanitarian agencies led UNAMSIL to seek ways to enable the military do some humanitarian work on its own, and it soon became common practice for the military contingents to have humanitarian units. Staff at UN headquarters in New York debated whether this should be allowed, as some argued that humanitarian work fell outside the mission's mandate. These planners were concerned about the health of the humanitarian-military-political interface in Sierra Leone (later improved significantly with the arrival of Alan Doss as DSRSG for Governance and Stabilization). Yet the irony is that Sierra Leoneans are the first to identify quick-impact initiatives as part of the success story of UNAMSIL.

*   *   *

By the end of 2001, UNAMSIL's fortunes had undergone a surprising turnaround on many levels. Militarily, the force was now more competent and empowered, a more genuine deterrent than had been the case in May 2000. Politically, high-level political dialogue and openness had helped move the peace process along, and the RUF seemed genuinely engaged. And publicly, UNAMSIL was no longer derided as futile and weak. This turn of events, surprising even to UN optimists, had been brought about by a rare confluence of factors: a galvanized Security Council, a Secretariat undergoing a period of self-criticism, and a mission leadership that gelled and produced an astute political strategy. The mission derided as a failure in 2000 was on its way toward becoming a success story.

∎ Notes

1. See *Fifth Report of the Secretary-General on the United Nations Mission in Sierra Leone*, UN Doc. S/2000/751, 31 July 2000, paras. 53–54.

2. Secretariat reports that are made public and deal with politically sensitive issues are often carefully crafted so as not to offend the sensitivities of key member states upon whose cooperation the bureaucracy depends.

3. See *Report of the Panel on United Nations Peace Operations*, UN Doc. A/55/305-S/2000/809, 21 August 2000.

4. The Brahimi Report defines spoilers as "groups (including signatories) who renege on their commitments or otherwise seek to undermine a peace accord by violence." See *Report of the Panel.*

5. See *Report of the Panel*, p. x.

6. See *UN Security Council Resolution 1289*, UN Doc. S/RES/1289, 7 February 2000 (see text of Resolution 1289 in this volume).

7. See *UN Security Council Resolution 1299*, UN Doc. S/RES/1299, 19 May 2000.

8. See *Fourth Report of the Secretary-General on the United Nations Mission in Sierra Leone*, UN Doc. S/2000/455, 19 May 2000; and *Eighth Report of the Secretary-General on the United Nations Mission in Sierra Leone*, UN Doc. S/2000/1199, 15 December 2000.

9. See *UN Security Council Resolution 1346*, UN Doc. S/RES/1346, 30 March 2001.

10. See ibid., para. 3.

11. See *Eighth Report of the Secretary-General*, para. 60.

12. See *UN Security Council Resolution 1313*, UN Doc. S/RES/1313, 4 August 2000.

13. See *Sixth Report of the Secretary-General on the United Nations Mission in Sierra Leone*, UN Doc. S/2000/832/Add-1, 12 September 2000.

14. John L. Hirsch, *Sierra Leone: Diamonds and the Struggle for Democracy* (Boulder: Lynne Rienner, 2001), p. 102.

15. Holbrooke was sworn in on 25 August 1999 at the US mission in New York.

16. Interview with a UN staff member, New York, December 2005.

17. See Tim Weiner, "G.O.P. Senator Frees Millions for U.N. Mission in Sierra Leone," *New York Times*, 7 June 2000, p. A10.

18. Telephone interviews with Adriaan Verhuel, September 2006.

19. See *Report of the Panel of Experts Pursuant to Security Council Resolution 1306 (2000), Paragraph 19, Concerning Sierra Leone*, UN Doc. S/2000/1195, 20 December 2000; and *UN Security Council Resolution 1343*, UN Doc. S/RES/1343, 7 March 2001.

20. Interview with Adriaan Verhuel.

21. See *Sixth Report of the Secretary-General.*

22. See David Keen, *Conflict and Collusion in Sierra Leone* (Oxford: Currey, 2005), p. 273.

23. Many of the West Side Boys were not former soldiers at all, but criminals who had been released from Pademba Road Prison as the AFRC/RUF junta retreated from Freetown in February 1998.

24. See Keen, *Conflict and Collusion in Sierra Leone*, pp. 284–285.

25. See United Nations, *Lessons Learned from United Nations Peacekeeping Experiences in Sierra Leone* (New York: Department of Peacekeeping Operations, Peacekeeping Best Practices Unit, September 2003), p. 10.

26. See *Eighth Report of the Secretary-General.*

27. Ibid.

28. Ibid.

29. See Amnesty International, "Guinea and Sierra Leone Border: Fighting

Continues to Endanger Civilian Lives," 4 May 2001, Amnesty International Index: AFR 51/004/2001.

30. See *Tenth Report of the Secretary-General on the United Nations Mission in Sierra Leone*, UN Doc. S/2001/627, 25 June 2001.

31. See Keen, *Conflict and Collusion in Sierra Leone*, pp. 256–260.

32. Oluyemi Adeniji, "End of Assignment Report of Special Representative of the Secretary-General for Sierra Leone," United Nations Secretariat, 2003.

7 | UNAMSIL: The Model Mission?

IN THE YEARS THAT FOLLOWED the Abuja cease-fire, UNAMSIL was able to build on its recovery to become what many have described as a model peacekeeping mission. At its 2002 peak, it was the largest and most expensive UN mission on the ground, with over 17,000 troops and a large civilian staff, at a total cost of nearly US$700 million a year.[1] This mission was able to carry out a massive disarmament program, successfully organize elections, and most important, provide a secure environment. When it left Sierra Leone at the end of 2005, there was much for the UN to celebrate.

This chapter documents the last years of UNAMSIL and its journey toward the status of a model mission. It outlines the mission's achievements in the "postconflict" phase of Sierra Leone's story, but also the limitations imposed by its mandate and withdrawal. It takes stock of all that still needed to be done, even after UNAMSIL departed in December 2005, to prevent a relapse into conflict, and assesses recent UN innovations in this area.

■ Disarmament and Elections

On 18 January 2002, President Ahmad Tejan Kabbah declared disarmament complete and the Sierra Leone civil war over. At a symbolic ceremony in Lungi, weapons were burned to represent the 47,000 former combatants who had turned in their weapons, mostly from the RUF and the CDF, between May 2001, when the disarmament program resumed, and January 2002.[2] For the first time since the conflict started, there was a real possibility that important tasks like elections and the consolidation of peace could take place.

UN peacekeepers intervene during clashes between supporters of the Revolutionary United Front Party (RUFP) and the Sierra Leone People's Party (SLPP) in Freetown, May 2002.

Georges Gobet/AFP/Getty Images

The first half of 2002 was dominated by preparations for the upcoming parliamentary and presidential elections, scheduled for May. Voter registration began in January, and political parties began to announce their candidates. Within the new political party formed by the RUF, called the Revolutionary United Front Party (RUFP), this was especially difficult. With Foday Sankoh awaiting trial and Issa Sesay too young to meet the presidential age requirement, the party's interim secretary-general, Alimamy Pallo Bangura, was eventually put forward following a tortuous process. Meanwhile, former AFRC junta chairman Johnny Paul Koroma resigned from his position as chairman of the government's Commission for the Consolidation of Peace, and announced that he too would contest the presidency as a candidate for the Peace and Liberation Party.

Held on 14 May, the elections were largely peaceful, notwithstanding some clashes on 11 May between members of the Sierra Leone People's Party and the former rebels of the RUFP in central Freetown, condemned by both parties. Observers from the European Union and Commonwealth deemed the elections as free and fair as possible given the circumstances,

A UNAMSIL soldier stands guard as Sierra Leoneans queue at a polling station in Freetown, May 2002.

Georges Gobet/AFP/Getty Images

and said that none of the problems reported were serious enough to have affected the outcome. With more than 70 percent of the presidential vote, President Kabbah won by a landslide, while the SLPP also won the majority of seats in the parliament. Bangura managed to secure only 1.7 percent of the presidential vote, and the RUFP failed to win a single parliamentary seat.[3]

UNAMSIL, mandated by the Security Council to help the government conduct the elections, assisted in the registration of more than 2.3 million voters, conducted mass voter education campaigns through the Public Information section, and set up offices in each electoral region to monitor the process and assist international election observers. During the elections themselves, it provided security for high-risk areas as well as logistical support, including the procurement of ballot boxes and communications equipment.[4] With military, civilian police, military observer, and civilian staff engaged, it was a truly joint effort, coordinated by a newly established electoral unit. It was the crowning glory for a mission that two years before had faced the wrath of Sierra Leoneans.

■ The Liberia Question and Conflict Diamonds

At the same time, concerns mounted that tensions in neighboring Liberia—and to some extent in Côte d'Ivoire—could have spillover effects in Sierra Leone. In early 2002, the United Nations High Commissioner for Refugees (UNHCR) began repatriating Sierra Leonean refugees from Liberia, many of whom were eager to return to vote in the election but also to escape Liberia, where clashes between government forces and insurgents were intensifying. By March 2002, the situation had worsened, and Liberian refugees were now entering Sierra Leone by the thousands, stretching the capacities of the UNHCR to the brink.[5] The UNHCR appealed for donor funding to meet these needs, but the response was slow.

In addition to causing a humanitarian crisis, the situation in Liberia risked undermining the peace in Sierra Leone, as an International Crisis Group report argued in April 2002.[6] In June, Liberian rebels attacked a refugee camp near the border with Sierra Leone, forcing some 11,000 Sierra Leonean refugees to flee.[7] During July, Liberian combatants were said to have abducted forty-six Sierra Leonean villagers during two separate raids on the town of Kokobu in Kailahun district.[8] Secretary-General Kofi Annan, echoed by SRSG Oluyemi Adeniji, warned that the escalating fighting posed a threat to the Sierra Leonean peace.[9] The Security Council also voiced concerns and called for dialogue between Mano River Union countries. But having already extended the life of UNAMSIL beyond the elections, the Council was now eager to start discussing the plan for withdrawal.[10]

As ever, Charles Taylor was at the center of the Liberian issue. In March 2003, a report by the nongovernmental organization Global Witness alleged that rebel groups fighting in Côte d'Ivoire's civil war consisted largely of Liberian and Sierra Leonean mercenaries who were being recruited, armed, trained, and directed by the Liberian government.[11] Among them was former RUF figure Sam "Mosquito" Bockarie, a close ally of Taylor's who had fled to Liberia in 1999 after breaking with Sankoh. Both of them hoped to destabilize Sierra Leone. But in 2003, Taylor's luck turned, as the Security Council extended sanctions against Liberia,[12] rumors circulated of a possible indictment by Sierra Leone's Special Court, and international efforts to end the Liberian civil war intensified. At the beginning of August, the Security Council passed a US-sponsored resolution[13] authorizing a multinational force in Liberia,[14] which was replaced by a UN mission in September under the leadership of SRSG Jacques Paul Klein. In August, a peace agreement was signed, by which time Taylor had stepped down to accept an offer of safe haven in Nigeria.[15]

The removal of Taylor from the West African stage also coincided with increasing attention on that arena in relation to the war on terror, in the aftermath of the September 2001 terrorist attacks in the United States. In a *Washington Post* article in November 2001, it was alleged that RUF leaders had been selling diamonds to Al-Qaida representatives since 1998, using a safe house in Liberia to conduct the transactions.[16] In February 2002, former US ambassador to Sierra Leone Joseph Melrose told a Senate Governmental Affairs subcommittee that there was evidence of such activity, even as the RUF, preparing to register as a legitimate political party, denied it.[17]

In May 2000, the first steps toward a process for certifying the origin of diamonds were taken at a meeting of diamond-producing countries in Kimberley, South Africa. In March 2002, the "Kimberley Process Certification Scheme" was approved by the UN General Assembly, which would come into fruition in November.[18] Participating countries were required to ensure that all exported diamonds had a Kimberley Process certificate, proving that trade in these diamonds would not help finance a rebel group or other entity seeking to overthrow a UN-recognized government, and that these diamonds had not been imported from, or exported to, a nonmember of the scheme. Human rights groups welcomed the initiative, though in subsequent years raised concerns that its implementation had been weakened by the essentially self-enforced nature of the scheme.

▍ A Fashionable Mission

Meanwhile, UNAMSIL had now become a fashionable mission, with a reputation for innovation and genuine impact. UNAMSIL's premises at Mammy Yoko Hotel were rapidly filled with a wide array of UN staff across multiple civilian issue areas. With much to do, the mission buzzed with life and there was an enormous flow of traffic up and down the steep staircases of UNAMSIL's four floors.

For a long time, the Political Affairs section was the most prominent civilian part of the mission. But as the security situation stabilized and the mission grew in capacity, attention was gradually focused on other aspects of UNAMSIL's role and that of the UN Country Team, such as long-term reintegration of demobilized combatants, extension of civil authority, and broader issues of national recovery, including poverty reduction, youth vulnerability and exclusion, women's rights, HIV/AIDS, health and education, environmental management, and child protection.[19]

In these areas, the dual Deputy Special Representative structure had significant impact. The SRSG was now free to get on with the business of diplomacy, safe in the knowledge that his DSRSG for Governance and

Stabilization, Alan Doss, was addressing critical gaps and improving inter-action with the rest of the UN family and Sierra Leonean civil society. Both of these groups acknowledged Alan Doss's dynamism in this role and the importance of his double-hatting, including Mohamed Farah, the FAO's country representative in Sierra Leone:

> The UN Country Team and UNAMSIL have worked closely together. At the beginning it was a difficult relationship. The practice of having Resident Coordinator as DSRSG means each has a seat with the other and the flow of information is better. When you need support for security, UNAMSIL is there. They have all sorts of support facility and are a fantastic resource to depend on. There is a spill over of the mission's huge amount of resources into the development and humani-tarians and therefore there is a spill over of good relations and a lot of convergence. . . . It was not a happy story initially. The link of the heart of the UN to the heart of the military was very useful. The view that we are all "UN," whether military or not, has penetrated and it makes it easier for coordination.[20]

This close cooperation was further demonstrated by the participation of UNAMSIL in the preparation of the United Nations Development Assistance Framework (UNDAF) for Sierra Leone, a framework docu-ment prepared by the UN Country Team in cooperation with the Sierra Leone government and the World Bank. The benefit of an integrated effort was immediately apparent in 2002, when the draft framework doc-ument was presented in task force meetings in New York by Doss. The key message in the framework was an overwhelming shift from emer-gency and relief operations to longer-term initiatives aimed at addressing the root causes of the Sierra Leone war, with particular emphasis on poverty reduction and reintegration, human rights and reconciliation, good governance, peace and stability, and economic recovery for the peri-od 2004–2007.[21]

But even as UNAMSIL grew increasingly competent, it continued like all UN missions to deal with new threats to its reputation and internal morale. In May 2002, the Pakistani government announced that it had begun the process of recalling over 4,000 soldiers from Sierra Leone so that they could be available at home, as tensions were escalating between Pakistan and India.[22] In August that same year, an independent inquiry conducted by Sierra Leonean civil society and human rights groups blamed UN peacekeepers for fatally shooting two people while trying to

Alan Doss, Deputy SRSG
for Governance and
Stabilization, at UN
headquarters, 2004.
UN photo/Eskinder Debebe

quell an anti-Nigerian riot in central Freetown the previous month,[23] although UNAMSIL claimed that the peacekeepers were not responsible for the deaths.[24] June 2004 was a particularly dark moment, when a Russian helicopter leased by the UN crashed into the jungle near Yengema, killing twenty-four people, among them UN staff and aid workers.[25]

Meanwhile, in February 2002, allegations surfaced that aid workers from NGOs and UN agencies in Sierra Leone, Liberia, and Guinea had sexually exploited refugee children, most of them girls aged thirteen to eighteen, according to a study commissioned by the UNHCR and the United Kingdom–based charity Save the Children.[26] Agency workers allegedly used "the very humanitarian aid and services intended to benefit the refugee population as a tool of exploitation," trading food and commodities for sex with girls.[27] While most of the perpetrators were said to be locally hired aid workers, in Sierra Leone UN peacekeepers were also implicated. The report claimed that despite UNAMSIL's efforts to enforce a code of conduct, sexual exploitation by peacekeepers was widespread throughout the country and especially ubiquitous in Freetown.[28] The UN immediately reiterated its policy of zero tolerance for such behavior and began planning initiatives to educate its peacekeepers and hold them accountable.

At the UNHCR's request, an investigation was conducted later in 2002 by the UN's Office of Internal Oversight Services (OIOS). The OIOS investigation found the allegations in the Save the Children report difficult to confirm, as many were based on third-hand accounts and lacked substantial evidence. The OIOS did confirm that "the problem of sexual exploitation of refugees is real," and made recommendations for various preventive measures.[29] However, the issue continued to undermine the UN's image, both in Sierra Leone and farther afield.[30]

In July 2003, SRSG Adeniji stepped down after he was appointed foreign minister of his homeland, Nigeria.[31] Alan Doss filled his shoes until December, when Daudi Ngelautwa Mwakawago of Tanzania was appointed to the job.[32] Mwakawago had been Permanent Representative of the United Republic of Tanzania to the UN since 1994 and was seen as a safe choice—if less inspiring compared to Adeniji—to steer the mission in its last phase. UNAMSIL was then in the drawdown phase and needed a day-to-day manager more than an astute political player. Mwakawago remained until the mission withdrew completely in December 2005, by which time much of UNAMSIL's early dynamism had dissipated and many staff had left to join the UN mission in Liberia.

■ In Pursuit of Justice

Another UN innovation tested in Sierra Leone was the establishment of a Special Court to try those accused of having committed the most serious crimes against humanity during the conflict. In previous years, a precedent had emerged for the Security Council to establish independent judicial mechanisms to address impunity in the aftermath of conflicts, notably the tribunals for Rwanda and the former Yugoslavia. But those courts had the full authority of the Security Council behind them, including authority under Chapter VII of the UN Charter to require cooperation from states. The Special Court, by contrast, was established on the basis of an agreement between the UN and the government of Sierra Leone. The court, to be based in-country and combine elements of both domestic and international law, was intended to provide a more efficient and cost-effective model for the achievement of justice than the ad hoc UN tribunals.

Talk of a Special Court actually dated from June 2000, when President Kabbah wrote a letter to the UN Secretary-General requesting assistance in prosecuting those who committed crimes against humanity during the civil war. Part of Kabbah's motivation for requesting UN assistance was that Sierra Leonean national law did not allow for the prosecution of war crimes or crimes against humanity, and in any case, his government could not afford to finance the prosecution of crimes on this scale.[33] In Sierra Leone and UN circles, it was widely believed that the letter had been orchestrated by the United States, where there was a keen interest in the issue of impunity. Some rumors even suggested that it had been drafted in the US ambassador's residence in Freetown.

Within a few months, the request for assistance was being given serious consideration. The Secretariat's Office of Legal Affairs busied itself drafting possible statutes, and a new hybrid arrangement was proposed—a Special Court with both international and Sierra Leonean characteristics. There was great interest across the UN community. Some were worried that the threat of indictment would discourage rebels from disarming, and therefore hinder the peace process. The prosecutor ultimately indicted only thirteen people, ten of whom were arrested. But then questions about funding began to be asked, such as whether spending US$25 million a year on trials for just a handful of people was justifiable.[34] The legal status of those under the age of eighteen was also controversial. Article 7 of the enabling statute allowed for those aged fifteen to eighteen to be indicted, but Prosecutor David Crane of the United States stated that he would not indict anyone for crimes committed while under the age of eighteen.[35]

The Security Council saw the Special Court as an important tool in the pursuit of justice and reconciliation, but was careful to balance these goals against "the need to minimize any potential disincentive to entering the disarmament, demobilization and reintegration process that the threat of prosecution may present—especially to child combatants."[36] In the end, however, the Council's decision that the court's funding would not come from assessed contributions to the UN, but rather from voluntary contributions, meant that the court was saddled with a long fundraising process. To manage the contributions, a committee representing a group of "interested states"—all contributors to the court—was established. Inadvertently, this resolved the DDR issue, as protracted discussions over funding stalled the court's operations until after the DDR process was completed.

Eventually, the funding shortfall caused the Secretary-General to move forward with scaled-down plans for the Special Court in January 2002, and an agreement between the government of Sierra Leone and the UN was signed on 16 January 2002. This paved the way for the appointment of American David M. Crane to the post of chief prosecutor, after which the first staff began to arrive and construction began on a complex of court buildings and a detention center in Freetown. In March 2003, the Special Court handed down its first indictments, six to former RUF and AFRC junta leaders (including Sankoh, Koroma, Bockarie, and Sesay) and one to CDF leader Sam Hinga Norman, who was serving as the minister

A UN soldier stands guard in front of the Special Court for Sierra Leone in Freetown, March 2006.

of internal affairs at the time. Meanwhile, the Truth and Reconciliation Commission (TRC), agreed to at Lomé, was finally inaugurated in July 2002, when commissioners were sworn in. It too was forced to scale back its budget significantly and suffered from continual financial and management problems into its operational phase in late 2002.[37]

Unlike the TRC, the Special Court, having been approved by both the Security Council and the General Assembly, was UN-endorsed, albeit judicially independent. But its relationship to the rest of the UN system would prove tense. Although the Security Council welcomed the indictments, the fact that the court had been established under a treaty between the UN and Sierra Leone, rather than a Chapter VII resolution of the Security Council, meant that cooperation by member states in arresting indictees and gathering evidence was voluntary, rather than mandatory. This became an issue after Taylor was indicted in June 2003 and the court called for him to be arrested in Ghana and then unsuccessfully sought a Security Council resolution obliging UN member states to cooperate. Ultimately, the court secured custody of Taylor nonetheless, in March 2006.

Meanwhile, there were concerns within UNAMSIL that the Special Court's activities would destabilize the security situation and the mission's political strategy. Some regional leaders felt that the court was compromising efforts to secure peace, as Taylor, fearful of being handed over for trial, was refusing to relinquish office. Adeniji, now Nigeria's foreign minister, also implied that the court's expectations concerning regional governments and the Taylor question were insensitive and even offensive.[38] The UNAMSIL leadership was well aware of these issues, which were compounded by additional tensions regarding the roles of the court and the mission—which had its own human rights section—with respect to broader questions on rule of law in Sierra Leone. A de facto division of labor emerged, however, when it became clear that the court had limited capacity to deal with such issues.

As of this writing, of the thirteen people indicted so far—for war crimes, crimes against humanity, and other serious violations of international humanitarian law—ten remain. Sankoh died in custody in 2003 and Norman died in custody in 2007. Bockarie and Koroma both fled the country seeking protection from Taylor; Bockarie later died, while Koroma's whereabouts remain unknown (and his indictment therefore stands). The first verdicts were announced on 20 June 2007, though most attention is on Taylor, who was finally arrested in March 2006. Upon a formal request from newly elected Liberian president Ellen Johnson-Sirleaf for Taylor to be transferred from Nigeria to the Special Court in Sierra Leone, Taylor fled his guarded residence for the Cameroon border. He was apprehended a few days later, however, and was subsequently arrested by Nigerian authorities. He was then taken to headquarters of the UN mission in Liberia, which transferred him into the custody of the Special Court in Freetown. However, his presence in the country was thought to be so inflammatory that it constituted a threat to regional peace and security. By authorization of the Security Council,[39] he was moved to The Hague in June 2006. The Special Court will continue to conduct the proceedings of his trial, which began in June 2007.

The Special Court has had an important role in achieving justice in Sierra Leone, and at a lower cost than the tribunals. There is no doubt of its mixed political impact, however. As well as inciting resentment among supporters of indictees and increasingly among ordinary Sierra Leoneans, who consider the court's continued presence as a waste of valuable resources, its defense teams have become highly politicized; Charles Margai, son of former prime minister Albert Margai and one of the CDF's defense counsels, became the main opposition candidate, representing the People's Movement for Democratic Change (PMDC) in the presidential elections of August 2007. For this reason, the court's relationship with UNAMSIL toward the end of the mission—one of polite separation—was

Charles Taylor is escorted by UN personnel to a plane departing for The Hague from Freetown, June 2006.
© Special Court for Sierra Leone Handout/epa/CORBIS

probably the best it had ever been. This did not reflect any specific failure on either side, but the reality that the principles of the UN—peace, security, human rights, justice—are not always compatible, even when they are each particularly desirable.

■ Establishing Benchmarks for UNAMSIL's Withdrawal

Perhaps the most innovative development within UNAMSIL was the set of benchmarks developed for UNAMSIL's withdrawal. In many previous cases, the Security Council had regarded elections as the key element of its exit strategy from a conflict zone. In Sierra Leone, although the Security Council began reducing UNAMSIL's troop strength as early as September 2002, it understood that a full disengagement could not occur until the domestic security sector had been adequately strengthened and state authority had been consolidated throughout the country.[40] Across the border, Liberia provided powerful evidence of that fact. In 1997, the international community (including the key ECOWAS states that had borne the major costs of peacemaking) had been desperate to shed the burden. But

failure to resolve fundamental security issues and to address the root causes of the crisis had led to another outbreak of war, practically negating the
international community's investment.

The exit strategy in Sierra Leone was linked to a number of issues,
related to the reasons for UNAMSIL's deployment in the first place and the
extent to which its objectives had been met. There was every indication
that the armed conflict had entirely stopped, notwithstanding sporadic incidents, such as an attack on a military supply depot near Freetown in
January 2003 thought to have involved Johnny Paul Koroma. But the
extension of state authority throughout the country—especially its control
of revenue sources such as diamond and gold mining—would prove more
challenging. During 2002 and 2003, the Security Council expressed concerns about the slow pace of government efforts in this respect,[41] clearly
concerned by rumors of the government's "dependency" on the mission.
Meanwhile, the SRSG and Secretary-General also appealed for withdrawal plans to reflect actual conditions on the ground rather than Security
Council aspirations. The result was a series of six-month extensions for
UNAMSIL leading up to the final withdrawal in December 2005, a system
inconvenient for mission planners but one to which UN staff were well
accustomed.

In his fifteenth report to the Security Council on UNAMSIL, in
September 2002, the Secretary-General underscored the importance of setting "specific benchmarks" to guide UNAMSIL's withdrawal from Sierra
Leone, the greatest concern being to avoid creating a "security vacuum" in
the country. Progress in building the capacity of the police and army was
to constitute the key security benchmark; others included completing the
reintegration of former combatants, consolidating state authority throughout the country, and restoring effective government control over diamond
mining.[42] The result was an adjustment, drawdown, and withdrawal
(ADW) plan that called for a gradual and systematic transfer of responsibility for security in Sierra Leone from UNAMSIL to Sierra Leone's new
army, which Kabbah named the Republic of Sierra Leone Armed Forces
(RSLAF) in January 2002, and the police force. The country was divided
into four zones, which corresponded to provinces, with security to be
handed over zone by zone.

The withdrawal, over a period of two years, was surprisingly successful. Before handover in each province, exercises were conducted to test the
readiness and capacity of the government security agencies to take over.
These began in the Northern province, considered the most benign part of
the country, and then moved, consecutively, to the Southern, Eastern, and
Western provinces. With the transfer of primary responsibility for security

in the Western area, which included Freetown, on 23 September 2004, UNAMSIL had successfully concluded the transfer of overall responsibility for security to the government of Sierra Leone.[43] Meanwhile, with a peace agreement in Liberia in 2003, the Security Council mandated UNAMSIL to assist in the initial deployment of the ECOWAS Mission in Liberia (ECOMIL),[44] and redeployed one of UNAMSIL's Nigerian battalions (NiBatt-15) to Liberia from Sierra Leone, renaming it NiBatt-1.[45]

The role of the UK in supporting several years of security-sector reform was vital for the drawdown phase. Its International Military Advisory and Training Team provided training for the RSLAF. It also provided technical assistance for other security agencies, including in the area of intelligence, where it was involved in creating the Office of National Security. Combined with UN Police, the UK also led a Commonwealth effort to train the Sierra Leone Police.

■ The Transition to "Peacebuilding"

Through the withdrawal period, the international community was well aware that Sierra Leone faced an array of challenges beyond security. In July 2002, a report released by the Brussels-based International Crisis Group outlined multiple political threats to stability, including a strong north-south divide exposed by the elections, a failure by President Kabbah to form a cabinet sufficiently broad-based to promote national reconciliation, and an ongoing culture of "winner take all" politics. Notwithstanding the existence of the Anticorruption Commission, official corruption—a major issue for donor governments—remained widespread, and there were also allegations of government interference in elections for paramount chieftancies.[46] Meanwhile, the victims of conflict, particularly organized groups of amputees, complained consistently that they were being treated far more poorly than the perpetrators of the conflict.

Poverty and a general lack of opportunity were also clear for all to see in Sierra Leone. In the UNDP's 2003 Human Development Index (HDI), an index of composite country rankings based on health, education, and income measurements, Sierra Leone was given a rank of 175 out of 175 countries, marking its third consecutive year of ranking last on the HDI. At 34.5 years, Sierra Leone's average life expectancy was the second lowest in the world.[47] As in other parts of West Africa, an enormous number of unemployed youths roamed the streets with nothing to do. Meanwhile, the infrastructure of the country and institutions of central government had effectively collapsed during the conflict, such that the government lacked the proper capacity to address even basic needs like health and education.

There was growing recognition that a failure to address some of the root causes of the conflict, such as poverty and a lack of opportunity, risked undermining the investment of the international community in Sierra Leone.

The problem, as ever, was one of funding. As a peacekeeping mission, UNAMSIL was funded from the peacekeeping budget agreed to by the Security Council, which focused primarily on the costs of staffing and operating a military operation and its civilian counterparts. Within the UN system, money for humanitarian work, and for the transition to recovery and development, was located in the agencies and programs. But these had no funds of their own, and instead relied on voluntary funds from donors. The consolidation of peace required the commitment of donors, including foreign governments and international financial institutions.

Relatively speaking, Sierra Leone was a lucky case. It had the commitment of the UK, which, in addition to funding security-sector reform, signed a memorandum of understanding with the Sierra Leone government in November 2002 committing itself to ten years of development assistance. Sierra Leone also benefited from low-interest loans, grants, and debt relief from financial institutions such as the World Bank, the International Monetary Fund, and the African Development Bank, which were broadly impressed by the country's economic performance in the aftermath of war. Also in November, the "Consultative Group" for Sierra Leone, designed to foster dialogue between the Sierra Leone government, international agencies, and donor governments, met in Paris for two days of talks convened by the UNDP and the World Bank.[48] Pledges of financial and technical support were made in areas such as security, governance and anticorruption action, public-sector reform, private-sector promotion, control of diamond resources, and aid coordination.

However, like so many other postconflict countries, Sierra Leone found that, now that the period of emergency was over, the international communtity's generosity was diminishing. The UN—including UNAMSIL, the Country Team, and also the Security Council—frequently complained about funding shortfalls across multiple areas. But just as Sierra Leone had earlier benefited from changes in peacekeeping arising from the Brahimi Report, it was to benefit again, in 2005, from a growing recognition of the importance of continuity beyond the peacekeeping phase. A new emphasis on peacebuilding arose partly as a result of the High-Level Panel on Threats, Challenges, and Change, appointed by the Secretary-General in 2003 to take stock of major security threats and the UN's responses to them. In light of the stark fact that half of all countries emerging from civil war tend to relapse back into conflict within five years of a peace agreement,[49] the panel claimed in its report that international support to such countries was often too short-term, poorly coordinated, and insufficiently focused on building the capacity of core institutions.[50]

The panel's recommendations, incorporated into Secretary-General Annan's own reform initiative,[51] catalyzed a new interest in peacebuilding and the establishment at UN headquarters of the Peacebuilding Commission, an intergovernmental body intended to help the Security Council focus on longer-term peacebuilding needs, including a postconflict country's needs once the troops have gone home, and engage international financial institutions on the issue of recovery. Sierra Leone, with its myriad problems, seemed a case ripe for the attentions of such a body.

▌ UNAMSIL to UNIOSIL

Indicative of the same recognition of longer-term needs, in December 2004, UNAMSIL and the UN Country Team began developing a transition plan (see Figure 7.1) to move international involvement from peacekeeping to peacebuilding in 2005.[52] The plan, completed in March 2005, listed tasks to be implemented in five key areas: security; consolidation of peace and political stability; consolidation of state authority and governance; reintegration of former combatants; and national recovery and economic and social development.[53] It was an ambitious plan, but it lacked a proper implementation strategy and seemed most concerned with establishing benchmarks and ticking them off before December 2005 in order to demonstrate UNAMSIL's success. That time period was of course hopelessly unrealistic.

In the end, security was the only withdrawal benchmark achieved with a high degree of satisfaction by the time UNAMSIL's mandate formally ended in December 2005. Despite sporadic incidents, such as a clash between the supporters of rival political groups in November 2005 in Bo, concerns that the security situation would deteriorate rapidly as soon as the bulk of UN troops left proved unfounded. Although some illicit mining of diamonds continued, the scale was not equivalent to earlier years and official exports of diamonds increased significantly. Moreover, despite problems with the DDR process, UNAMSIL, over the course of its mandate, successfully disarmed and demobilized over 75,000 combatants and collected more than 42,000 weapons,[54] thereby detaching former fighters from the command structures of their armed groups and dismantling RUF military structures.

Figure 7.1 The UNAMSIL Transition Plan

Security

- Strengthen the Office of National Security.
- Build capacity of Republic of Sierra Leone Armed Forces (RSLAF) to maintain security.
- Return the Sierra Leone Police to its prewar strength and build its capacity through training and infrastructure development.

Consolidation of Peace and Political Stability

- Promote national reconciliation through facilitation of dialogue and capacity building for parliament, political parties, and civil society.
- Enhance regional cooperation, including through support for reactivation of the Mano River Union.

Consolidation of State Authority and Governance

- Support electoral reform through restructuring of the National Electoral Commission.
- Decentralize governance through capacity building for district offices and local councils.
- Reform and strengthen the justice sector through training of additional magistrates and new prison officers.
- Strengthen the Anticorruption Commission through an improved national anticorruption strategy.
- Strengthen government control over diamond mining through cooperation from the private sector.

Reintegration of Former Combatants

- Promote community-based reintegration programs at the district level, with particular focus on skills development for youth; monitor the impact of reintegration on former combatants, children, and communities.
- Facilitate cross-border repatriation and reintegration of former Sierra Leonean and Liberian combatants and refugees.
- Address cross-border disarmament, demobilization, and reintegration by monitoring and curbing illicit traffic and trade of small arms and light weapons in the Mano River region.

National Recovery and Economic and Social Development

- Improve economic and financial management through development of a poverty reduction strategy, improved systems for revenue collection and procurement, and support to the civil service.

(continues)

(Figure 7.1 continued)

- Promote job creation and microenterprise among youth through capacity-building programs and establishment of nationwide youth structures.
- Support increased participation of women in local government, provide skills development for women entrepreneurs, and increase women's access to microcredit.
- Strengthen the capacity of national child protection institutions, including social welfare programs and legislative frameworks.
- Implement health-sector reform through capacity building and decentralization of health services; build capacity of educational institutions, including through teacher training.
- Expand HIV/AIDS prevention and treatment to highly vulnerable populations, and reduce the rate of infection.

As is common in peacekeeping environments, serious questions surrounded the reintegration aspect of DDR. Although the majority of disarmed and demobilized combatants registered by Sierra Leone's National Commission for Disarmament, Demobilization, and Reintegration were offered reintegration opportunities, the reintegration program suffered from a shortfall in funding that slowed the pace as early as September 2002. In Resolution 1436 of September 2002, the Security Council urged the government of Sierra Leone, which was barely able to function, to "seek actively the urgently needed additional resources for reintegration."[55] Adeniji pointed out that the original budget had been based on vastly underestimated numbers of combatants. But an additional problem was that UNAMSIL's Civil Affairs section was unable to tend to much of the country when the government had little or no authority outside the capital.

Likewise, even as UNAMSIL's presence increased around the countryside, the task of supporting the reinstatement of state authority throughout Sierra Leone proved very difficult, given the sheer magnitude of the collapse of institutional and physical infrastructure. There was an obvious lack of progress, for example, in the development of a system for domestic revenue collection, let alone the bigger tasks of poverty reduction and development. Within government ministries unable to tap the funding available for security-sector reform, it was common to find only a handful of staff who, having just a few old computers and desks, were barely capable of taking stock of the country's needs, let alone addressing them.

In this context, questions were raised by Sierra Leoneans as to why the UN was leaving while poverty was still so rampant. The answer provided by UNAMSIL's leadership was that UNAMSIL was a peacekeeping mis-

Workers pan for diamonds in a government-controlled diamond mine near Kenema, June 2001.

Chris Hondros/Getty Images

sion and that the work of peacekeeping—the establishment of security—was done, and a lot more than that as well. The UN Country Team, international financial institutions, and international donors would stay on to address the root causes and put the country on a more normal development track. But to preserve a semblance of continuity, the Security Council decided to create a successor mission to assist with peacebuilding, the United Nations Integrated Office in Sierra Leone (UNIOSIL). Now the DSRSG, serving as both Resident/Humanitarian Coordinator and UNDP Resident Representative—a post occupied since September 2004 by Victor da Silva Angelo—was, in addition, named head of the mission, with the title "Executive Representative of the Secretary-General."[56]

UNAMSIL's mandate ended in the same month—December 2005—that the Peacebuilding Commission was established at UN headquarters in New York.[57] UNIOSIL took over from UNAMSIL on 1 January 2006. In 2006, at the request of the governments in question, the Peacebuilding Commission selected Sierra Leone and Burundi as its first cases. The achievements of the commission to date—agreeing on priority areas and $35 million for Sierra Leone from a special "peacebuilding fund"—have been less expansive than its adherents might have hoped, largely because the body has been sidetracked by procedural issues and a lack of clarity about its role. But it is still too early to judge whether the international community's awareness of the importance of peacebuilding can be translated into sustained commitments on the ground well beyond the signing of a peace agreement.

The irony of UNAMSIL's legacy is that the peacebuilding community has come to see Sierra Leone as its "easy" case, a country in which there was a successful peacekeeping mission and a lot of international assistance. In 2007, the environment remained stable, the RSLAF was in control of security, and in August and September Sierra Leoneans had the opportunity to participate meaningfully in choosing the leadership of their country. But livelihoods and opportunity structures had not improved significantly, and the political environment was tense in the lead-up to elections.

Although the story of UNAMSIL—one of deep crisis followed by a painful recovery and ultimately a celebrated withdrawal—may be over, it remains to be seen whether the peace the troops fought for will be consolidated. The events of the coming years will be key to determining whether UNAMSIL retains its status as a success story.

▌ Notes

1. See *Fifteenth Report of the Secretary-General on the United Nations Mission in Sierra Leone*, UN Doc. S/2002/987, 5 September 2002.

2. See *Thirteenth Report of the Secretary-General on the United Nations Mission in Sierra Leone*, UN Doc. S/2002/267, 14 March 2002; and UNAMSIL, "Sierra Leone War Is Over, Declares President," press release, 18 January 2002, http://www.un.org/depts/dpko/unamsil/db/180102.htm.

3. See "Sierra Leone's Kabbah Urges Unity," *BBC World News*, 20 May 2002, http://news.bbc.co.uk/2/hi/africa/1997843.stm.

4. See *Fourteenth Report of the Secretary-General on the United Nations Mission in Sierra Leone*, UN Doc. S/2002/679, 19 June 2002, paras. 8–9.

5. See *Thirteenth Report of the Secretary-General*.

6. See International Crisis Group, *Liberia: The Key to Ending Regional Instability*, Africa Report no. 43 (Freetown, 24 April 2002).

7. See "Sierra Leone: Liberian Rebels Attack on Refugee Camp, Abduct Relief Workers," *BBC Monitoring Africa*, 23 June 2002.

8. See "Sierra Leone: Armed Men from Liberia Abduct Civilians," *Africa News*, 29 July 2002.

9. See *Fourteenth Report of the Secretary-General*.

10. See *UN Security Council Resolution 1436*, UN Doc. S/RES/1436, 24 September 2002.

11. See Global Witness, "The Usual Suspects: Liberia's Weapons and Mercenaries in Côte d'Ivoire and Sierra Leone," March 2003.

12. See *UN Security Council Resolution 1478*, UN Doc. S/RES/1478, 6 May 2003.

13. See *UN Security Council Resolution 1497*, UN Doc. S/RES/1497, 1 August 2003.

14. The deployment of the ECOWAS Mission in Liberia (ECOMIL), support-ed by UNAMSIL and the United States, began in August 2003.

15. See *UN Security Council Resolution 1509*, UN Doc. S/RES/1509, 19 September 2003; and *Report of the Secretary-General to the Security Council on Liberia*, UN Doc. S/2003/875, 11 September 2003.

16. See Douglas Farah, "Al Qaeda Cash Tied to Diamond Trade: Sale of Gems from Sierra Leone Rebels Raised Millions, Sources Say," *Washington Post*, 2 November 2001, p. A1.

17. See Joseph Melrose, "Testimony of Hon. Joseph Melrose, Former U.S. Ambassador to Sierra Leone," *Illicit Diamonds, Conflict, and Terrorism: The Role of U.S. Agencies in Fighting the Conflict Diamond Trade*, hearing before the Committee on Governmental Affairs, Subcommittee on Oversight of Government Management, Restructuring, and the District of Columbia, US Senate, Washington, DC, 13 February 2002.

18. See *UN General Assembly Resolution 57/302*, UN Doc. A/RES/57/302, 13 March 2002.

19. In January 2000, UNAMSIL became the first peacekeeping mission to deploy a Child Protection Adviser. See Office of the Special Representative of the Secretary-General for Children and Armed Conflict, "Briefing by Special Representative for Children and Armed Conflict," press release, 22 February 2000.

20. Interview with Mohamed Farrah, representative of the Food and Agriculture Organization, Sierra Leone, December 2005.

21. United Nations, *Sierra Leone: Peace, Recovery, and Development—UN Development Assistance Framework, 2004–2007* (UN Country Team, March 2003).

22. See Zahid Hussain, "Pakistan Is Ready to Call Peace Troops Home to War," *The Times* (London), 24 May 2002.

23. See "UN Soldiers Killed Victims in Freetown Riot: Report," *Agence France Presse*, 25 August 2002.

24. UNAMSIL established a fact-finding committee to investigate the deaths of two civilians during the anti-Nigerian riots on 18 July, and concluded that, although peacekeepers had fired warning shots into the air as a crowd-dispersal tactic, this firing was never directed at the crowd itself. See UNAMSIL, "Statement by the United Nations Mission in Sierra Leone on Events of 18 July 2002," press release, 9 August 2002.

25. See Warren Hoge and Steven Lee Myers, "U.N. Helicopter Crash Kills 24 During Mission in Sierra Leone," *New York Times*, 30 June 2004, p. A8.

26. See United Nations High Commissioner for Refugees and Save the Children–UK, "Sexual Violence and Exploitation: The Experience of Refugee Children in Guinea, Liberia, and Sierra Leone," February 2002, http://www.unhcr.org/cgi-bin/texis/vtx/news/opendoc.pdf?id=3c7cf89a4&tbl=partners.

27. Ibid., p. 4.

28. Ibid., pp. 6–7.

29. See "Report of the Office of Internal Oversight Services on the Investigation into Sexual Exploitation of Refugees by Aid Workers in West Africa," in *General Assembly Resolution 57/465*, UN Doc. A/57/465, 11 October 2002.

30. In March 2002, the Inter-Agency Standing Committee (IASC), composed of UN and non-UN humanitarian partners, established the Task Force on Protection from Sexual Exploitation and Abuse in Humanitarian Crises. However,

over the next few years, reports surfaced of widespread sexual exploitation of refugees by UN peacekeepers in Haiti, Liberia, and the Democratic Republic of Congo.

31. See "Secretary-General 'Very Pleased' at Appointment of Oluyemi Adeniji as Foreign Minister of Nigeria," press release, UN Doc. SG/SM/8782, 17 July 2003.

32. See "Secretary-General Appoints New Special Representative for Sierra Leone," press release, UN Doc. SG/A/858, 1 December 2003.

33. See International Center for Transitional Justice, New York, *The Special Court for Sierra Leone Under Scrutiny* (March 2006), p. 13.

34. However, the Special Court's annual budget was significantly smaller than the budgets of the International Criminal Tribunals for the former Yugoslavia and Rwanda, which were approximately $120 million each. See International Center for Transitional Justice, *The Special Court for Sierra Leone Under Scrutiny*, p. 29.

35. See International Center for Transitional Justice, *The Special Court for Sierra Leone Under Scrutiny*, pp. 13–14.

36. See *Report of the Security Council Mission to Sierra Leone*, UN Doc. S/2000/992, 16 October 2000, para. 54(b).

37. The Truth and Reconciliation Commission completed its proceedings and issued its final report in October 2004.

38. In addition, there were serious questions regarding how the court would deal with the role of ECOWAS in the conflict. Ultimately, the indictments largely sidestepped the involvement of Nigerian troops.

39. In contrast to the Security Council's refusal to issue a Chapter VII resolution to facilitate Taylor's arrest in Ghana following his indictment in 2003, in this case the Council obliged the Special Court by issuing a resolution under Chapter VII to ensure that Taylor could be transferred to the Netherlands for trial. See *UN Security Council Resolution 1688*, UN Doc. S/RES/1688, 16 June 2006.

40. See *UN Security Council Resolution 1436*, UN Doc. S/RES/1436, 24 September 2002.

41. See "Press Statement by Security Council President on Sierra Leone," UN Doc. SC/7629, 10 January 2003.

42. See *Fifteenth Report of the Secretary-General*, paras. 12–13.

43. See *Twenty-fourth Report of the Secretary-General on the United Nations Mission in Sierra Leone*, UN Doc. S/2004/965, 10 December 2004, para. 2.

44. See *Report of the Secretary-General to the Security Council on Liberia*, para. 12.

45. See UNAMSIL, "UNAMSIL Officer-in-Charge Bids Farewell to Nigerian Troops to Be Deployed in Liberia," press release, 4 August 2003.

46. International Crisis Group, *Sierra Leone After Elections: Politics as Usual?* Africa Report no. 49 (Freetown, 15 July 2002).

47. See United Nations Development Programme, *Millennium Development Goals: A Compact Among Nations to End Human Poverty* (New York: Oxford University Press, 2003).

48. See World Bank, "Sierra Leone: Partners Support the Country's Plan for Peace, Recovery, and Development," press release, 14 November 2002.

49. See Paul Collier et al., *Breaking the Conflict Trap: Civil War and Development Policy* (Washington, DC: World Bank and Oxford University Press, 2003), p. 7.

50. See *A More Secure World: Our Shared Responsibility*, report of the High-Level Panel on Threats, Challenges, and Change, UN Doc. A/59/565, 2 December 2004.

51. See *In Larger Freedom: Towards Development, Security, and Human Rights for All*, report of the Secretary-General, UN Doc. A/59/2005, 21 March 2005.

52. See *Twenty-fourth Report of the Secretary-General*, para. 12.

53. UNAMSIL/UNCT, "Transition Strategy: Laying a Foundation for Durable Peace and Sustainable Development in Sierra Leone," revised version, 1 March 2005.

54. "United Nations Mission in Sierra Leone, Fact Sheet 1: Disarmament, Demobilization, and Reintegration," UNAMSIL End of Mission Press Kit, Peace and Security Section of the United Nations Department of Public Information, DPI/2412B, December 2005.

55. See *UN Security Council Resolution 1436*, UN Doc. S/RES/1436, 24 September 2002, para. 5.

56. See *Twenty-seventh Report of the Secretary-General on the United Nations Mission in Sierra Leone*, UN Doc. S/2005/777, 12 December 2005.

57. On the establishment and mandate of UNIOSIL, see *UN Security Council Resolution 1620*, UN Doc. S/RES/1620, 31 August 2005 (see text of Resolution 1620 in this volume). On the Peacebuilding Commission, see *UN Security Council Resolution 1645*, UN Doc. S/RES/1645, 20 December 2005.

Chronology of Sierra Leone and the Conflict

1961	Independence is declared on 27 April. Having led the country to independence, Sir Milton Margai becomes head of the postindependence government following elections.
1964	Albert Margai becomes prime minister following the death of his brother Sir Milton.
1967	Siaka Stevens wins elections, leading to a power tussle and coup d'état.
1968	Countercoup reinstates Siaka Stevens, who begins the process of consolidating power over political opponents as well as the security establishment.
1977–1978	Under Stevens, Sierra Leone becomes a one-party state. Stevens declares himself president-for-life.
1985	Stevens steps down and hands over power to the commander of the armed forces, General Joseph Momoh.
1989	Outbreak of civil war in neighboring Liberia in December.
1990	A referendum is planned for a return to multiparty rule.
1991	In March, Liberian rebels (members of Charles Taylor's National Patriotic Front of Liberia [NPFL]) and Sierra Leonean dissidents invade Sierra Leone from the Liberian border. Revolutionary United Front (RUF) leader Foday Sankoh takes credit for the attacks. An Economic Community of West African States (ECOWAS) force is deployed to counter the RUF rebellion, which slowly spreads across the country.
1992	In April, General Momoh is ousted in a military coup by junior Sierra Leone Army (SLA) officers. One month later, Captain Valentine Strasser, leader of the new National Provisional Ruling Council (NPRC), is sworn in as head of state.
1995	Berhanu Dinka from Ethiopia is appointed Special Envoy of the Secretary-General to work in collaboration with the Organization of African Unity (OAU) and ECOWAS to negotiate a settlement to the conflict.

135

To make up for a weak military, Strasser's government recruits the mercenary firm Executive Outcomes to assist traditional hunting militias, most notably the Kamajors of the Mende group, in waging the war against the rebels.

1996

January   Brigadier-General Maada Bio takes over power from Strasser in a bloodless coup; he is overwhelmed by widespread demand for democratic elections.

February   Presidential and legislative elections are marred by extreme rebel violence against civilians in the countryside. The practice of chopping off the limbs of innocent Sierra Leoneans as punishment for voting is widespread.

March   In a run-off election, Ahmad Tejan Kabbah of the Sierra Leone People's Party (SLPP) is elected president. Bio's military government peacefully relinquishes power.

September   Following an alleged coup attempt, President Kabbah fires some twenty officers, including Strasser and Bio, from the armed forces.

November   UN Special Envoy Dinka assists in negotiating a peace agreement between the government and the RUF, known as the Abidjan Accord.

1997

January   Under a new Secretary-General, Kofi Annan, the UN becomes more actively involved in trying to find a solution to the civil war in Sierra Leone.

              Executive Outcomes departs Sierra Leone, as the government is unable to meet the mercenary firm's rising costs.

March   Foday Sankoh flies to Nigeria to acquire weapons and is arrested by Nigerian authorities for illegal possession of ammunition. At President Kabbah's request, Sankoh is held in Nigerian custody.

May   Segments of the army collude with rebels to oust President Kabbah. The Armed Forces Revolutionary Council (AFRC) assumes power, with Major Johnny Paul as its chairman. President Kabbah and his government go into exile in neighboring Guinea.

June   Nigeria-led forces attempt to reverse the coup, without success.

July   The ECOWAS Committee of Four, with members from Nigeria, Côte d'Ivoire, Guinea, and Ghana, urges the junta to relinquish power during a series of negotiations.

August   ECOWAS members gathered at the Heads of State summit in Abuja agree to impose a total embargo on all supplies of oil and weapons to the junta, as well as a travel ban on junta leaders.

September   Francis G. Okelo of Uganda replaces Dinka as Special Envoy of the Secretary-General for Sierra Leone.

              The UN Security Council imposes an oil and arms embargo and authorizes ECOWAS to ensure its implementation using ECOMOG troops (UN Security Council Resolution 1132).

October   In Conakry, ECOWAS and the AFRC junta agree on a cease-fire, to be monitored by the ECOWAS Cease-Fire Monitoring Group (ECOMOG) and UN military observers. The AFRC also agrees to withdraw and allow the restoration of Kabbah's government within six months. The AFRC junta publicly commits to implementing the agreement, but quickly reneges after criticizing key provisions; the agreement is never implemented.

1998

February   Following fierce fighting in January, ECOMOG troops overwhelm rebel forces in Freetown and retake the capital. The AFRC/RUF junta flees the Freetown area and retreats to the countryside.

March   President Kabbah's government is reinstated in Freetown. Kabbah declares a state of emergency and charges dozens of people with treason, including former president Joseph Momoh, for collaborating with the AFRC. Kabbah formalizes the Kamajors and other civil militias fighting alongside ECOMOG into the Civil Defense Forces (CDF).

April   President Kabbah appoints Maxwell Khobe, Nigerian commander of the ECOMOG task force in Sierra Leone, as chief of defense of the Sierra Leone Armed Forces, and promotes him to brigadier-general. Restructuring of the armed forces begins under Khobe's leadership.

May   Following rampant media reports that President Kabbah had contracted Sandline International, in violation of the UN arms embargo, to help him regain power, the British government withdraws its High Commissioner in Sierra Leone, Peter Penfold.

June   Following the sudden death of General Sani Abacha, the Nigerian government becomes less enthusiastic about its military involvement in Sierra Leone and more interested in a negotiated settlement.

July   The United Nations Observer Mission in Sierra Leone (UNOMSIL) is established (UN Security Council Resolution 1181), consisting of seventy observers and with an initial six-month mandate. Special Envoy Francis G. Okelo becomes Special Representative of the Secretary-General and head of the mission.

                 Sankoh returns to Sierra Leone from detention in Nigeria.

October   Twenty-four Sierra Leonean military officers are executed for their role in the junta. Sankoh is sentenced to death for treason.

1999

January   AFRC/RUF forces overwhelm ECOMOG troops in Freetown in a surprise attack. Throughout the month, hundreds of ECOMOG troops are killed, thousands of children are abducted by rebel forces, and mutilation, torture, and murder of civilians are widespread. All UNOMSIL personnel are evacuated and Kabbah's government again goes into exile. ECOMOG undertakes a counterattack, supported by the CDF and civil society intelligence.

April	ECOMOG confirms involvement of the Liberian and Burkinabe governments in delivering weapons to the rebels. The ECOMOG commander threatens air strikes into neighboring Liberia and Burkina Faso unless the flow of weapons stops.
May	In Nigeria, the newly elected civilian government of President Olusegun Obasanjo starts to put more emphasis on the need for a negotiated settlement amid rising costs and the unpopularity of Nigeria's participation in ECOMOG in Sierra Leone.
	President Kabbah and Foday Sankoh sign a cease-fire agreement in Lomé, Togo. Negotiations begin for a new peace agreement.
July	The peace process between the Sierra Leone government and the RUF, assisted by international mediators from the United Nations, the OAU, ECOWAS, the Commonwealth, the United Kingdom, and the United States, ends with the signing of the Lomé Peace Agreement. As part of the agreement, the Sierra Leone government accedes to RUF demands for blanket amnesty, while Foday Sankoh is made chairman of the Strategic Mineral Resources Commission, and the RUF is allocated a further eight cabinet posts. The RUF promises to release abducted civilians, to disarm and be reintegrated into the Sierra Leone Armed Forces, and to reconstitute itself into a political organization.
October	Foday Sankoh and Johnny Paul Koroma return to Freetown.
	The United Nations Mission to Sierra Leone (UNAMSIL) is established and replaces UNOMSIL (UN Security Council Resolution 1270). The framework for UNAMSIL had been provided by the Lomé Agreement.
November	Oluyemi Adeniji of Nigeria is appointed Special Representative of the Secretary-General for Sierra Leone, replacing Okelo, and becomes head of UNAMSIL.
	UNAMSIL, initially planned to consist of 6,000 troops, begins deploying in Sierra Leone.

2000

February	UNAMSIL's mandate is revised to include a number of additional tasks, an expansion of its military personnel to 11,100, and an increase in its civil affairs, civilian police, administrative, and technical components (UN Security Council Resolution 1289).
April	The UN takes over control of peacekeeping operations from ECOMOG. The sudden death of Brigadier-General Maxwell Khobe, chief of defense, throws the leadership of the Sierra Leone Army into confusion.
May	ECOMOG completes its withdrawal by 2 May. Nearly 500 UN peacekeepers are kidnapped in the first week of the month. On 8 May, the RUF shoots and kills some twenty people outside Sankoh's house in Freetown who were demonstrating against the RUF's violations of the Lomé Agreement. Sankoh flees, but is apprehended and arrested in Freetown on 17 May.

The British government dispatches an 800-strong paratrooper rescue mission to Freetown, ostensibly to evacuate British citizens, supported by naval ships and air force planes. They retake control of the Freetown airport and subsequently deploy in defensive positions around the capital, providing logistical support to peacekeepers.

July

The UN Security Council adopts British-proposed sanctions on illegal diamond exports from Sierra Leone (UN Security Council Resolution 1306).

September

An internal report by UNAMSIL's Force Commander, Major-General Vijay Jetley, is leaked, sparking controversy. In it, Jetley accuses UNAMSIL's Nigerian contingents and senior leadership of conspiring with rebels and deliberately subverting the UN mission.

Kenyan lieutenant-general Daniel Opande is appointed as UNAMSIL Force Commander, replacing General Jetley.

November

The RUF and the Sierra Leone government sign a new cease-fire agreement in Abuja, which obliges the RUF to return captured weapons and to undertake a thorough disarmament, demobilization, and reintegration (DDR) process.

2001

March

The UN Security Council bans Liberian diamond exports, strengthens the arms embargo, and bans key Liberian regime members from international travel (UN Security Council Resolution 1343).

November

More than twenty political associations assemble at the National Consultative Forum to discuss electoral issues and agree to a constituency system rather than proportional representation.

Alarm spreads over a *Washington Post* article linking Al-Qaida terrorists to RUF diamond smuggling.

2002

January

The UN and the Sierra Leone government formally agree to establish a Special Court.

March

UNAMSIL reaches nearly 17,500 peacekeepers in Sierra Leone, making it the largest and most expensive UN peacekeeping operation ever.

May

Kabbah is overwhelmingly elected and sworn in as president. The candidate for the newly formed Revolutionary United Front Party (RUFP) receives less than 2 percent of the vote.

July

The Truth and Reconciliation Commission for Sierra Leone is inaugurated.

2003

March

The Special Court for Sierra Leone indicts former RUF leaders Foday Sankoh, Issa Sesay, Morris Kallon, and Sam Bockarie, as well as AFRC leaders Johnny Paul Koroma and Alex Timba Brima, and CDF leader Sam Hinga Norman. The Special Court also indicts Charles Taylor for his involvement in the Sierra Leone conflict.

April	The Special Court for Sierra Leone indicts RUF leader Augustine Gbao.
July	Foday Sankoh dies in prison in Freetown from a heart attack, hindering any further court case against him (and also preventing disclosure of further information on Charles Taylor's involvement).
December	Daudi Mwakawago of Tanzania is appointed Special Representative of the Secretary-General for Sierra Leone, replacing Adeniji, and becomes head of UNAMSIL until the termination of the mission.

2004

February	The national disarmament and rehabilitation process concludes, with over 72,000 combatants, including over 6,800 child soldiers, demobilized.

2005

August	The United Nations Integrated Office in Sierra Leone (UNIOSIL) is established (with its twelve-month period of operations set to begin 1 January 2006) to further address root causes of conflict (UN Security Council Resolution 1620).
December	Termination of the UNAMSIL mission; full withdrawal completed.

2006

January	UNIOSIL begins its work, aimed at helping the country consolidate peace; strengthening the capacity of state institutions, rule of law, human rights, and the security sector; accelerating the Millennium Development Goals; improving transparency; and building capacity to hold free and fair elections in 2007.
March	Charles Taylor is flown from exile in Nigeria back to Monrovia, where he is arrested and quickly sent across the border into custody at the Special Court in Freetown. The UN Security Council authorizes his extradition to The Hague for trial.

2007

June	The trial of Charles Taylor begins at The Hague.
	The UN Security Council refers Sierra Leone to the newly created UN Peacebuilding Commission, which subsequently puts it on its agenda.
August	Presidential and parliamentary elections held in Sierra Leone.
December	The UN Peacebuilding Commission activates the newly created Peacebuilding Fund, which is intended to fill critical gaps in financing for peacebuilding activities, especially in the very early stages of recovery. Sierra Leone is a designated recipient.

The Lomé Peace Agreement

The Government of the Republic of Sierra Leone and the Revolutionary United Front of Sierra Leone (RUF/SL)

Having met in Lomé, Togo, from May 25, 1999, to July 7, 1999, under the auspices of the current chairman of ECOWAS, President Gnassingbe Eyadema;

Recalling earlier initiatives undertaken by the countries of the subregion and the international community, aimed at bringing about a negotiated settlement of the conflict in Sierra Leone, and culminating in the Abidjan Peace Agreement of November 30, 1996, and the ECOWAS Peace Plan of October 23, 1997;

Moved by the imperative need to meet the desire of the people of Sierra Leone for a definitive settlement of the fratricidal war in their country and for genuine national unity and reconciliation;

Committed to promoting full respect for human rights and humanitarian law;

Committed to promoting popular participation in the governance of the country and the advancement of democracy in a sociopolitical framework free of inequality, nepotism, and corruption;

Concerned with the socioeconomic well-being of all the people of Sierra Leone;

Determined to foster mutual trust and confidence between themselves;

Determined to establish sustainable peace and security; to pledge forthwith, to settle all past, present, and future differences and grievances by peaceful means; and to refrain from the threat and use of armed force to bring about any change in Sierra Leone;

Reaffirming the conviction that sovereignty belongs to the people, and that government derives all its powers, authority, and legitimacy from the people;

Recognizing the imperative that the children of Sierra Leone, especially those affected by armed conflict, in view of their vulnerability, are entitled to special care and the protection of their inherent right to life, survival, and development, in accordance with the provisions of the International Convention on the Rights of the Child;

Guided by the Declaration in the Final Communiqué of the Meeting in Lomé of the ministers of foreign affairs of ECOWAS of May 25, 1999, in which they stressed the importance of democracy as a factor of regional peace and security, and as essential to the socioeconomic development of ECOWAS member states; and in which they pledged their commitment to the consolidation of democracy and respect of human rights while reaffirming the need for all member states to consolidate their democratic base, observe the principles of good governance and good economic management in order to ensure the emergence and development of a democratic culture that takes into account the interests of the peoples of West Africa;

Recommitting themselves to the total observance and compliance with the Cease-Fire Agreement signed in Lomé on May 18, 1999, and appended as Annex 1 until the signing of the present Peace Agreement.

Hereby agree as follows:

Part One: Cessation of Hostilities

Article I: Cease-Fire

The armed conflict between the government of Sierra Leone and the RUF/SL is hereby ended with immediate effect. Accordingly, the two sides shall ensure that a total and permanent cessation of hostilities is observed forthwith.

Article II: Cease-Fire Monitoring

1. A Cease-Fire Monitoring Committee (hereinafter termed the CMC) to be chaired by the United Nations Observer Mission in Sierra Leone (hereinafter termed UNOMSIL) with representatives of the government of Sierra Leone, RUF/SL, the Civil Defense Forces (hereinafter termed the CDF) and ECOMOG shall be established at provincial and district levels with immediate effect to monitor, verify, and report all violations of the cease-fire.

2. A Joint Monitoring Commission (hereinafter termed the JMC) shall be established at the national level to be chaired by UNOMSIL with representatives of the government of Sierra Leone, RUF/SL, CDF, and ECOMOG. The JMC shall receive, investigate, and take appropriate action on reports of violations of the cease-fire from the CMC. The parties agree to the definition of cease-fire violations as contained in Annex 2, which constitutes an integral part of the present agreement.

3. The parties shall seek the assistance of the international community in providing funds and other logistics to enable the JMC to carry out its mandate.

Part Two: Governance

The government of Sierra Leone and the RUF/SL, recognizing the right of the people of Sierra Leone to live in peace, and desirous of finding a transitional mechanism to incorporate the RUF/SL into governance within the spirit and letter of the constitution, agree to the following formulas for structuring the government for the duration of the period before the next elections, as prescribed by the constitution, managing scarce public resources for the benefit of the development of the people of Sierra Leone and sharing the responsibility of implementing the peace. Each of these formulas (not in priority order) is contained in a separate article of this part of the present agreement; and may be further detailed in protocols annexed to it.

Article III—Transformation of the RUF/SL into a Political Party

Article IV—Enabling Members of the RUF/SL to Hold Public Office

Article V—Enabling the RUF/SL to Join a Broad-Based Government of National Unity Through Cabinet Appointments

Article VI—Commission for the Consolidation of Peace

Article VII—Commission for the Management of Strategic Resources, National Reconstruction and Development

Article VIII—Council of Elders and Religious Leaders

Article III: Transformation of the RUF/SL into a Political Party

1. The government of Sierra Leone shall accord every facility to the RUF/SL to transform itself into a political party and enter the mainstream of the democratic process. To that end:

2. Immediately upon the signing of the present agreement, the RUF/SL shall commence to organize itself to function as a political movement, with the rights, privileges, and duties accorded to all political parties in Sierra Leone. These include the freedom to publish, unhindered access to the media, freedom of association, freedom of expression, freedom of assembly, and the right to mobilize and associate freely.

3. Within a period of thirty days, following the signing of the present agreement, the necessary legal steps shall be taken by the government of Sierra Leone to enable the RUF/SL to register as a political party.

4. The parties shall approach the international community with a view to mobilizing resources for the purposes of enabling the RUF/SL to function as a political party. These resources may include but shall not be limited to:

(i) Setting up a trust fund;

(ii) Training for RUF/SL membership in party organization and functions; and

(iii) Providing any other assistance necessary for achieving the goals of this section.

Article IV: Enabling Members of the RUF/SL to Hold Public Office

1. The government of Sierra Leone shall take the necessary steps to enable those RUF/SL members nominated by the RUF/SL to hold public office, within the time-frames agreed and contained in the present agreement for the integration of the various bodies named herein.

2. Accordingly, necessary legal steps shall be taken by the government of Sierra Leone, within a period of fourteen days following the signing of the present agreement, to amend relevant laws and regulations that may constitute an impediment or bar to RUF/SL and AFRC personnel holding public office.

3. Within seven days of the removal of any such legal impediments, both parties shall meet to discuss and agree on the appointment of RUF/SL members to positions in parastatals, diplomacy, and any other public sector.

Article V: Enabling the RUF/SL to Join a Broad-Based Government of National Unity Through Cabinet Appointments

1. The government of Sierra Leone shall accord every opportunity to the RUF/SL to join a broad-based government of national unity through cabinet appointments. To that end:

2. The chairmanship of the board of the Commission for the Management of Strategic Resources, National Reconstruction, and Development (CMRRD) as provided for in Article VII of the present agreement shall be offered to the leader of the RUF/SL, Corporal Foday Sankoh. For this purpose he shall enjoy the status of vice president and shall therefore be answerable only to the president of Sierra Leone.

3. The government of Sierra Leone shall give ministerial positions to the RUF/SL in a moderately expanded cabinet of eighteen, bearing in mind that the interests of other political parties and civil society organizations should also be taken into account, as follows:

(i) One of the senior cabinet appointments such as finance, foreign affairs, and justice;

(ii) Three other cabinet positions.

4. In addition, the Government of Sierra Leone shall, in the same spirit, make available to the RUF/SL the following senior government positions: Four posts of Deputy Minister.

5. Within a period of fourteen days following the signing of the present Agreement, the necessary steps shall be taken by the Government of Sierra Leone to remove any legal impediments that may prevent RUF/SL members from holding cabinet and other positions.

Article VI: Commission for the Consolidation of Peace

1. A Commission for the Consolidation of Peace (hereinafter termed the CCP), shall be established within two weeks of the signing of the present agreement to implement a postconflict program that ensures reconciliation and the welfare of all parties to the conflict, especially the victims of war. The CCP shall have the overall goal and responsibility for supervising and monitoring the implementation of and compliance with the provisions of the present agreement relative to the promotion of national reconciliation and the consolidation of peace.

2. The CCP shall ensure that all structures for national reconciliation and the consolidation of peace already in existence and those provided for in the present Agreement are operational and given the necessary resources for realizing their respective mandates. These structures shall comprise:

(i) the Commission for the Management of Strategic Resources, National Reconstruction, and Development;

(ii) the Joint Monitoring Commission;

(iii) the Provincial and District Cease-Fire Monitoring Committees;

(iv) the Committee for the Release of Prisoners of War and Non-Combatants;

(v) the Committee for Humanitarian Assistance;

(vi) the National Commission on Disarmament, Demobilization, and Reintegration;

(vii) the National Commission for Resettlement, Rehabilitation, and Reconstruction;

(viii) the Human Rights Commission; and

(ix) the Truth and Reconciliation Commission.

3. The CCP shall have the right to inspect any activity or site connected with the implementation of the present agreement.

4. The CCP shall have full powers to organize its work in any manner it deems appropriate and to appoint any group or subcommittee that it deems necessary in the discharge of its functions.

5. The commission shall be composed of the following members:

(i) Two representatives of the civil society;

(ii) One representative each named by the government, the RUF/SL, and the parliament.

6. The CCP shall have its own offices, adequate communication facilities, and secretarial support staff.

7. Recommendations for improvements or modifications shall be made to the president of Sierra Leone for appropriate action. Likewise, failures of the structures to perform their assigned duties shall also be brought to the attention of the president.

8. Disputes arising out of the preceding paragraph shall be brought to the Council of Elders and Religious Leaders for resolution, as specified in Article VIII of the present agreement.

9. Should protocols be needed in furtherance of any provision in the present agreement, the CCP shall have the responsibility for their preparation.

10. The mandate of the CCP shall terminate at the end of the next general elections.

Article VII: Commission for the Management of Strategic Resources, National Reconstruction and Development

1. Given the emergency situation facing the country, the parties agree that the government shall exercise full control over the exploitation of gold, diamonds, and other resources, for the benefit of the people of Sierra Leone. Accordingly, a Commission for the Management of Strategic Resources, National Reconstruction, and Development (hereinafter termed the CMRRD) shall be established and charged with the responsibility of securing and monitoring the legitimate exploitation of Sierra Leone's gold and diamonds, and other resources that are determined to be of strategic importance for national security and welfare as well as cater for postwar rehabilitation and reconstruction, as provided for under Article XXVIII of the present agreement.

2. The government shall take the necessary legal action within a period not exceeding two weeks from the signing of the present agreement to the effect that all exploitation, sale, export, or any other transaction of gold and diamonds shall be forbidden except those sanctioned by the CMRRD. All previous concessions shall be null and void.

3. The CMRRD shall authorize licensing of artisanal production of diamonds

and gold, in accordance with prevailing laws and regulations. All gold and diamonds extracted or otherwise sourced from any Sierra Leonean territory shall be sold to the government.

4. The CMRRD shall ensure, through the appropriate authorities, the security of the areas covered under this article, and shall take all necessary measures against unauthorized exploitation.

5. For the export or local resale of gold and diamonds by the government, the CMRRD shall authorize a buying and selling agreement with one or more reputable international and specialized mineral companies. All exports of Sierra Leonean gold and diamonds shall be transacted by the government, under these agreements.

6. The proceeds from the transactions of gold and diamonds shall be public monies that shall enter a special treasury account to be spent exclusively on the development of the people of Sierra Leone, with appropriations for public education, public health, infrastructural development, and compensation for incapacitated war victims as well as postwar rehabilitation and reconstruction. Priority spending shall go to rural areas.

7. The government shall, if necessary, seek the assistance and cooperation of other governments and their instruments of law enforcement to detect and facilitate the prosecution of violations of this article.

8. The management of other natural resources shall be reviewed by the CMRRD to determine if their regulation is a matter of national security and welfare, and recommend appropriate policy to the government.

9. The functions of the Ministry of Mines shall continue to be carried out by the current authorized ministry. However, in respect of strategic mineral resources, the CMRRD shall be an autonomous body in carrying out its duties concerning the regulation of Sierra Leone's strategic natural resources.

10. All agreements and transactions referred to in this article shall be subject to full public disclosure and records of all correspondence, negotiations, business transactions, and any other matters related to exploitation, management, local or international marketing, and any other matter shall be public documents.

11. The commission shall issue monthly reports, including the details of all the transactions related to gold and diamonds, and other licenses or concessions of natural resources, and its own administrative costs.

12. The commission shall be governed by a board whose chairmanship shall be offered to the leader of the RUF/SL, Corporal Foday Sankoh. The board shall also comprise:

(i) Two representatives of the government appointed by the president;

(ii) Two representatives of the political party to be formed by the RUF/SL;

(iii) Three representatives of the civil society; and

(iv) Two representatives of other political parties appointed by parliament.

13. The government shall take the required administrative actions to implement the commitments made in the present agreement; and in the case of enabling legislation, it shall draft and submit to parliament within thirty days of the signature of the present agreement, the relevant bills for their enactment into law.

14. The government commits itself to propose and support an amendment to the constitution to make the exploitation of gold and diamonds the legitimate domain of the people of Sierra Leone, and to determine that the proceeds be used for the development of Sierra Leone, particularly public education, public health, infrastructure development, and compensation of incapacitated war victims as well as postwar reconstruction and development.

Article VIII: Council of Elders and Religious Leaders

1. The signatories agree to refer any conflicting differences of interpretation of this article or any other article of the present agreement or its protocols, to a Council of Elders and Religious Leaders comprised as follows:
(i) Two members appointed by the Inter-Religious Council;
(ii) One member each appointed by the government and the RUF/SL; and
(iii) One member appointed by ECOWAS.
2. The council shall designate its own chairperson from among its members. All of its decisions shall be taken by the concurrence of at least four members, and shall be binding and public, provided that an aggrieved party may appeal to the supreme court.

Part Three: Other Political Issues

The third part of the present agreement consists of the following articles:
Article IX—Pardon and Amnesty
Article X—Review of the Present Constitution
Article XI—Date of Next Elections
Article XII—National Electoral Commission

Article IX: Pardon and Amnesty

1. In order to bring lasting peace to Sierra Leone, the government of Sierra Leone shall take appropriate legal steps to grant Corporal Foday Sankoh absolute and free pardon.
2. After the signing of the present agreement, the government of Sierra Leone shall also grant absolute and free pardon and reprieve to all combatants and collaborators in respect of anything done by them in pursuit of their objectives, up to the time of the signing of the present agreement.
3. To consolidate the peace and promote the cause of national reconciliation, the government of Sierra Leone shall ensure that no official or judicial action is taken against any member of the RUF/SL, ex-AFRC, ex-SLA, or CDF in respect of anything done by them in pursuit of their objectives as members of those organizations, since March 1991, up to the time of the signing of the present agreement. In addition, legislative and other measures necessary to guarantee immunity to former combatants, exiles, and other persons currently outside the country for reasons related to the armed conflict shall be adopted ensuring the full exercise of their civil and political rights, with a view to their reintegration within in a framework of full legality.

Article X: Review of the Present Constitution

In order to ensure that the 1991 Constitution of Sierra Leone represents the needs and aspirations of the people of Sierra Leone and that no constitutional or any other legal provision prevents the implementation of the present agreement, the government of Sierra Leone shall take the necessary steps to establish a Constitutional Review Committee to review the provisions of the present constitution, and where deemed appropriate, recommend revisions and amendments, in accordance with Part V, Section 108 of the Constitution of 1991.

Article XI: Date of Next Elections

The next national elections in Sierra Leone shall be held in accordance with the present constitution of Sierra Leone.

Article XII: National Electoral Commission

1. A new independent National Electoral Commission (hereinafter termed the NEC) shall be set up by the government, not later than three months after the signing of the present agreement.

2. In setting up the new NEC the president shall consult all political parties, including the RUF/SL, to determine the membership and terms of reference of the commission, paying particular attention to the need for a level playing field in the nation's elections.

3. No member of the NEC shall be eligible for appointment to political office by any government formed as a result of an election he or she was mandated to conduct.

4. The NEC shall request the assistance of the international community, including the UN, the OAU, ECOWAS, and the Commonwealth of Nations, in monitoring the next presidential and parliamentary elections in Sierra Leone.

Part Four: Postconflict Military and Security Issues

1. The government of Sierra Leone and the RUF/SL, recognizing that the maintenance of peace and security is of paramount importance for the achievement of lasting peace in Sierra Leone and for the welfare of its people, have agreed to the following formulas for dealing with postconflict military and security matters. Each of these formulas (not in priority order) is contained in separate articles of this part of the present agreement and may be further detailed in protocols annexed to the agreement.

Article XIII—Transformation and New Mandate of ECOMOG
Article XIV—New Mandate of UNOMSIL
Article XV—Security Guarantees for Peace Monitors
Article XVI—Encampment, Disarmament, Demobilization and Reintegration
Article XVII—Restructuring and Training of the Sierra Leone Armed Forces
Article XVIII—Withdrawal of Mercenaries
Article XIX—Notification to Joint Monitoring Commission
Article XX—Notification to Military Commands

Article XIII: Transformation and New Mandate of ECOMOG

1. Immediately upon the signing of the present agreement, the parties shall request ECOWAS to revise the mandate of ECOMOG in Sierra Leone as follows:

(i) Peacekeeping;
(ii) Security of the State of Sierra Leone;
    i. Protection of UNOMSIL.
    ii. Protection of Disarmament, Demobilization and Reintegration personnel.

2. The government shall, immediately upon the signing of the present agreement, request ECOWAS for troop contributions from at least two additional countries. The additional contingents shall be deployed not later than thirty days from the date of signature of the present agreement. The Security Council shall be requested to provide assistance in support of ECOMOG.

3. The parties agree to develop a timetable for the phased withdrawal of ECOMOG, including measures for securing all of the territory of Sierra Leone by the restructured armed forces. The phased withdrawal of ECOMOG will be linked to the phased creation and deployment of the restructured armed forces.

Article XIV: New Mandate of UNOMSIL

1. The UN Security Council is requested to amend the mandate of UNOMSIL to enable it to undertake the various provisions outlined in the present agreement.

Article XV: Security Guarantees for Peace Monitors

1. The government of Sierra Leone and the RUF/SL agree to guarantee the safety, security, and freedom of movement of UNOMSIL military observers throughout Sierra Leone. This guarantee shall be monitored by the Joint Monitoring Commission.

2. The freedom of movement includes complete and unhindered access for UNOMSIL military observers in the conduct of their duties throughout Sierra Leone. Before and during the process of disarmament, demobilization, and reintegration, officers and escorts to be provided by both parties shall be required to facilitate this access.

3. Such freedom of movement and security shall also be accorded to nonmilitary UNOMSIL personnel such as human rights officers in the conduct of their duties. These personnel shall, in most cases, be accompanied by UNOMSIL military observers.

4. The provision of security to be extended shall include United Nations aircraft, vehicles, and other property.

Article XVI: Encampment, Disarmament, Demobilization, and Reintegration

1. A neutral peacekeeping force comprised of UNOMSIL and ECOMOG shall disarm all combatants of the RUF/SL, CDF, SLA, and paramilitary groups. The encampment, disarmament, and demobilization process shall commence within six weeks of the signing of the present agreement in line with the deployment of the neutral peacekeeping force.

2. The present SLA shall be restricted to the barracks and their arms in the armory and their ammunitions in the magazines and placed under constant surveil-

lance by the neutral peacekeeping force during the process of disarmament and demobilization.

3. UNOMSIL shall be present in all disarmament and demobilization locations to monitor the process and provide security guarantees to all ex-combatants.

4. Upon the signing of the present agreement, the government of Sierra Leone shall immediately request the international community to assist with the provision of the necessary financial and technical resources needed for the adaptation and extension of the existing Encampment, Disarmament, Demobilization, and Reintegration Program in Sierra Leone, including payment of retirement benefits and other emoluments due to former members of the SLA.

Article XVII: Restructuring and Training of the Sierra Leone Armed Forces

1. The restructuring, composition, and training of the new Sierra Leone armed forces will be carried out by the government with a view to creating truly national armed forces, bearing loyalty solely to the state of Sierra Leone, and able and willing to perform their constitutional role.

2. Those ex-combatants of the RUF/SL, CDF, and SLA who wish to be integrated into the new restructured national armed forces may do so provided they meet established criteria.

3. Recruitment into the armed forces shall reflect the geopolitical structure of Sierra Leone within the established strength.

Article XVIII: Withdrawal of Mercenaries

All mercenaries, in any guise, shall be withdrawn from Sierra Leone immediately upon the signing of the present agreement. Their withdrawal shall be supervised by the Joint Monitoring Commission.

Article XIX: Notification to Joint Monitoring Commission

Immediately upon the establishment of the JMC provided for in Article II of the present agreement, each party shall furnish to the JMC information regarding the strength and locations of all combatants as well as the positions and descriptions of all known unexploded bombs (UXBs), explosive ordnance devices (EODs), minefields, booby traps, wire entanglements, and all other physical or military hazards. The JMC shall seek all necessary technical assistance in mine clearance and the disposal or destruction of similar devices and weapons under the operational control of the neutral peacekeeping force. The parties shall keep the JMC updated on changes in this information so that it can notify the public as needed, to prevent injuries.

Article XX: Notification to Military Commands

Each party shall ensure that the terms of the present agreement, and written orders requiring compliance, are immediately communicated to all of its forces.

Part Five: Humanitarian, Human Rights, and Socioeconomic Issues

1. The Government of Sierra Leone and the RUF/SL, recognizing the importance of upholding, promoting and protecting the human rights of every Sierra Leonean as well as the enforcement of humanitarian law, agree to the following formulas for the achievement of these laudable objectives. Each of these formulas (not in priority order) is contained in separate Articles of this Part of the present Agreement.

Article XXI—Release of Prisoners and Abductees
Article XXII—Refugees and Displaced Persons
Article XXIII—Guarantee of the Security of Displaced Persons and Refugees
Article XXIV—Guarantee and Promotion of Human Rights
Article XXV—Human Rights Commission
Article XXVI—Human Rights Violations
Article XXVII—Humanitarian Relief
Article XXVIII—Postwar Rehabilitation and Reconstruction
Article XXIX—Special Fund for War Victims
Article XXX—Child Combatants
Article XXXI—Education and Health

Article XXI: Release of Prisoners and Abductees

All political prisoners of war as well as all noncombatants shall be released immediately and unconditionally by both parties, in accordance with the Statement of June 2, 1999, which is contained in Annex 3 and constitutes an integral part of the present agreement.

Article XXII: Refugees and Displaced Persons

The parties through the National Commission for Resettlement, Rehabilitation, and Reconstruction agree to seek funding from and the involvement of the UN and other agencies, including friendly countries, in order to design and implement a plan for voluntary repatriation and reintegration of Sierra Leonean refugees and internally displaced persons, including noncombatants, in conformity with international conventions, norms, and practices.

Article XXIII: Guarantee of the Security of Displaced Persons and Refugees

As a reaffirmation of their commitment to the observation of the conventions and principles of human rights and the status of refugees, the parties shall take effective and appropriate measures to ensure that the right of Sierra Leoneans to asylum is fully respected and that no camps or dwellings of refugees or displaced persons are violated.

Article XXIV: Guarantee and Promotion of Human Rights

1. The basic civil and political liberties recognized by the Sierra Leone legal system and contained in the declarations and principles of human rights adopted

by the UN and OAU, especially the Universal Declaration of Human Rights and the African Charter on Human and People's Rights, shall be fully protected and promoted within Sierra Leonean society.

2. These include the right to life and liberty, freedom from torture, the right to a fair trial, freedom of conscience, expression, and association, and the right to take part in the governance of one's country.

Article XXV: Human Rights Commission

1. The parties pledge to strengthen the existing machinery for addressing grievances of the people in respect of alleged violations of their basic human rights by the creation, as a matter of urgency and not later than ninety days after the signing of the present agreement, of an autonomous quasi-judicial national Human Rights Commission.

2. The parties further pledge to promote human rights education throughout the various sectors of Sierra Leonean society, including the schools, the media, the police, the military and the religious community.

3. In pursuance of the above, technical and material assistance may be sought from the UN High Commissioner for Human Rights, the African Commission on Human and Peoples Rights, and other relevant international organizations.

4. A consortium of local human rights and civil society groups in Sierra Leone shall be encouraged to help monitor human rights observance.

Article XXVI: Human Rights Violations

1. A Truth and Reconciliation Commission shall be established to address impunity, break the cycle of violence, provide a forum for both the victims and perpetrators of human rights violations to tell their story, and get a clear picture of the past in order to facilitate genuine healing and reconciliation.

2. In the spirit of national reconciliation, the commission shall deal with the question of human rights violations since the beginning of the Sierra Leonean conflict in 1991. This commission shall, among other things, recommend measures to be taken for the rehabilitation of victims of human rights violations.

3. Membership of the commission shall be drawn from a cross-section of Sierra Leonean society with the participation and some technical support of the international community. This commission shall be established within ninety days after the signing of the present agreement and shall, not later than twelve months after the commencement of its work, submit its report to the government for immediate implementation of its recommendations.

Article XXVII: Humanitarian Relief

1. The parties reaffirm their commitment to their Statement on the Delivery of Humanitarian Assistance in Sierra Leone of June 3, 1999, which is contained in Annex 4 and constitutes an integral part of the present agreement. To this end, the government shall request appropriate international humanitarian assistance for the people of Sierra Leone who are in need all over the country.

2. The parties agree to guarantee safe and unhindered access by all humanitarian organizations throughout the country in order to facilitate delivery of humanitarian assistance, in accordance with international conventions, principles, and norms that govern humanitarian operations. In this respect, the parties agree to guarantee the security of the presence and movement of humanitarian personnel.

3. The parties also agree to guarantee the security of all properties and goods transported, stocked or distributed by humanitarian organizations, as well as the security of their projects and beneficiaries.

4. The government shall set up at various levels throughout the country, the appropriate and effective administrative or security bodies that will monitor and facilitate the implementation of these guarantees of safety for the personnel, goods, and areas of operation of the humanitarian organizations.

Article XXVIII: Postwar Rehabilitation and Reconstruction

1. The government, through the National Commission for Resettlement, Rehabilitation, and Reconstruction and with the support of the international community, shall provide appropriate financial and technical resources for postwar rehabilitation, reconstruction, and development.

2. Given that women have been particularly victimized during the war, special attention shall be accorded to their needs and potentials in formulating and implementing national rehabilitation, reconstruction, and development programs, to enable them to play a central role in the moral, social, and physical reconstruction of Sierra Leone.

Article XXIX: Special Fund for War Victims

The government, with the support of the international community, shall design and implement a program for the rehabilitation of war victims. For this purpose, a special fund shall be set up.

Article XXX: Child Combatants

The government shall accord particular attention to the issue of child soldiers. It shall, accordingly, mobilize resources, both within the country and from the international community, and especially through the office of the UN Special Representative for Children in Armed Conflict, UNICEF, and other agencies, to address the special needs of these children in the existing disarmament, demobilization, and reintegration processes.

Article XXXI: Education and Health

The government shall provide free compulsory education for the first nine years of schooling (Basic Education) and shall endeavor to provide free schooling for a further three years. The government shall also endeavor to provide affordable primary health care throughout the country.

Part Six: Implementation of the Agreement

Article XXXII: Joint Implementation Committee

A Joint Implementation Committee consisting of members of the Commission for the Consolidation of Peace (CCP) and the Committee of Seven on Sierra Leone, as well as the moral guarantors, provided for in Article XXXIV of the present agreement, and other international supporters, shall be established. Under the chairmanship of ECOWAS, the Joint Implementation Committee shall be responsible for reviewing and assessing the state of implementation of the agreement, and shall meet at least once every three months. Without prejudice to the functions of the Commission for the Consolidation of Peace as provided for in Article VI, the Joint Implementation Committee shall make recommendations deemed necessary to ensure effective implementation of the present agreement according to the Schedule of Implementation, which appears as Annex 5.

Article XXXIII: Request for International Involvement

The parties request that the provisions of the present agreement affecting the United Nations shall enter into force upon the adoption by the UN Security Council of a resolution responding affirmatively to the request made in this agreement. Likewise, the decisionmaking bodies of the other international organizations concerned are requested to take similar action, where appropriate.

Part Seven: Moral Guarantors and International Support

Article XXXIV: Moral Guarantors

The government of the Togolese Republic, the United Nations, the OAU, ECOWAS, and the Commonwealth of Nations shall stand as moral guarantors that this peace agreement is implemented with integrity and in good faith by both parties.

Article XXXV: International Support

Both parties call on the international community to assist them in implementing the present agreement with integrity and good faith. The international organizations mentioned in Article XXXIV and the governments of Benin, Burkina Faso, Côte d'Ivoire, Ghana, Guinea, Liberia, Libyan Arab Jamahiriya, Mali, Nigeria, Togo, the United Kingdom, and the United States of America are facilitating and supporting the conclusion of this agreement. These states and organizations believe that this agreement must protect the paramount interests of the people of Sierra Leone in peace and security.

Part Eight: Final Provisions

Article XXXVI: Registration and Publication

The Sierra Leone government shall register the signed agreement not later than fifteen days from the date of the signing of this agreement. The signed agreement shall also be published in the *Sierra Leone Gazette* not later than forty-eight hours after the date of registration of this agreement. This agreement shall be laid before the parliament of Sierra Leone not later than twenty-one days after the signing of this agreement.

Article XXXVII: Entry into Force

The present agreement shall enter into force immediately upon its signing by the parties.

Done in Lomé this seventh day of the month of July 1999 in twelve (12) original texts in English and French, each text being equally authentic.

Alhaji Ahmad Tejan Kabbah
    President of the Republic of Sierra Leone
Corporal Foday Saybana Sankoh
    Leader of the Revolutionary United Front of Sierra Leone
His Excellency Gnassingbe Eyadema
    President of the Togolese Republic, Chairman of ECOWAS
His Excellency Blaise Compaoré
    President of Burkina Faso
His Excellency Dahkpanah Dr. Charles Ghankey Taylor
    President of the Republic of Liberia
His Excellency Olusegun Obasanjo
    President and Commander-in-Chief of the Armed Forces of the
    Federal Republic of Nigeria
His Excellency Youssoufou Bamba
    Secretary of State at the Foreign Mission in Charge of International
    Cooperation of Côte d'Ivoire
His Excellency Victor Gbeho
    Minister of Foreign Affairs of the Republic of Ghana
Mr. Roger Laloupo
    Representative of the ECOWAS Special Representative
Ambassador Francis G. Okelo
    Executive Secretary of the United Nations Secretary-General
Ms. Adwoa Coleman
    Representative of the Organization of African Unity
Dr. Moses K. Z. Anafu
    Representative of the Commonwealth of Nations

Annex 1: Agreement on Cease-Fire in Sierra Leone

President Ahmed Tejan Kabbah and Rev. Jesse Jackson met on May 18, 1999, with Corporal Foday Saybana Sankoh, under the auspices of President Gnassingbe Eyadema. At that meeting, the question of the peace process for Sierra Leone was discussed.

*   *   *

The government of the Republic of Sierra Leone and the Revolutionary United Front of Sierra Leone (RUF/SL),

Desirous to promote the ongoing dialogue process with a view to establishing durable peace and stability in Sierra Leone; and

Wishing to create an appropriate atmosphere conducive to the holding of peace talks in Lomé, which began with the RUF internal consultations to be followed by dialogue between the government and the RUF;

Have jointly decided to:

1. Agree to cease-fire as from May 24, 1999, the day that President Eyadema invited foreign ministers of ECOWAS to discuss problems pertaining to Sierra Leone. It was further agreed that the dialogue between the government of Sierra Leone and RUF would commence on May 25, 1999;

2. Maintain their present and respective positions in Sierra Leone as of May 24, 1999; and refrain from any hostile or aggressive act that could undermine the peace process;

3. Commit to start negotiations in good faith, involving all relevant parties in the discussions, not later than May 25 in Lomé;

4. Guarantee safe and unhindered access by humanitarian organizations to all people in need; establish safe corridors for the provision of food and medical supplies to ECOMOG soldiers behind RUF lines, and to RUF combatants behind ECOMOG lines;

5. Immediate release of all prisoners of war and noncombatants;

6. Request the United Nations, subject to the Security Council's authorization, to deploy military observers as soon as possible to observe compliance by the government forces (ECOMOG and Civil Defense Forces) and the RUF, including former AFRC forces, with this cease-fire agreement.

This agreement is without prejudice to any other agreement or additional protocols that may be discussed during the dialogue between the government and the RUF.

Signed in Lomé (Togo) May 18, 1999, in six (6) originals in English and French.

For the government of Sierra Leone
    Alhadji Dr. Ahmad Tejan Kabbah
    President of the Republic of Sierra Leone
For the Revolutionary United Front of Sierra Leone
    Corporal Foday Saybana Sankoh
    Leader of the Revolutionary United Front (RUF)
Witnessed By:
For the Government of Togo and Current Chairman of ECOWAS
    Gnassingbe Eyadema
    President of the Republic of Togo
For the United Nations
    Francis G. Okelo
    Special Representative of the Secretary General
For the Organization of African Unity (OAU)
    Adwoa Coleman
    Representative of the Organization of African Unity
U.S. Presidential Special Envoy for the Promotion of Democracy in Africa
    Rev. Jesse Jackson

Annex 2: Definition of Cease-Fire Violations

1. In accordance with Article II of the present agreement, both parties agree that the following constitute cease-fire violations and a breach of the Cease-Fire

Agreement:

    a. The use of weapons of any kind in any circumstance including:

        (i) Automatic and semi-automatic rifles, pistols, machine guns and any other small arms weapon systems.

        (ii) Heavy machine guns and any other heavy weapon systems.

        (iii) Grenades and rocket-propelled grenade weapon systems.

        (iv) Artillery, rockets, mortars, and any other indirect fire weapon systems.

        (v) All types of mine, explosive devices, and improvised booby traps.

        (vi) Air defense weapon systems of any nature.

        (vii) Any other weapon not included in the above paragraphs.

    b. Troop movements of any nature outside of the areas recognized as being under the control of respective fighting forces without prior notification to the Cease-Fire Monitoring Committee of any movements at least forty-eight hours in advance.

    c. The movement of arms and ammunition. To be considered in the context of Security Council Resolution 1171 (1998).

    d. Troop movements of any nature.

    e. The construction and/or the improvement of defensive works and positions within respective areas of control, but outside a geographical boundary of 500 meters from existing similar positions.

    f. Reconnaissance of any nature outside of respective areas of control.

    g. Any other offensive or aggressive action.

    2. Any training or other military activities not provided for in Articles XIII to XIX of the present agreement, constitute a cease-fire violation.

    3. In the event of a hostile external force threatening the territorial integrity or sovereignty of Sierra Leone, military action may be undertaken by the Sierra Leone government.

Annex 3: Statement by the Government of Sierra Leone and the Revolutionary United Front of Sierra Leone on the Release of Prisoners of War and Noncombatants

The Government of Sierra Leone (GOSL) and the Revolutionary United Front (RUF/SL) have agreed to implement as soon as possible the provision of the Cease-Fire Agreement that was signed on May 18, 1999, in Lomé, relating to the immediate release of prisoners of war and noncombatants.

    Both sides reaffirmed the importance of the implementation of this provision in the interest of the furtherance of the talks.

    They therefore decided that an appropriate committee be established to handle the release of all prisoners of war and noncombatants.

    Both the Government of Sierra Leone and the Revolutionary United Front of Sierra Leone decided that such a committee be established by the UN and chaired by the UN Chief Military Observer in Sierra Leone and comprising representatives of the International Committee of the Red Cross (ICRC), UNICEF, and other relevant UN agencies and NGOs.

    This committee should begin its work immediately by contacting both parties to the conflict with a view to effecting the immediate release of these prisoners of war and noncombatants.

—Lomé, June 2, 1999

Annex 4: Statement by the Government of Sierra Leone and the Revolutionary United Front of Sierra Leone on the Delivery of Humanitarian Assistance in Sierra Leone

The parties to the conflict in Sierra Leone, meeting in Lomé, Togo, on June 3, 1999, in the context of the dialogue between the Government of Sierra Leone (GOSL) and the Revolutionary United Front of Sierra Leone (RUF/SL):

Reaffirm their respect for international convention, principles, and norms that govern the right of people to receive humanitarian assistance and the effective delivery of such assistance.

Reiterate their commitment to the implementation of the Cease-Fire Agreement signed by the two parties on May 18, 1999, in Lomé.

Aware of the fact that the protracted civil strife in Sierra Leone has created a situation whereby the vast majority of Sierra Leoneans in need of humanitarian assistance cannot be reached.

Hereby agree as follows:

1. That all duly registered humanitarian agencies shall be guaranteed safe and unhindered access to all areas under the control of the respective parties in order that humanitarian assistance can be delivered safely and effectively, in accordance with international conventions, principles, and norms governing humanitarian operations.

2. In this respect the two parties shall:

a. guarantee safe access and facilitate the fielding of independent assessment missions by duly registered humanitarian agencies.

b. identify, in collaboration with the UN Humanitarian Coordinator in Sierra Leone and UNOMSIL, mutually agreed routes (road, air, and waterways) by which humanitarian goods and personnel shall be transported to the beneficiaries to provide needed assistance.

c. allow duly registered humanitarian agencies to deliver assistance according to needs established through independent assessments.

d. guarantee the security of all properties and of any goods transported, stocked, or distributed by the duly registered humanitarian agencies, as well as the security of their project areas and beneficiaries.

3. The two parties undertake to establish with immediate effect, and not later than seven days, an Implementation Committee formed by appropriately designated and mandated representatives from the Government of Sierra Leone, the Revolutionary United Front of Sierra Leone, the civil society, the NGO community, and UNOMSIL; and chaired by the United Nations Humanitarian Coordinator, in coordination with the special representative of the Secretary-General in Sierra Leone.

The Implementation Committee will be mandated to:

a. Ascertain and assess the security of proposed routes to be used by the humanitarian agencies, and disseminate information on routes to interested humanitarian agencies.

b. Receive and review complaints which may arise in the implementation of this arrangement, in order to reestablish full compliance.

4. The parties agree to set up at various levels in their areas of control, the appropriate and effective administrative and security bodies that will monitor and facilitate the effective delivery of humanitarian assistance in all approved points of delivery, and ensure the security of the personnel, goods, and project areas of the humanitarian agencies as well as the safety of the beneficiaries.

—Issued in Lomé, June 3, 1999

Annex 5: Draft Schedule of Implementation of the Peace Agreement

1. Activities with specific timing:

Timing	Activities	Action Required	Follow-up Action
Day 1	Signing of the Peace Agreement		
	Amnesty	The Government to grant absolute and free pardon to the RUF leader Foday Sankoh through appropriate legal steps	
	Transformation and new mandate of ECOMOG	Request to ECOWAS by the parties for revision of the mandate of ECOMOG in Sierra Leone	
		Request to the UN Security Council to amend the mandate of UNOMSIL to enable it to undertake the various provisions outlined in the present Agreement	
		Request to the international community to provide substantial financial and logistical assistance to facilitate implementation of the Peace Agreement	
		Request to ECOWAS by the parties for contributions of additional troops	
	Transformation of the RUF into a political party	RUF/SL to commence to organize itself to function as a political party	
	Encampment, disarmament, demobilization and reintegration (DDR)	Request for international assistance in adapting and extending the existing DDR program	
	Withdrawal of mercenaries	Supervision by Joint Monitoring Commission	
	Notification to Joint Monitoring Commission	Communication by the parties of positions and description of all known warlike devices/materials	
	Notification to Military Commands	Communication by the parties of written orders requiring compliance	

(continues)

Day 15	Enabling members of the RUF/SL to hold public office, and to join a broad-based Government of National Unity through Cabinet appointments	Removal by the Government of all legal impediments	
	Commission for the Consolidation of Peace (CCP)	Creation of the Commission to implement a post-conflict reconciliation and welfare	Mandate of the Commission to terminate at the program end of next general elections Jan.–Feb. 2001
	Commission for the Management of Strategic Resources, National Reconstruction and Development (CMRRD)	Ban on all exploitation, sale, export, or any transaction of gold and diamonds except those sanctioned by the CMRDD	
Day 22	Enabling members of the RUF/SL to hold public office	Discussion and agreement between both parties on the appointment of RUF/SL members to positions of parastatal, diplomacy and any other public sector	For a period of fourteen days
Day 31	Transformation of the RUF into a political party	Necessary legal steps by the Government for the registration of the RUF as a political party	
	Commission for the Management of Strategic Resources, National Reconstruction and Development (CMRRD)	Preparation and submission by Government to the Parliament of relevant bills for enabling legislation commitments made under the peace agreement	
	Transformation, new mandate, and phased withdrawal of ECOMOG	Deployment of troops from at least two additional countries	
Day 60	Completion of encampment, disarmament and demobilization	Restriction of SLA soldiers to the barracks and storage of their arms and ammunition under constant surveillance by the Neutral Peace-Keeping Force during the disarmament process	
		Monitoring of disarmament and demobilization by UNOMSIL	
Day 90	Human Rights Commission	Creation of an autonomous quasi-judicial national Human Rights Commission	

		Request for technical and material assistance from the UN High Commissioner for Human Rights, the African Commission on Human Rights and Peoples Rights and other relevant organizations
		Creation of a Truth and Reconciliation Commission
	Elections	Establishment of a new independent National Electoral Commission (NEC) in consultation with all political parties including the RUF/SL
		Request for financial and logistical support for the operations of the NEC
		Request for assistance from the international community in monitoring the next presidential and parliamentary elections in Sierra Leone
Day 456	Human Rights Violations	Submission by the Truth and Reconciliation Commission of its report and recommendation to the Government for immediate implementation

2. Activities without specific timing (short/medium/long term):

Serial No.	Activities	Action Required	Follow-up Action
1.	Cease-fire monitoring	Establishment of a Cease-Fire Monitoring Committee at provincial and district levels	JMC already established and operational
	(Cease-Fire Agreement signed on 18 May 1999)	Request for international assistance in providing funds and other logistics for the operations of the JMC	
2.	Review of the present Constitution	Establishment of a Constitutional Review Committee	
3.	Mediation by the Council of Elders and Religious Leaders	Appointment of members of the Council by the Interreligious Council, the Government, the RUF and ECOWAS	

(continues)

4.	Timetable for the phased withdrawal of ECOMOG	Formulation of the timetable in connection with the phased creation and deployment of the restructured Armed Forces
5.	Security guarantees for peace monitors	Communication, in writing, of security guarantees to UNMILOBs [UN Military Observers]
6.	Restructuring and training of the SLA	Creation by the Government of truly national armed forces reflecting the geo-political structure of Sierra Leone within the established guidelines

Selected
UN Security Council
Resolutions

Resolution 1181 (1998)

**Adopted by the Security Council
at its 3902nd meeting, on 13 July 1998**

The Security Council,

Recalling its previous relevant resolutions and the statements of its President,

Welcoming the continued efforts of the Government of Sierra Leone to restore peaceful and secure conditions in the country, to re-establish effective administration and the democratic process and to embark on the task of national reconciliation, reconstruction and rehabilitation,

Recognizing the important contribution of the Economic Community of West African States (ECOWAS) in support of these objectives,

Having considered the report of the Secretary-General of 9 June 1998 (S/1998/486 and Add.1),

Noting the objectives set by ECOWAS for its Military Observer Group (ECOMOG) as described in paragraph 17 of the report of Secretary-General,

Gravely concerned at the loss of life and immense suffering undergone by the people of Sierra Leone, including refugees and displaced persons, as a result of the continuing rebel attacks, and in particular at the plight of children affected by the conflict,

1. *Condemns* the continued resistance of remnants of the ousted junta and members of the Revolutionary United Front (RUF) to the authority of the legitimate government and the violence they are perpetrating against the civilian population of Sierra Leone, and *demands* that they lay down their arms immediately;

2. *Emphasizes* the need to promote national reconciliation in Sierra Leone, encourages all parties in the country to work together towards this objective, and welcomes the assistance of the Secretary-General and his Special Envoy in that regard;

3. *Welcomes* the proposal in the report of the Secretary-General of 9 June

1998 on the establishment of the United Nations Observer Mission in Sierra Leone (UNOMSIL);

4. *Notes* that the Government of Sierra Leone has adopted a disarmament, demobilization and reintegration plan agreed with the International Bank for Reconstruction and Development, the United Nations Development Programme and other donors;

5. *Commends* the positive role of ECOWAS and ECOMOG in their efforts to restore peace, security and stability throughout the country at the request of the Government of Sierra Leone, and *notes* the role of ECOMOG in assisting the implementation of the disarmament, demobilization and reintegration plan adopted by the Government of Sierra Leone, including the provision of security and responsibility for arms collection and destruction;

6. *Decides* to establish UNOMSIL for an initial period of six months until 13 January 1999, and *further decides* that it shall include up to 70 military observers as well as a small medical unit, with the necessary equipment and civilian support staff, with the following mandate:

(a) To monitor the military and security situation in the country as a whole, as security conditions permit, and to provide the Special Representative of the Secretary-General with regular information thereon in particular with a view to determining when conditions are sufficiently secure to allow subsequent deployments of military observers beyond the first phase described in paragraph 7 below;

(b) To monitor the disarmament and demobilization of former combatants concentrated in secure areas of the country, including monitoring of the role of ECOMOG in the provision of security and in the collection and destruction of arms in those secure areas;

(c) To assist in monitoring respect for international humanitarian law, including at disarmament and demobilization sites, where security conditions permit;

(d) To monitor the voluntary disarmament and demobilization of members of the Civil Defense Forces (CDF), as security conditions permit;

7. *Decides further* that the elements of UNOMSIL referred to in paragraph 6 above shall be deployed as outlined in the Secretary-General's report, with approximately 40 military observers deployed in the first phase to ECOMOG-secured areas, and that subsequent deployments shall take place as soon as security conditions permit, and subject to progress on the implementation of the disarmament, demobilization and reintegration plan and the availability of the necessary equipment and resources;

8. *Decides further* that UNOMSIL shall be led by the Special Envoy of the Secretary-General, who will be designated Special Representative for Sierra Leone, that UNOMSIL shall subsume the office of the Special Envoy and its civilian staff, and that the augmented civilian staff, as recommended by the Secretary-General in paragraphs 74 and 75 of his report, shall perform, *inter alia,* the following tasks:

(a) To advise, in coordination with other international efforts, the Government of Sierra Leone and local police officials on police practice, training, re-equipment and recruitment, in particular on the need to respect internationally accepted standards of policing in democratic societies, to advise on the planning of the reform and restructuring of the Sierra Leone police force, and to monitor progress in that regard;

(b) To report on violations of international humanitarian law and human rights in Sierra Leone, and, in consultation with the relevant United Nations agencies, to assist the Government of Sierra Leone in its efforts to address the country's human rights needs;

9. *Welcomes* the commitment of ECOMOG to ensure the security of United Nations personnel, and in this regard *welcomes also* the intention of the Secretary-General to establish security arrangements for United Nations personnel with the Chairman of ECOWAS and to conclude a status of mission agreement with Government of Sierra Leone;

10. *Decides* that the elements of UNOMSIL referred to in paragraph 6 above shall be deployed when the Secretary-General informs the Council that security arrangements and the status of mission agreement have been concluded, and *further decides* to keep the deployment of UNOMSIL under review in the light of the prevailing security conditions;

11. *Stresses* the need for full cooperation and close coordination between UNOMSIL and ECOMOG in their respective operational activities;

12. *Demands* that all factions and forces in Sierra Leone strictly respect the status of UNOMSIL personnel, as well as organizations and agencies delivering humanitarian assistance throughout Sierra Leone, and that they respect human rights and abide by applicable rules of international humanitarian law;

13. *Expresses* its serious concern at the reports of cross-border arms flows and support to the rebels in Sierra Leone, *welcomes* the intention of the Secretary-General, as indicated in his report, to pursue with all parties concerned steps to eliminate these activities, and in that regard *reaffirms* the obligation of all States to comply strictly with the terms of the embargo on the sale or supply of arms and related *matériel* to Sierra Leone imposed by resolution 1171 (1998) of 5 June 1998, and to bring all instances of violations of the arms embargo before the Committee established by resolution 1132 (1997) of 8 October 1997;

14. *Welcomes* the efforts of the Government of Sierra Leone to coordinate an effective national response to the needs of children affected by armed conflict, and the recommendation of the Special Representative of the Secretary-General for Children in Armed Conflict that Sierra Leone be made one of the pilot projects for a more concerted and effective response to the needs of children in the context of post-conflict peace-building;

15. *Further welcomes* the decision of the Secretary-General to convene a high-level conference to mobilize assistance for peacekeeping activities, emergency and humanitarian needs and reconstruction and rehabilitation in Sierra Leone;

16. *Reiterates* its urgent appeal to States to make contributions to the Trust Fund which has been established to support peacekeeping and related activities in Sierra Leone, to provide technical and logistical support to assist ECOMOG to carry out its peacekeeping role, and to help facilitate other ECOWAS member States to provide additional troops to strengthen the deployment of ECOMOG in Sierra Leone;

17. *Urges* all States and international organizations to provide urgent humanitarian assistance to Sierra Leone, in response to the consolidated inter-agency appeal launched on 24 June 1998;

18. *Encourages* all States and international organizations to assist and participate in the longer term tasks of reconstruction and economic and social recovery and development in Sierra Leone;

19. *Requests* the Secretary-General to submit an initial report to the Council within 30 days of the adoption of this resolution and every 60 days thereafter on the deployment of UNOMSIL and on the progress of UNOMSIL in carrying out its mandate, and also to inform the Council on plans for the later phases of the deployment of UNOMSIL when security conditions permit these to be implemented;

20. *Decides* to remain seized of the matter.

Resolution 1270 (1999)

Adopted by the Security Council
at its 4054th meeting, on 22 October 1999

The Security Council,

Recalling its resolutions 1171 (1998) of 5 June 1998, 1181 (1998) of 13 July 1998, 1231 (1999) of 11 March 1999 and 1260 (1999) of 20 August 1999 and other relevant resolutions and the statement of its President of 15 May 1999 (S/PRST/1999/13),

Recalling also the report of the Secretary-General of 8 September 1999 (S/1999/957) and its resolution 1265 (1999) of 17 September 1999 on the protection of civilians in armed conflict,

Affirming the commitment of all States to respect the sovereignty, political independence and territorial integrity of Sierra Leone,

Having considered the report of the Secretary-General of 23 September 1999 (S/1999/1003),

Determining that the situation in Sierra Leone continues to constitute a threat to international peace and security in the region,

1. *Welcomes* the important steps taken by the Government of Sierra Leone, the leadership of the Revolutionary United Front of Sierra Leone (RUF), the Military Observer Group (ECOMOG) of the Economic Community of West African States (ECOWAS) and the United Nations Observer Mission in Sierra Leone (UNOMSIL) towards implementation of the Peace Agreement (S/1999/777) since its signing in Lomé on 7 July 1999, and *recognizes* the important role of the Joint Implementation Committee established by the Peace Agreement under the chairmanship of the President of Togo;

2. *Calls upon* the parties to fulfill all their commitments under the Peace Agreement to facilitate the restoration of peace, stability, national reconciliation and development in Sierra Leone;

3. *Takes note* of the preparations made for the disarmament, demobilization and reintegration of ex-combatants, including child soldiers, by the Government of Sierra Leone through the National Committee for Disarmament, Demobilization and Reintegration, and *urges* all concerned to make every effort to ensure that all designated centers begin to function as soon as possible;

4. *Calls upon* the RUF, the Civil Defense Forces, former Sierra Leone Armed Forces/Armed Forces Revolutionary Council (AFRC) and all other armed groups

in Sierra Leone to begin immediately to disband and give up their arms in accordance with the provisions of the Peace Agreement, and to participate fully in the disarmament, demobilization and reintegration program;

5. *Welcomes* the return to Freetown of the leaders of the RUF and AFRC, and calls upon them to engage fully and responsibly in the implementation of the Peace Agreement and to direct the participation of all rebel groups in the disarmament and demobilization process without delay;

6. *Deplores* the recent taking of hostages, including UNOMSIL and ECOMOG personnel, by rebel groups and *calls upon* those responsible to put an end to such practices immediately and to address their concerns about the terms of the Peace Agreement peacefully through dialogue with the parties concerned;

7. *Reiterates* its appreciation for the indispensable role which ECOMOG forces continue to play in the maintenance of security and stability in and the protection of the people of Sierra Leone, and *approves* the new mandate for ECOMOG (S/1999/1073, annex) adopted by ECOWAS on 25 August 1999;

8. *Decides* to establish the United Nations Mission in Sierra Leone (UNAMSIL) with immediate effect for an initial period of six months and with the following mandate:

(a) To cooperate with the Government of Sierra Leone and the other parties to the Peace Agreement in the implementation of the Agreement;

(b) To assist the Government of Sierra Leone in the implementation of the disarmament, demobilization and reintegration plan;

(c) To that end, to establish a presence at key locations throughout the territory of Sierra Leone, including at disarmament/reception centers and demobilization centers;

(d) To ensure the security and freedom of movement of United Nations personnel;

(e) To monitor adherence to the cease-fire in accordance with the cease-fire agreement of 18 May 1999 (S/1999/585, annex) through the structures provided for therein;

(f) To encourage the parties to create confidence-building mechanisms and support their functioning;

(g) To facilitate the delivery of humanitarian assistance;

(h) To support the operations of United Nations civilian officials, including the Special Representative of the Secretary-General and his staff, human rights officers and civil affairs officers;

(i) To provide support, as requested, to the elections, which are to be held in accordance with the present constitution of Sierra Leone;

9. *Decides also* that the military component of UNAMSIL shall comprise a maximum of 6,000 military personnel, including 260 military observers, subject to periodic review in the light of conditions on the ground and the progress made in the peace process, in particular in the disarmament, demobilization and reintegration program, and *takes note* of paragraph 43 of the report of the Secretary-General of 23 September 1999;

10. *Decides further* that UNAMSIL will take over the substantive civilian and military components and functions of UNOMSIL as well as its assets, and to that end decides that the mandate of UNOMSIL shall terminate immediately on the establishment of UNAMSIL;

11. *Commends* the readiness of ECOMOG to continue to provide security for

the areas where it is currently located, in particular around Freetown and Lungi, to provide protection for the Government of Sierra Leone, to conduct other operations in accordance with their mandate to ensure the implementation of the Peace Agreement, and to initiate and proceed with disarmament and demobilization in conjunction and full coordination with UNAMSIL;

12. *Stresses* the need for close cooperation and coordination between ECOMOG and UNAMSIL in carrying out their respective tasks, and welcomes the intended establishment of joint operations centers at headquarters and, if necessary, also at subordinate levels in the field;

13. *Reiterates* the importance of the safety, security and freedom of movement of United Nations and associated personnel, notes that the Government of Sierra Leone and the RUF have agreed in the Peace Agreement to provide guarantees in this regard, and *calls upon* all parties in Sierra Leone to respect fully the status of United Nations and associated personnel;

14. *Acting* under Chapter VII of the Charter of the United Nations, decides that in the discharge of its mandate UNAMSIL may take the necessary action to ensure the security and freedom of movement of its personnel and, within its capabilities and areas of deployment, to afford protection to civilians under imminent threat of physical violence, taking into account the responsibilities of the Government of Sierra Leone and ECOMOG;

15. *Underlines* the importance of including in UNAMSIL personnel with appropriate training in international humanitarian, human rights and refugee law, including child and gender related provisions, negotiation and communication skills, cultural awareness and civilian-military coordination;

16. *Requests* the Government of Sierra Leone to conclude a status-of-forces agreement with the Secretary-General within 30 days of the adoption of this resolution, and *recalls* that pending the conclusion of such an agreement the model status-of-forces agreement dated 9 October 1990 (A/45/594) should apply provisionally;

17. *Stresses* the urgent need to promote peace and national reconciliation and to foster accountability and respect for human rights in Sierra Leone, underlines in this context the key role of the Truth and Reconciliation Commission, the Human Rights Commission and the Commission for the Consolidation of Peace established under the Peace Agreement, and *urges* the Government of Sierra Leone to ensure the prompt establishment and effective functioning of these bodies with the full participation of all parties and drawing on the relevant experience and support of Member States, specialized bodies, other multilateral organizations and civil society;

18. *Emphasizes* that the plight of children is among the most pressing challenges facing Sierra Leone, welcomes the continued commitment of the Government of Sierra Leone to work with the United Nations Children's Fund, the Office of the Special Representative of the Secretary-General for Children and Armed Conflict and other international agencies to give particular attention to the long-term rehabilitation of child combatants in Sierra Leone, and *reiterates* its encouragement of those involved to address the special needs of all children affected by the conflict;

19. *Urges* all parties concerned to ensure that refugees and internally displaced persons are protected and are enabled to return voluntarily and in safety to their homes, and *encourages* States and international organizations to provide urgent assistance to that end;

20. *Stresses* the urgent need for substantial additional resources to finance the

disarmament, demobilization and reintegration process, and *calls upon* all States, international and other organizations to contribute generously to the multidonor trust fund established by the International Bank for Reconstruction and Development for this purpose;

21. *Stresses* also the continued need for urgent and substantial humanitarian assistance to the people of Sierra Leone, as well as for sustained and generous assistance for the longer term tasks of peace-building, reconstruction, economic and social recovery and development in Sierra Leone, and *urges* all States and international and other organizations to provide such assistance as a priority;

22. *Calls upon* all parties to ensure safe and unhindered access of humanitarian assistance to those in need in Sierra Leone, to guarantee the safety and security of humanitarian personnel and to respect strictly the relevant provisions of international humanitarian and human rights law;

23. *Urges* the Government of Sierra Leone to expedite the formation of professional and accountable national police and armed forces, including through their restructuring and training, without which it will not be possible to achieve long-term stability, national reconciliation and the reconstruction of the country, and *underlines* the importance of support and assistance from the international community in this regard;

24. *Welcomes* the continued work by the United Nations on the development of the Strategic Framework for Sierra Leone aimed at enhancing effective collaboration and coordination within the United Nations system and between the United Nations and its national and international partners in Sierra Leone;

25. *Notes* the intention of the Secretary-General to keep the situation in Sierra Leone under close review and to revert to the Council with additional proposals if required;

26. *Requests* the Secretary-General to report to the Council every 45 days to provide updates on the status of the peace process, on security conditions on the ground and on the continued level of deployment of ECOMOG personnel, so that troop levels and the tasks to be performed can be evaluated as outlined in paragraphs 49 and 50 of the report of the Secretary-General of 23 September 1999;

27. *Decides* to remain actively seized of the matter.

Resolution 1289 (2000)

Adopted by the Security Council
at its 4099th meeting, on 7 February 2000

The Security Council,

Recalling its resolutions 1171 (1998) of 5 June 1998, 1181 (1998) of 13 July 1998, 1231 (1999) of 11 March 1999, 1260 (1999) of 20 August 1999, 1265 (1999) of 17 September 1999 and 1270 (1999) of 22 October 1999 and other relevant resolutions and the statement of its President of 15 May 1999 (S/PRST/1999/13),

Affirming the commitment of all States to respect the sovereignty, political independence and territorial integrity of Sierra Leone,

Recalling the relevant principles contained in the Convention on the Safety of United Nations and Associated Personnel adopted on 9 December 1994,

Welcoming and encouraging efforts by the United Nations to sensitize peace-keeping personnel in the prevention and control of HIV/AIDS and other communicable diseases in all its peacekeeping operations,

Taking note of the letter to its President from the Minister of Foreign Affairs and International Cooperation of Sierra Leone of 17 January 2000 (S/2000/31),

Having considered the reports of the Secretary-General of 23 September 1999 (S/1999/1003), 6 December 1999 (S/1999/1223) and 11 January 2000 (S/2000/13) and the letter of the Secretary-General to its President of 23 December 1999 (S/1999/1285),

Determining that the situation in Sierra Leone continues to constitute a threat to international peace and security in the region,

1. *Notes* that the deployment of the United Nations Mission in Sierra Leone (UNAMSIL) as established by resolution 1270 (1999) is in the process of completion;

2. *Welcomes* the efforts made by the Government of Sierra Leone, the leadership of the Revolutionary United Front Party of Sierra Leone, the Military Observer Group (ECOMOG) of the Economic Community of West African States and UNAMSIL towards the implementation of the Peace Agreement signed in Lomé on 7 July 1999 (S/1999/777);

3. *Reiterates* its call upon the parties to fulfill all their commitments under the Peace Agreement to facilitate the restoration of peace, stability, national reconciliation and development in Sierra Leone, and *stresses* that the responsibility for the success of the peace process ultimately lies with the people and leaders of Sierra Leone;

4. *Notes* with concern that, despite the progress that has been made, the peace process thus far has been marred by the limited and sporadic participation in the disarmament, demobilization and reintegration program, by the lack of progress on the release of abductees and child soldiers, and by continued hostage-taking and attacks on humanitarian personnel, and *expresses* its conviction that the expansion of UNAMSIL as provided for in paragraphs 9 to 12 below will create conditions under which all parties can work to ensure that the provisions of the Peace Agreement are implemented in full;

5. *Notes also* with concern the continuing human rights violations against the civilian population of Sierra Leone, and *emphasizes* that the amnesty extended under the Peace Agreement does not extend to such violations committed after the date of its signing;

6. *Calls upon* the parties and all others involved to take steps to ensure that the disarmament, demobilization and reintegration program is fully implemented throughout the country, and in particular *urges* the Revolutionary United Front (RUF), the Civil Defense Forces, the former Sierra Leone Armed Forces/Armed Forces Revolutionary Council (AFRC) and all other armed groups to participate fully in the program and cooperate with all those responsible for its implementation;

7. *Takes note* of the decision of the Governments of Nigeria, Guinea and Ghana to withdraw their remaining ECOMOG contingents from Sierra Leone, as reported in the letter of the Secretary-General of 23 December 1999;

8. *Expresses* its appreciation to ECOMOG for its indispensable contribution towards the restoration of democracy and the maintenance of peace, security and stability in Sierra Leone, *commends* highly the forces and the Governments of its contributing States for their courage and sacrifice, and *encourages* all States to

assist the contributing States further in meeting the costs they have incurred in making possible the deployment of ECOMOG forces in Sierra Leone;

9. *Decides* that the military component of UNAMSIL shall be expanded to a maximum of 11,100 military personnel, including the 260 military observers already deployed, subject to periodic review in the light of conditions on the ground and the progress made in the peace process, in particular in the disarmament, demobilization and reintegration program, and *takes note* of paragraph 33 of the report of the Secretary-General of 11 January 2000;

10. *Acting* under Chapter VII of the Charter of the United Nations, *decides further* that the mandate of UNAMSIL shall be revised to include the following additional tasks, to be performed by UNAMSIL within its capabilities and areas of deployment and in the light of conditions on the ground:

(a) To provide security at key locations and Government buildings, in particular in Freetown, important intersections and major airports, including Lungi airport;

(b) To facilitate the free flow of people, goods and humanitarian assistance along specified thoroughfares;

(c) To provide security in and at all sites of the disarmament, demobilization and reintegration program;

(d) To coordinate with and assist, in common areas of deployment, the Sierra Leone law enforcement authorities in the discharge of their responsibilities;

(e) To guard weapons, ammunition and other military equipment collected from ex-combatants and to assist in their subsequent disposal or destruction, *authorizes* UNAMSIL to take the necessary action to fulfill the additional tasks set out above, and *affirms* that, in the discharge of its mandate, UNAMSIL may take the necessary action to ensure the security and freedom of movement of its personnel and, within its capabilities and areas of deployment, to afford protection to civilians under imminent threat of physical violence, taking into account the responsibilities of the Government of Sierra Leone;

11. *Decides further* that the mandate of UNAMSIL, as revised, shall be extended for a period of six months from the date of adoption of this resolution;

12. *Authorizes* the increases in the civil affairs, civilian police, administrative and technical personnel of UNAMSIL proposed by the Secretary-General in his report of 11 January 2000;

13. *Welcomes* the intention of the Secretary-General, as indicated in his report of 11 January 2000, to establish within UNAMSIL a landmine action office responsible for awareness training of UNAMSIL personnel and for the coordination of mine action activities of nongovernmental organizations and humanitarian agencies operating in Sierra Leone;

14. *Stresses* the importance of a smooth transition between ECOMOG and UNAMSIL for the successful implementation of the Peace Agreement and the stability of Sierra Leone, and in that regard *urges* all those concerned to consult over the timing of troop movements and withdrawals;

15. *Reiterates* the importance of the safety, security and freedom of movement of United Nations and associated personnel, *notes* that the Government of Sierra Leone and the RUF have agreed in the Peace Agreement to provide guarantees in this regard, and *calls upon* all parties in Sierra Leone to respect fully the status of United Nations and associated personnel;

16. *Reiterates* its request to the Government of Sierra Leone to conclude a status-of-forces agreement with the Secretary-General within 30 days of the adoption

of this resolution, and *recalls* that pending the conclusion of such an agreement the model status-of-forces agreement dated 9 October 1990 (A/45/594) should apply provisionally;

17. *Reiterates also* the continued need to promote peace and national reconciliation and to foster accountability and respect for human rights in Sierra Leone, and *urges* the Government of Sierra Leone, specialized agencies, other multilateral organizations, civil society and Member States to accelerate their efforts to establish the Truth and Reconciliation Commission, the Human Rights Commission and the Commission for the Consolidation of Peace as fully functioning and effective institutions, as provided for under the Peace Agreement;

18. *Emphasizes* the importance of the exercise by the Government of Sierra Leone of full control over the exploitation of gold, diamonds and other resources for the benefit of the people of the country and in accordance with Article VII, paragraph 6, of the Peace Agreement, and to that end *calls* for the early and effective operation of the Commission of the Management of Strategic Resources, National Reconstruction and Development;

19. *Welcomes* the contributions that have been made to the multidonor trust fund established by the International Bank for Reconstruction and Development to finance the disarmament, demobilization and reintegration process, and *urges* all States and international and other organizations which have not yet done so to contribute generously to the fund so that the process is adequately financed and the provisions of the Peace Agreement can be fully implemented;

20. *Underlines* the ultimate responsibility of the Government of Sierra Leone for the provision of adequate security forces in the country, *calls upon* it, in that regard, to take urgent steps towards the establishment of professional and accountable national police and armed forces, and *stresses* the importance to this objective of generous support and assistance from the international community;

21. *Reiterates* the continued need for urgent and substantial assistance to the people of Sierra Leone, as well as for sustained and generous assistance for the longer term tasks of peace-building, reconstruction, economic and social recovery and development in Sierra Leone, and *urges* all States and international and other organizations to provide such assistance as a priority;

22. *Requests* the Secretary-General to continue to report to the Council every 45 days to provide, *inter alia*, assessments of security conditions on the ground so that troop levels and the tasks to be performed by UNAMSIL can be kept under review, as indicated in the report of the Secretary-General of 11 January 2000;

23. *Decides* to remain actively seized of the matter.

Resolution 1306 (2000)

Adopted by the Security Council
at its 4168th meeting, on 5 July 2000

The Security Council,

Recalling its previous resolutions and the statements of its President concerning the situation in Sierra Leone, and in particular its resolutions 1132 (1997) of 8 October 1997, 1171 (1998) of 5 June 1998 and 1299 (2000) of 19 May 2000,

Affirming the commitment of all States to respect the sovereignty, political independence and territorial integrity of Sierra Leone,

Having considered the report of the Secretary-General of 19 May 2000 (S/2000/455), and in particular its paragraph 94,

Determining that the situation in Sierra Leone continues to constitute a threat to international peace and security in the region,

Acting under Chapter VII of the Charter of the United Nations,

A

Expressing its concern at the role played by the illicit trade in diamonds in fueling the conflict in Sierra Leone, and at reports that such diamonds transit neighboring countries, including the territory of Liberia,

Welcoming ongoing efforts by interested States, the International Diamond Manufacturers Association, the World Federation of Diamond Bourses, the Diamond High Council, other representatives of the diamond industry and non-governmental experts to improve the transparency of the international diamond trade, and encouraging further action in this regard,

Emphasizing that the legitimate diamond trade is of great economic importance for many States, and can make a positive contribution to prosperity and stability and to the reconstruction of countries emerging from conflict, and *emphasizing further* that nothing in this resolution is intended to undermine the legitimate diamond trade or to diminish confidence in the integrity of the legitimate diamond industry,

Welcoming the decision taken by the member States of the Economic Community of West African States (ECOWAS) at their Abuja summit on 28–29 May 2000 to undertake a regional inquiry into the illegal trade in diamonds,

Taking note of the letter of 29 June 2000 to its President from the Permanent Representative of Sierra Leone to the United Nations and of its enclosure (S/2000/641),

1. *Decides* that all States shall take the necessary measures to prohibit the direct or indirect import of all rough diamonds from Sierra Leone to their territory;

2. *Requests* the Government of Sierra Leone to ensure, as a matter of urgency, that an effective Certificate of Origin regime for trade in diamonds is in operation in Sierra Leone;

3. *Also requests* States, relevant international organizations and other bodies in a position to do so to offer assistance to the Government of Sierra Leone to facilitate the full operation of an effective Certificate of Origin regime for Sierra Leone rough diamonds;

4. *Further requests* the Government of Sierra Leone to notify the Committee established by resolution 1132 (1997) ("the Committee") of the details of such a Certificate of Origin regime when it is fully in operation;

5. *Decides* that rough diamonds controlled by the Government of Sierra Leone through the Certificate of Origin regime shall be exempt from the measures

imposed in paragraph 1 above when the Committee has reported to the Council, taking into account expert advice obtained at the request of the Committee through the Secretary-General, that an effective regime is fully in operation;

6. *Decides* that the measures referred to in paragraph 1 above are established for an initial period of 18 months, and *affirms* that, at the end of this period, it will review the situation in Sierra Leone, including the extent of the Government's authority over the diamond-producing areas, in order to decide whether to extend these measures for a further period and, if necessary, to modify them or adopt further measures;

7. *Further decides* that the Committee shall also undertake the following tasks:

(a) To seek from all States further information regarding the action taken by them with a view to implementing effectively the measures imposed by paragraph 1 above;

(b) To consider information brought to its attention concerning violations of the measures imposed by paragraph 1 above, identifying, where possible, persons or entities, including vessels, reported to be engaged in such violations;

(c) To make periodic reports to the Security Council on information submitted to it regarding alleged violations of the measures imposed by paragraph 1 above, identifying, where possible, persons or entities, including vessels, reported to be engaged in such violations;

(d) To promulgate such guidelines as may be necessary to facilitate the implementation of the measures imposed by paragraph 1 above;

(e) To continue its cooperation with other relevant sanctions committees in particular that established pursuant to resolution 985 (1995) of 13 April 1995 concerning Liberia and that established pursuant to resolution 864 (1993) of 15 September 1993 concerning the situation in Angola;

8. *Requests* all States to report to the Committee established by resolution 1132 (1997), within 30 days of the adoption of this resolution, on the actions they have taken to implement the measures imposed by paragraph 1 above;

9. *Calls upon* all States, in particular those through which rough diamonds from Sierra Leone are known to transit, and all relevant international and regional organizations to act strictly in accordance with the provisions of this resolution notwithstanding the existence of any rights or obligations conferred or imposed by any international agreement or any contract entered into or any license or permit granted prior to the date of adoption of this resolution;

10. *Encourages* the International Diamond Manufacturers Association, the World Federation of Diamond Bourses, the Diamond High Council and all other representatives of the diamond industry to work with the Government of Sierra Leone and the Committee to develop methods and working practices to facilitate the effective implementation of this resolution;

11. *Invites* States, international organizations, members of the diamond industry and other relevant entities in a position to do so to offer assistance to the Government of Sierra Leone to contribute to the further development of a well-structured and well-regulated diamond industry that provides for the identification of the provenance of rough diamonds;

12. *Requests* the Committee to hold an exploratory hearing in New York no later than 31 July 2000 to assess the role of diamonds in the Sierra Leone conflict and the link between trade in Sierra Leone diamonds and trade in arms and related *matériel* in violation of resolution 1171 (1998), involving representatives of

interested States and regional organizations, the diamond industry and other relevant experts, *requests* the Secretary-General to provide the necessary resources, and *further requests* the Committee to report on the hearing to the Council;

13. *Welcomes* the commitments made by certain members of the diamond industry not to trade in diamonds originating from conflict zones, including in Sierra Leone, *urges* all other companies and individuals involved in trading in rough diamonds to make similar declarations in respect of Sierra Leone diamonds, and *underlines* the importance of relevant financial institutions encouraging such companies to do so;

14. *Stresses* the need for the extension of government authority to the diamond-producing areas for a durable solution to the problem of illegal exploitation of diamonds in Sierra Leone;

15. *Decides* to conduct a first review on the measures imposed by paragraph 1 above no later than 15 September 2000, and further such reviews every six months after the date of adoption of the resolution, and to consider at those times what further measures may be necessary;

16. *Urges* all States, relevant United Nations bodies and, as appropriate, other organizations and interested parties to report to the Committee information on possible violations of the measures imposed by paragraph 1 above;

B

Stressing the need to ensure effective implementation of the measures concerning arms and related *matériel* imposed by paragraph 2 of resolution 1171 (1998),

Stressing the obligation of all Member States, including those neighboring Sierra Leone, to comply fully with the measures imposed by the Council,

Recalling the ECOWAS Moratorium on the Importation, Exportation and Manufacture of Light Weapons in West Africa adopted in Abuja on 31 October 1998 (S/1998/1194, annex),

17. *Reminds* States of their obligation to implement fully the measures imposed by resolution 1171 (1998), and *calls upon* them, where they have not already done so, to enforce, strengthen or enact, as appropriate, legislation making it a criminal offense under domestic law for their nationals or other persons operating on their territory to act in violation of the measures imposed by paragraph 2 of that resolution, and to report to the Committee not later than 31 July 2000 on the implementation of those measures;

18. *Urges* all States, relevant United Nations bodies and, as appropriate, other organizations and interested parties to report to the Committee information on possible violations of the measures imposed by the Council;

19. *Requests* the Secretary-General, in consultation with the Committee, to establish a panel of experts, for an initial period of four months, consisting of no more than five members:

(a) To collect information on possible violations of the measures imposed by paragraph 2 of resolution 1171 (1998) and the link between trade in diamonds and trade in arms and related *matériel*, including through visits to Sierra Leone and other States as appropriate, and making contact with those they consider appropriate, including diplomatic missions;

(b) To consider the adequacy, for the purpose of detecting flights of aircraft suspected of carrying arms and related *matériel* across national borders in violation of the measures imposed by paragraph 2 of resolution 1171 (1998), of air traffic control systems in the region;

(c) To participate, if possible, in the hearing referred to in paragraph 12 above;

(d) To report to the Council through the Committee with observations and recommendations on strengthening the implementation of the measures imposed by paragraph 2 of resolution 1171 (1998), and of those imposed by paragraph 1 above, no later than 31 October 2000, and *further requests* the Secretary-General to provide the necessary resources;

20. *Expresses* its readiness, on the basis, *inter alia*, of the report produced pursuant to paragraph 19 (d) above, to consider appropriate action in relation to States that it determines to have violated the measures imposed by paragraph 2 of resolution 1171 (1998) and paragraph 1 above;

21. *Urges* all States to cooperate with the panel in the discharge of its mandate, and *underlines*, in this regard, the importance of the cooperation and technical expertise of the Secretariat and other parts of the United Nations system;

22. *Requests* the Committee to strengthen existing contacts with regional organizations, in particular ECOWAS and the Organization of African Unity, and relevant international organizations, including INTERPOL, with a view to identifying ways to improve effective implementation of the measures imposed by paragraph 2 of resolution 1171 (1998);

23. *Requests* the Committee to make information it considers relevant publicly available through appropriate media, including through the improved use of information technology;

24. *Requests* the Secretary-General to publicize the provisions of this resolution and the obligations imposed by it;

25. *Decides* to remain actively seized of the matter.

Resolution 1315 (2000)

Adopted by the Security Council
at its 4186th meeting, on 14 August 2000

The Security Council,

Deeply concerned at the very serious crimes committed within the territory of Sierra Leone against the people of Sierra Leone and United Nations and associated personnel and at the prevailing situation of impunity,

Commending the efforts of the Government of Sierra Leone and the Economic Community of West African States (ECOWAS) to bring lasting peace to Sierra Leone,

Noting that the Heads of State and Government of ECOWAS agreed at the 23rd Summit of the Organization in Abuja on 28 and 29 May 2000 to dispatch a regional investigation of the resumption of hostilities,

Noting also the steps taken by the Government of Sierra Leone in creating a national truth and reconciliation process, as required by Article XXVI of the Lomé Peace Agreement (S/1999/777) to contribute to the promotion of the rule of law,

Recalling that the Special Representative of the Secretary-General appended to his signature of the Lomé Agreement a statement that the United Nations holds the understanding that the amnesty provisions of the Agreement shall not apply to international crimes of genocide, crimes against humanity, war crimes and other serious violations of international humanitarian law,

Reaffirming the importance of compliance with international humanitarian law, and *reaffirming further* that persons who commit or authorize serious violations of international humanitarian law are individually responsible and accountable for those violations and that the international community will exert every effort to bring those responsible to justice in accordance with international standards of justice, fairness and due process of law,

Recognizing that, in the particular circumstances of Sierra Leone, a credible system of justice and accountability for the very serious crimes committed there would end impunity and would contribute to the process of national reconciliation and to the restoration and maintenance of peace,

Taking note in this regard of the letter dated 12 June 2000 from the President of Sierra Leone to the Secretary-General and the Suggested Framework attached to it (S/2000/786, annex),

Recognizing further the desire of the Government of Sierra Leone for assistance from the United Nations in establishing a strong and credible court that will meet the objectives of bringing justice and ensuring lasting peace,

Noting the report of the Secretary-General of 31 July 2000 (S/2000/751) and, in particular, *taking note* with appreciation of the steps already taken by the Secretary-General in response to the request of the Government of Sierra Leone to assist it in establishing a special court,

Noting further the negative impact of the security situation on the administration of justice in Sierra Leone and the pressing need for international cooperation to assist in strengthening the judicial system of Sierra Leone,

Acknowledging the important contribution that can be made to this effort by qualified persons from West African States, the Commonwealth, other Member States of the United Nations and international organizations, to expedite the process of bringing justice and reconciliation to Sierra Leone and the region,

Reiterating that the situation in Sierra Leone continues to constitute a threat to international peace and security in the region,

1. *Requests* the Secretary-General to negotiate an agreement with the Government of Sierra Leone to create an independent special court consistent with this resolution, and *expresses* its readiness to take further steps expeditiously upon receiving and reviewing the report of the Secretary-General referred to in paragraph 6 below;

2. *Recommends* that the subject matter jurisdiction of the special court should include notably crimes against humanity, war crimes and other serious violations of international humanitarian law, as well as crimes under relevant Sierra Leonean law committed within the territory of Sierra Leone;

3. *Recommends further* that the special court should have personal jurisdiction over persons who bear the greatest responsibility for the commission of the crimes referred to in paragraph 2, including those leaders who, in committing such crimes, have threatened the establishment of and implementation of the peace process in Sierra Leone;

4. *Emphasizes* the importance of ensuring the impartiality, independence and credibility of the process, in particular with regard to the status of the judges and the prosecutors;

5. *Requests*, in this connection, that the Secretary-General, if necessary, send

a team of experts to Sierra Leone as may be required to prepare the report referred to in paragraph 6 below;

6. *Requests* the Secretary-General to submit a report to the Security Council on the implementation of this resolution, in particular on his consultations and negotiations with the Government of Sierra Leone concerning the establishment of the special court, including recommendations, no later than 30 days from the date of this resolution;

7. *Requests* the Secretary-General to address in his report the questions of the temporal jurisdiction of the special court, an appeals process including the advisability, feasibility, and appropriateness of an appeals chamber in the special court or of sharing the Appeals Chamber of the International Criminal Tribunals for the Former Yugoslavia and Rwanda or other effective options, and a possible alternative host State, should it be necessary to convene the special court outside the seat of the court in Sierra Leone, if circumstances so require;

8. *Requests* the Secretary-General to include recommendations on the following:

(a) any additional agreements that may be required for the provision of the international assistance which will be necessary for the establishment and functioning of the special court;

(b) the level of participation, support and technical assistance of qualified persons from Member States of the United Nations, including in particular, member States of ECOWAS and the Commonwealth, and from the United Nations Mission in Sierra Leone that will be necessary for the efficient, independent and impartial functioning of the special court;

(c) the amount of voluntary contributions, as appropriate, of funds, equipment and services to the special court, including through the offer of expert personnel that may be needed from States, intergovernmental organizations and nongovernmental organizations;

(d) whether the special court could receive, as necessary and feasible, expertise and advice from the International Criminal Tribunals for the Former Yugoslavia and Rwanda;

9. *Decides* to remain actively seized of the matter.

Resolution 1620 (2005)

Adopted by the Security Council
at its 5254th meeting, on 31 August 2005

The Security Council,

Recalling its previous resolutions and the statements of its President concerning the situation in Sierra Leone,

Commending the valuable contribution the United Nations Mission in Sierra Leone (UNAMSIL) has made to the recovery of Sierra Leone from conflict and to the country's peace, security and development,

Having considered the report of the Secretary-General of 26 April 2005

(S/2005/273), and its addendum of 28 July 2005 (S/2005/273/Add.2), and welcoming his recommendation that a United Nations integrated office be established in Sierra Leone, after the withdrawal of UNAMSIL at the end of 2005, in order to continue to assist the Government of Sierra Leone to consolidate peace by enhancing political and economic governance, building the national capacity for conflict prevention, and preparing for elections in 2007,

Noting the letter of 21 June 2005 from the President of Sierra Leone to the Secretary-General (S/2005/419), that likewise emphasizes the need for an integrated United Nations office to support the above objectives,

Emphasizing the importance of a smooth transition between UNAMSIL and the new United Nations integrated office, and of the effective and efficient operation of the office,

Emphasizing the importance of the continued support of the United Nations and the international community for the long-term security and development of Sierra Leone, particularly in building the capacity of the Government of Sierra Leone,

Reiterating its appreciation for the essential work of the Special Court for Sierra Leone and its vital contribution to the establishment of rule of law in Sierra Leone and the subregion, underlining its expectation that the Court will finish its work in accordance with its Completion Strategy, and in this regard encouraging all States to cooperate fully with the Court and to provide it with the necessary financial resources,

Welcoming the publication of the report of the Sierra Leone Truth and Reconciliation Commission and encouraging the Government of Sierra Leone to take further steps to implement its recommendations,

1. *Requests* the Secretary-General to establish the United Nations Integrated Office in Sierra Leone (UNIOSIL), as recommended in the addendum to his report (S/2005/273/Add.2), for an initial period of 12 months beginning on 1 January 2006, with the following key tasks:

(a) to assist the Government of Sierra Leone in:

(i) building the capacity of State institutions to address further the root causes of the conflict, provide basic services and accelerate progress towards the Millennium Development Goals through poverty reduction and sustainable economic growth, including through the creation of an enabling framework for private investment and systematic efforts to address HIV/AIDS;

(ii) developing a national action plan for human rights and establishing the national human rights commission;

(iii) building the capacity of the National Electoral Commission to conduct a free, fair and credible electoral process in 2007;

(iv) enhancing good governance, transparency and accountability of public institutions, including through anti-corruption measures and improved fiscal management;

(v) strengthening the rule of law, including by developing the independence and capacity of the justice system and the capacity of the police and corrections system;

(vi) strengthening the Sierra Leonean security sector, in cooperation with the International Military Advisory and Training Team and other partners;

(vii) promoting a culture of peace, dialogue, and participation in critical national issues through a strategic approach to public information and communication, including through building an independent and capable public radio capacity;

(viii) developing initiatives for the protection and well-being of youth, women and children;

(b) to liaise with the Sierra Leonean security sector and other partners, to report on the security situation and make recommendations concerning external and internal security threats;

(c) to coordinate with United Nations missions and offices and regional organizations in West Africa in dealing with cross-border challenges such as the illicit movement of small arms, human trafficking and smuggling and illegal trade in natural resources;

(d) to coordinate with the Special Court for Sierra Leone;

2. *Emphasizes* the primary responsibility of the Government of Sierra Leone for the consolidation of peace and security in the country, and *urges* continued support from international donors for the Government's efforts in this regard;

3. *Underlines* the importance of establishing a fully integrated office with effective coordination of strategy and programs between the United Nations agencies, funds and programs in Sierra Leone, between the United Nations and other international donors, and between the integrated office, the Economic Community of West African States and other United Nations missions in the region;

4. *Welcomes* the Secretary-General's recommendation in the addendum to his report (S/2005/273/Add.2) that the integrated office should be headed by an Executive Representative of the Secretary-General and his intention that he/she should also serve as the Resident Representative of the United Nations Development Programme and United Nations Resident Coordinator;

5. *Requests* the Secretary-General to continue planning for security for the Special Court for Sierra Leone on the basis outlined in paragraphs 15 to 24 of the addendum to his report (S/2005/273/Add.2), and *looks forward* to further details on the proposed arrangements;

6. *Requests* the Secretary-General to keep the Council regularly informed of progress with establishing the United Nations integrated office in Sierra Leone, and thereafter with the implementation of this resolution;

7. *Decides* to remain actively seized of the matter.

List of Relevant UN Documents

Resolutions of the Security Council

1997
S/RES/1132, 3 October 1997
Imposed sanctions against the military junta and prevented the sale of petroleum and arms.

1998
S/RES/1156, 16 March 1998
Welcomed the return of the democratically elected president and terminated prohibitions on the sale or supply of petroleum.

S/RES/1162, 17 April 1998
Authorized the deployment of United Nations military liaison and security advisory personnel.

S/RES/1171, 5 June 1998
Prohibited the sale and supply of arms and related matériel to nongovernmental forces in Sierra Leone.

S/RES/1181, 13 July 1998
Established the United Nations Observer Mission in Sierra Leone (UNOMSIL).

1999
S/RES/1220, 12 January 1999
Extended UNOMSIL's mandate until 13 March 1999 and welcomed the intention of the Secretary-General to redeploy staff, subject to strict attention to the security situation.

S/RES/1231, 11 March 1999
Extended UNOMSIL's mandate until 13 June 1999 and noted the Secretary-General's intention to make recommendations on UNOMSIL's expansion.

S/RES/1245, 11 June 1999
Extended UNOMSIL's mandate until 13 December 1999 and welcomed the holding of talks in Lomé.

S/RES/1260, 20 August 1999
Authorized the expansion of UNOMSIL.
S/RES/1270, 22 October 1999
Established the United Nations Mission in Sierra Leone (UNAMSIL).

2000

S/RES/1289, 7 February 2000
Authorized further expansion of UNAMSIL.
S/RES/1299, 19 May 2000
Authorized an increase in the troop strength of UNAMSIL.
S/RES/1306, 5 July 2000
Prohibited the import of rough diamonds from Sierra Leone and called upon the government of Sierra Leone to establish a Certificate of Origin regime for trade in diamonds.
S/RES/1313, 4 August 2000
Extended UNAMSIL's mandate until 8 September 2000, expressed intention to strengthen UNAMSIL's mandate, and requested the Secretary-General to make recommendations on the restructuring and strengthening of UNAMSIL.
S/RES/1315, 14 August 2000
Requested the Secretary-General to negotiate an agreement with the government of Sierra Leone to create an independent Special Court.
S/RES/1317, 5 September 2000
Extended UNAMSIL's mandate until 20 September 2000.
S/RES/1321, 20 September 2000
Extended UNAMSIL's mandate until 31 December 2000.
S/RES/1334, 22 December 2000
Extended UNAMSIL's mandate until 31 March 2001.

2001

S/RES/1343, 7 March 2001
Authorized a ban on Liberian diamond exports, a ban on international travel by key regime members, and strengthening of the arms embargo.
S/RES/1346, 30 March 2001
Extended UNAMSIL's mandate until 30 September 2001 and increased its troop strength.
S/RES/1370, 18 September 2001
Extended UNAMSIL's mandate until 30 March 2002.
S/RES/1385, 19 December 2001
Extended the ban on the import of Sierra Leone diamonds, excluding those diamonds authorized by the government of Sierra Leone under the Certificate of Origin regime, until 5 December 2002.

2002

S/RES/1389, 16 January 2002
Authorized UNAMSIL to undertake election-related tasks.
S/RES/1400, 28 March 2002
Extended UNAMSIL's mandate until 30 September 2002.
S/RES/1436, 24 September 2002
Extended UNAMSIL's mandate until 30 March 2003.

S/RES/1446, 4 December 2002
Extended the ban on the import of Sierra Leone diamonds, excluding those diamonds authorized by the government of Sierra Leone under the Certificate of Origin regime, until 5 June 2003.

2003
S/RES/1470, 28 March 2003
Extended UNAMSIL's mandate until 30 September 2003.
S/RES/1492, 18 July 2003
Approved the recommendations for the Secretary-General for the drawdown of UNAMSIL.
S/RES/1508, 19 September 2003
Extended UNAMSIL's mandate until 31 March 2004.

2004
S/RES/1537, 30 March 2004
Extended UNAMSIL's mandate until 30 September 2004.
S/RES/1562, 17 September 2004
Extended UNAMSIL's mandate until 30 June 2005.

2005
S/RES/1610, 30 June 2005
Extended UNAMSIL's mandate for a final six months, until 31 December 2005.
S/RES/1620, 31 August 2005
Established the United Nations Integrated Office in Sierra Leone (UNIOSIL) for an initial period of twelve months beginning 1 January 2006.

2006
S/RES/1734, 22 December 2006
Extended UNIOSIL's mandate until 31 December 2007.

Statements by the President of the Security Council

1996
S/PRST/1996/7, 15 February 1996
Welcomed the decision to proceed with elections in Sierra Leone as scheduled.
S/PRST/1996/12, 19 March 1996
Welcomed the parliamentary and presidential elections.
S/PRST/1996/46, 4 December 1996
Welcomed the Abidjan Peace Agreement, signed by the government of Sierra Leone and the Revolutionary United Front.

1997
S/PRST/1997/29, 27 May 1997
Deplored the attempt to overthrow the democratically elected government of

Sierra Leone and called for an immediate restoration of constitutional order.
S/PRST/1997/36, 11 July 1997
> Called again for the immediate and unconditional restoration of constitutional order.
S/PRST/1997/42, 6 August 1997
> Condemned the overthrow of the democratically elected government.
S/PRST/1997/52, 17 November 1997
> Reiterated the condemnation of the overthrow of the democratically elected government.

1998
S/PRST/1998/5, 26 February 1998
> Expressed regret at the suffering undergone by the people of Sierra Leone and encouraged ECOMOG to proceed in its efforts to foster peace.
S/PRST/1998/13, 20 May 1998
> Condemned atrocities carried out against the civilian population, as gross violations of international humanitarian law.

1999
S/PRST/1999/1, 7 January 1999
> Expressed concern about attacks by armed rebels in Sierra Leone's capital.
S/PRST/1999/13, 15 May 1999
> Welcomed the intention of the Secretary-General to increase UNOMSIL's presence on the ground, within authorized levels.

2000
S/PRST/2000/14, 4 May 2000
> Strongly condemned armed attacks against UNAMSIL forces.
S/PRST/2000/24, 17 July 2000
> Expressed full support for the decision to mount a military operation to relieve surrounded peacekeepers and military observers.
S/2000/992, 16 October 2000
> Report on the Security Council Mission to Sierra Leone.
S/PRST/2000/31, 3 November 2000
> Expressed concern about the continued fragile situation in Sierra Leone and the related instability in the subregion, stressed a comprehensive regional approach in restoring security and stability, and reiterated the intent to strengthen UNAMSIL at the appropriate time.
S/PRST/2000/41, 21 December 2000
> Condemned incursions into Guinea along its borders by rebel groups from Liberia and Sierra Leone.

2002
S/PRST/2002/14, 22 May 2002
> Welcomed elections in Sierra Leone.

2005
S/PRST/2005/63, 20 December 2005
> Commended UNAMSIL's contribution to recovery in Sierra Leone as the mission approached its 31 December exit.

Reports of the Secretary-General

1995

S/1995/975, 21 November 1995
Covered the period since the good offices of the Secretary-General were formally requested by the government of Sierra Leone in November 1994.

1997

S/1997/80, 26 January 1997
Addressed United Nations assistance in implementation of the Abidjan Peace Agreement of 30 November 1996 (S/1996/1034, annex).

S/1997/80/Add.1, 31 January 1997
Addendum report; informed the Security Council about costs of establishing and maintaining of a peacekeeping operation in Sierra Leone.

S/1997/811, 21 October 1997
Report on the situation in Sierra Leone submitted pursuant to Security Council Resolution 1132 of 8 October 1997.

S/1997/958, 5 December 1997
Second report on the situation in Sierra Leone.

1998

S/1998/103, 5 February 1998
Third report on the situation in Sierra Leone.

S/1998/112, 10 February 1998
Report submitted pursuant to paragraph 13 of Security Council Resolution 1132 (1997), on mandatory sanctions.

S/1998/249, 18 March 1998
Fourth report on the situation in Sierra Leone; included proposals concerning the role of the United Nations and its future presence in Sierra Leone.

S/1998/112/Add.1, 31 March 1998
Report submitted pursuant to paragraph 13 of Security Council Resolution 1132 (1997).

S/1998/486, 9 June 1998
Fifth report on the situation in Sierra Leone.

S/1998/486/Add.1, 1 July 1998
Addendum to the fifth report on the situation in Sierra Leone; included estimated cost of establishing UNOMSIL.

S/1998/750, 12 August 1998
First report on UNOMSIL.

S/1998/960, 16 October 1998
Second report on UNOMSIL.

S/1998/1176, 16 December 1998
Third report on UNOMSIL.

1999

S/1999/20, 7 January 1999
Special report on UNOMSIL.

S/1999/237,4 March 1999
Fifth report on UNOMSIL.

S/1999/645, 4 June 1999
 Sixth report on UNOMSIL.
S/1999/836, 30 July 1999
 Seventh report on UNOMSIL.
S/1999/836/Add.1, 11 August 1999
 Addendum to the seventh report on UNOMSIL.
S/1999/1223, 6 December 1999
 First report on UNAMSIL.

2000

S/2000/13 + Add.1, 11 January 2000
 Second report on UNAMSIL.
S/2000/186, 7 March 2000
 Third report on UNAMSIL.
S/2000/455, 19 May 2000
 Fourth report on UNAMSIL.
S/2000/751, 31 July 2000
 Fifth report on UNAMSIL.
S/2000/832, 24 August 2000
 Sixth report on UNAMSIL.
S/2000/832/Add.1, 12 September 2000
 Addendum to the sixth report on UNAMSIL.
S/2000/915, 4 October 2000
 Report of on the establishment of a Special Court for Sierra Leone.
S/2000/1055, 31 October 2000
 Seventh report on UNAMSIL.
S/2000/1199, 15 December 2000
 Eighth report on UNAMSIL.

2001

S/2001/228, 14 March 2001
 Ninth report on UNAMSIL.
S/2001/513, 23 May 2001
 Report on the issue of refugees and internally displaced persons.
S/2001/627, 25 June 2001
 Tenth report on UNAMSIL.
S/2001/857, 7 September 2001
 Eleventh report on UNAMSIL.
S/2001/857/Add.1, 10 September 2001
 Addendum to the eleventh report on UNAMSIL; included an annex covering
 contributions as of 5 September 2001.
S/2001/1195, 13 December 2001
 Twelfth report on UNAMSIL.

2002

S/2002/267, 14 March 2002
 Thirteenth report on UNAMSIL.
S/2002/679, 19 June 2002
 Fourteenth report on UNAMSIL.

S/2002/987, 5 September 2002
Fifteenth report on UNAMSIL.
S/2002/1417, 24 December 2002
Sixteenth report on UNAMSIL.

2003

S/2003/321, 17 March 2003
Seventeenth report on UNAMSIL.
S/2003/663, 23 June 2003
Eighteenth report on UNAMSIL.
S/2003/863, 5 September 2003
Nineteenth report on UNAMSIL.
S/2003/1201, 23 December 2003
Twentieth report on UNAMSIL.

2004

S/2004/228, 19 March 2004
Twenty-first report on UNAMSIL.
S/2004/536, 6 July 2004
Twenty-second report on UNAMSIL.
S/2004/724, 9 September 2004
Twenty-third report on UNAMSIL.
S/2004/965, 10 December 2004
Twenty-fourth report on UNAMSIL.

2005

S/2005/135, 2 March 2005
Report on intermission cooperation and possible cross-border operations among UNAMSIL, the United Nations Mission in Liberia (UNMIL), and the United Nations Operation in Côte d'Ivoire (UNOCI).
S/2005/273, 26 April 2005
Twenty-fifth report on UNAMSIL.
S/2005/273/Add.1, 21 June 2005
Addendum to the twenty-fifth report on UNAMSIL; covered the budget for the mission from 1 July 2005 to 30 June 2006.
S/2005/273/Add.2, 28 July 2005
Addendum to the twenty-fifth report on UNAMSIL; included recommendations for the establishment of a modestly sized UN integrated office in Sierra Leone, following the withdrawal of UNAMSIL, to develop and implement a viable peace consolidation strategy for the country.
S/2005/596, 20 September 2005
Twenty-sixth report on UNAMSIL.
S/2005/777, 12 December 2005
Twenty-seventh report on UNAMSIL.

2006

S/2006/269, 28 April 2006
First report on the United Nations Integrated Office in Sierra Leone (UNIOSIL).

S/2006/695, 29 August 2006
Second report on UNIOSIL.
S/2006/922, 28 November 2006
Third report on UNIOSIL.

Documents on Establishment of the
Special Court for Sierra Leone

S/2000/915, 4 October 2000
Report of the Secretary-General on establishment of a Special Court for Sierra Leone.
S/RES/1315, 14 August 2000
Requested the Secretary-General to negotiate an agreement with the government of Sierra Leone to create an independent Special Court.
S/2001/40, 12 January 2001
Letter from the Secretary-General to the President of the Security Council concerning the Secretary-General's understanding of the meaning, scope, and legal effect of proposals made by members of the Council.
S/2001/95, 31 January 2001
Letter dated 31 January 2001 from the President of the Security Council to the Secretary-General referring to the Secretary-General's letter of 12 January 2001 (S/2001/40).
S/2001/693, 13 July 2001
Letter dated 12 July 2001 from the Secretary-General to the President of the Security Council regarding revised budget estimates for operation of the Special Court.
S/2001/722, 23 July 2001
Letter dated 23 July 2001 from the President of the Security Council to the Secretary-General referring to plans to move forward with establishment of a Special Court.
S/2001/1320, 28 December 2001
Letter dated 26 December 2001 from the Secretary-General to the President of the Security Council regarding contributions to commence establishment and operation of the Special Court.
S/2004/182, 10 March 2004
Letter dated 26 February 2004 from the Secretary-General to the President of the Security Council regarding the Special Court.

Note: See also Truth and Reconciliation Commission, Sierra Leone, "Witness to Truth: Report of the Sierra Leone Truth and Reconciliation Commission" (Accra, Ghana: Graphic Packaging, 2004).

Bibliography

Abdullah, Ibrahim, ed. *Between Democracy and Terror: The Sierra Leone Civil War.* Dakar: CODESRIA, 2003.

Abdullah, Ibrahim, and Patrick Muana. "The Revolutionary United Front of Sierra Leone: A Revolt of the Lumpenproletariat." In Christopher Clapham, ed., *African Guerrillas.* Bloomington: Indiana University Press, 1998.

Abraham, Arthur. "Dancing with the Chameleon: Sierra Leone and the Elusive Quest for Peace." *Journal of Contemporary African Studies* 19, no. 2 (July 2001): 205–228.

Adebajo, Adekeye, ed. *Building Peace in West Africa: Liberia, Sierra Leone, and Guinea Bissau.* Boulder: Lynne Rienner, 2002.

———. "Sierra Leone: A Feast for the Sobels." In Adekeye Adebajo, ed., *Building Peace in West Africa: Liberia, Sierra Leone, and Guinea Bissau.* Boulder: Lynne Rienner, 2002.

Alao, Abiodun, John Mackinlay, and 'Funmi Olonisakin. *Peacekeepers, Politicians, and Warlords.* Tokyo: United Nations University Press, 1999.

Alusala, Nelson, and Thokozani Thusi. *A Step Towards Peace: Disarmament in Africa.* Pretoria: ISS, 2004.

Amnesty International. "Guinea and Sierra Leone Border: Fighting Continues to Endanger Civilian Lives." 4 May 2001. Amnesty International Index: AFR 51/004/2001.

———. *Human Rights Abuses in a War Against Civilians.* 13 September 1995. Amnesty International Index: AFR 51/05/95.

———. *Sierra Leone: Towards a Future Founded on Human Rights.* 25 September 1996. Amnesty International Index: AFR 51/05/96.

Ayissi, Anatole, and Robin-Edward Poulton, eds. *Bound to Cooperate: Conflict, Peace, and People in Sierra Leone.* Geneva: United Nations Institute for Disarmament Research, 2000.

Bangura, Yusuf. "Strategic Policy Failure and State Fragmentation: Security, Peacekeeping, and Democratization in Sierra Leone." In Ricardo Reneì Laremont, ed., *The Causes of War and the Consequences of Peacekeeping in Africa.* Portsmouth, NH: Heinemann, 2002.

———. "Understanding the Political and Cultural Dynamics of the Sierra Leone

War: A Critique of Paul Richards' 'Fighting for the Rain Forest.'" *Africa Development* 22, nos. 3–4 (1997): 131. Published by CODESRIA.

Bazergan, Roxanne. "Analysis." *Conflict, Security, and Development* 3, no. 1 (April 2003): 27–50.

Bernarth, Clifford, and Sayre Nyce. *UNAMSIL: A Peacekeeping Success—Lessons Learned.* Report on the United Nations Mission in Sierra Leone. Washington, DC: Refugees International, October 2002.

Bones, Alan. "Case Study: Peacekeeping in Sierra Leone." In Rob McRae and Don Hubert, eds., *Human Security and the New Diplomacy: Protecting People, Promoting Peace.* Montreal: McGill-Queen's University Press, 2001.

Clapham, Christopher. "Problems of Peace Enforcement: Lessons to Be Drawn from Multinational Peacekeeping Operations in On-Going Conflicts in Africa." In Tunde Zack-Williams, Diane Frost, and Alex Thomson, eds., *Africa in Crisis: New Challenges and Possibilities.* London: Pluto, 2002.

Collier, Paul, et al. *Breaking the Conflict Trap: Civil War and Development Policy.* Washington, DC: World Bank and Oxford University Press, 2003.

Conciliation Resources. *Implementing the Lomé Peace Agreement.* London: CR, September 2000.

Dahrendorf, Nicola, ed. *A Review of Peace Operations: A Case for Change.* London: King's College London, 2003.

Dobbins, James, et al. "Sierra Leone." In James Dobbins et al., *The UN's Role in Nation-Building: From the Congo to Iraq.* Santa Monica: RAND, 2005.

Economist Intelligence Unit. *Guinea, Sierra Leone, Liberia: Country Report, September 2005.* London, 2005.

———. *Sierra Leone: Country Profile, 2005.* London, 2005.

Ellis, Stephen. *The Mask of Anarchy: The Destruction of Liberia and the Religious Dimension of an African Civil War.* London: Hurst, 1999.

Ero, Comfort. "The Future of ECOMOG in West Africa." In Jakkie Cilliers and Greg Mills, eds., *From Peacekeeping to Complex Emergencies: Peace Support Missions in Africa.* Johannesburg: SAIIA/ISS, 1999.

Fawole, W. Alade. *Military Power and Third-Party Conflict Mediation in West Africa: The Liberia and Sierra Leone Case Studies.* Ile-Ife: Obafemi Awolowo University Press, 2001.

Francis, David J., et al. "UN-ECOWAS-ECOMOG Co-deployment in Sierra Leone." In David J. Francis et al., *Dangers of Co-deployment: UN Co-operative Peacekeeping in Africa.* Aldershot: Ashgate, 2005.

Gberie, Lansana. *A Dirty War in West Africa: The R.U.F. and the Destruction of Sierra Leone.* London: Hurst, 2005.

Gberie, Lansana, Ralph Hazleton, and Ian Smillie. *The Heart of The Matter: Sierra Leone, Diamonds, & Human Security.* Ottawa: Partnership Africa Canada, January 2000. http://www.sierra-leone.org/heartmatter.html.

Gbla, Osman. "Security Sector Reform Under International Tutelage in Sierra Leone." *International Peacekeeping* 13, no. 1 (March 2006): 78–93.

Ginifer, Jeremy, and Kaye Oliver. *Evaluation of the Conflict Prevention Pools: Sierra Leone.* Evaluation Report no. EV647. London: DFID, March 2004.

Global Witness. *The Usual Suspects: Liberia's Weapons and Mercenaries in Côte d'Ivoire and Sierra Leone.* London: Global Witness, March 2003.

Grabish, Beatrice. "Peacewatch: Return of President Ahmad Tejan Ahmad Kabbah to Power." *UN Chronicle,* Summer 1998.

Higate, Paul. "Peacekeeping and Gender Relations in Sierra Leone." In Paul

Higate, *Gender and Peacekeeping: Case Studies: The Democratic Republic of the Congo and Sierra Leone.* Pretoria: ISS, 2004.

Hirsch, John L. "Sierra Leone." In David M. Malone, ed., *The UN Security Council: From the Cold War to the 21st Century.* Boulder: Lynne Rienner, 2004.

————. *Sierra Leone: Diamonds and the Struggle for Democracy.* International Peace Academy Occasional Paper series. Boulder: Lynne Rienner, 2001.

Human Rights Watch. *Sierra Leone: Getting Away with Murder, Mutilation, Rape.* New York, July 1999.

International Center for Transitional Justice. *The Special Court for Sierra Leone Under Scrutiny.* Prosecutions Case Studies series. Written by Tom Perriello and Marieke Wierda. New York, March 2006.

International Crisis Group. *Liberia: The Key to Ending Regional Instability.* Africa Report no. 43. Freetown, 24 April 2002.

————. *Liberia and Sierra Leone: Rebuilding Failed States.* Africa Report no. 87. Dakar, 8 December 2004.

————. *Sierra Leone: The State of Security and Governance.* Africa Report no. 67. Freetown, 2 September 2003.

————. *Sierra Leone After Elections: Politics as Usual?* Africa Report no. 49. Freetown, 15 July 2002.

Jonah, James O. C. "The United Nations." In Adekeye Adebayo and Ismail Rashid, eds., *West Africa's Security Challenges: Building Peace in a Troubled Region.* Boulder: Lynne Rienner, 2004.

Kandeh, Jimmy D. "Subaltern Terror in Sierra Leone." In Tunde Zack-Williams, Diane Frost, and Alex Thomson, eds., *Africa in Crisis: New Challenges and Possibilities.* London: Pluto, 2002.

Keen, David. *Conflict and Collusion in Sierra Leone.* Oxford: Currey, 2005.

King's College London. *A Case for Change: Review of UN Peace Operations.* London: Conflict Security and Development Group, 2003.

Krasno, Jean. *Public Opinion Survey of UNAMSIL's Work in Sierra Leone.* New York: United Nations Department of Peacekeeping Operations, Peacekeeping Best Practices Section, July 2005.

Langholtz, Harvey, Boris Kondoch, and Alan Wells, eds. *International Peacekeeping: Yearbook of International Peace Operations.* Vol. 10. Leiden: Nijhoff, 2004.

Le Billon, Philippe. *Fuelling War: Natural Resources and Armed Conflict.* Adelphi Paper no. 373. London: IISS, 2005.

————."The Geopolitical Economy of Resource Wars." *Geopolitics* 9, no. 1 (2004): 1–28.

————, ed. *Geopolitics of Resource Wars: Resource Dependence, Governance and Violence.* London; Portland: Frank Cass Publishers, 2004.

Legg, Sir Thomas, and Sir Robin Ibbs. *Report of the Sierra Leone Arms Investigation.* London: Stationery Office, 27 July 1998.

Lord, David, ed. "Paying the Price: The Sierra Leone Peace Process." In *Accord: An International Review of Peace Initiatives,* vol. 9. London: Conciliation Resources, 2000.

Malan, Mark, Sarah Meek, Thokozani Thusi, Jeremy Ginifer, and Patrick Coker. *Sierra Leone: Building the Road to Recovery.* Monograph no. 80. Pretoria: ISS, March 2003.

Malan, Mark, Phenyo Rakate, and Angela McIntyre. *Peacekeeping in Sierra*

Leone: UNAMSIL Hits Home Straight. Monograph no. 68. Pretoria: ISS, 2002.

Montague, Dena. "The Business of War and the Prospect of Peace in Sierra Leone." *Brown Journal of World Affairs* 9, no. 1 (Spring 2002): 236.

Musah, Abdel-Fatau, and J. 'Kayode Fayemi, eds. *Mercenaries: An African Security Dilemma.* London: Press, 2000.

Oloniskan, 'Funmi. *Reinventing Peacekeeping in Africa: Conceptual and Legal Issues in ECOMOG Operations.* The Hague: Kluwer Law International, 2000.

―――. "Sierra Leone." In Jane Boulden, ed., *Dealing with Conflict in Africa: The United Nations and Regional Organizations.* New York: Palgrave Macmillan, 2003.

Oloniskan, 'Funmi, and Comfort Ero. "Africa and the Regionalization of Peace Operations." In Michael Pugh and Waheguru Pal Singh Sidhu, eds., *The United Nations & Regional Security: Europe and Beyond.* Boulder: Lynne Rienner, 2003.

Pham, J. Peter. *The Sierra Leonean Tragedy: History and Global Dimensions.* Hauppauge, NY: Nova Science, 2006.

Rashid, Ismail. "Student Radicals, Lumpen Youth, and the Origins of the Revolutionary Groups in Sierra Leone, 1977–1996." In Ibrahim Abdullah, ed., *Between Democracy and Terror: The Sierra Leone Civil War.* Dakar: CODESRIA, 2003.

Richards, Paul, ed. *No Peace, No War: An Anthropology of Contemporary Armed Conflicts.* Athens: Ohio University Press, 2005.

Rupert, James. "Diamond Hunters Fuel Africa's Brutal Wars." *Washington Post,* 16 October 1999.

Smillie, Ian, Lansana Gberie, and Ralph Hazleton. *The Heart of the Matter: Sierra Leone, Diamonds, and Human Security.* Ottawa: Partnership Africa Canada, 2000.

Sorenson, David S., and Pia Christina Wood, eds. *The Politics of Peacekeeping in the Post–Cold War Era.* Peacekeeping no. 17. New York: Cass, 2005.

Sriram, Chandra Lekha, and Karin Wermester, eds. *From Promise to Practice: Strengthening UN Capacities for the Prevention of Violent Conflict.* Project of the International Peace Academy. Boulder: Lynne Rienner, 2003.

Synge, Richard. "Recent History (of Sierra Leone)." In Iain Frame and Katharine Murison, eds., *Africa South of the Sahara 2006,* 35th ed. London: Europa, 2005.

United Nations. *In Larger Freedom: Towards Development, Security, and Human Rights for All.* Report of the Secretary-General. UN Doc. A/59/2005, 21 March 2005.

―――. *Lessons Learned from United Nations Peacekeeping Experiences in Sierra Leone.* New York: Department of Peacekeeping Operations, Peacekeeping Best Practices Unit, September 2003.

―――. *A More Secure World: Our Shared Responsibility.* Report of the High-Level Panel on Threats, Challenges, and Change. UN Doc. A/59/565, 2 December 2004.

―――. *Peace Agreement Between the Government of the Republic of Sierra Leone and the Revolutionary United Front of Sierra Leone.* UN Doc. S/1996/1034, 30 November 1996.

―――. *Report of the Panel on United Nations Peace Operations.* UN Doc. A/55/305-S/2000/809, 21 August 2000.

————. *Sierra Leone: Peace, Recovery, and Development—UN Development Assistance Framework, 2004–2007.* UN Country Team, March 2003.

United Nations Development Programme. *Millennium Development Goals: A Compact Among Nations to End Human Poverty.* New York: Oxford University Press, 2003.

United Nations High Commissioner for Refugees and Save the Children–UK. "Sexual Violence and Exploitation: The Experience of Refugee Children in Guinea, Liberia, and Sierra Leone." February 2002. http://www.unhcr .org/cgi-bin/texis/vtx/news/opendoc.pdf?id=3c7cf89a4&tbl=partners.

US House of Representatives. *Elections in Sierra Leone: A Step Toward Regional Stability?* Hearing before the Committee on International Relations, Subcommittee on Africa, US House of Representatives. 107th Congress, 2nd sess., May 16, 2002. Washington, DC: Government Printing Office.

Vines, Alex. "Combating Light Weapons Proliferation in West Africa." *International Affairs* 81, no. 2 (March 2005): 341–360.

Index

About the Book

THE FIRST IN A SERIES of "inside" histories, *Peacekeeping in Sierra Leone* relates how a small country—one insignificant in the strategic considerations of the world powers—propelled the United Nations to center stage in a crisis that called its very authority into serious question; and how the UN mission in Sierra Leone was transformed from its nadir into what is now widely considered one of the most successful peacekeeping missions in UN history.

'Funmi Olonisakin tells the story of this experience, highlighting the key moments and the reasoning behind strategic decisions. She also captures UNAMSIL's internal struggle as it fought to regain some honor after the May 2000 crisis, when the UN had to rely on the infamous Charles Taylor to broker the release of 500 peacekeeper hostages.

Olonisakin's rich narrative not only illuminates the ins and outs of the UNAMSIL mission, but also reflects on its meaning for current and future peace operations in Africa and beyond.

'Funmi Olonisakin is director of the Conflict, Security, and Development Group of the School of Social Science and Public Policy at King's College London. She is also founding member of the International Governing Council of the London- and Lagos-based Center for Democracy and Development. Her numerous publications include *The Challenges of Security Sector Governance in West Africa* and *Reinventing Peacekeeping in Africa: Conceptual and Legal Issues in the ECOMOG Operations.*